FOR YOU
TO SAY

A GRECIAN MEMOIR

BY

JOHN P. MANUEL

Tzatziki For You to Say
Copyright © 2010 by John P. Manuel

First published 2010 by Lulu.com

Typeset in Janson Text 9pt
...with tons of mistakes no doubt!

Further copies of this book may be purchased from:

http://www.lulu.com/
Plus good on-line book stores

...Go on, support a struggling writer!

1st Edition. November 2010

ISBN: 978-1-4466-4709-7

Greece is a very poor country
..inhabited by very rich people.
- *Anon*
This works on several levels,
think about it!

"When you go measuring a man's success,
don't count money - count happiness."
- *Ken Dodd*

A FEW WORDS, BY WAY OF EXPLANATION...

Firstly, my wife's name is Yvonne Susan Maria. To all our friends back in the UK she's known as Yvonne. She felt that it seemed like a good idea when we moved to Rhodes to be known as Maria, a decision which has led to endless confusion. So bear with me when I call her Yvonne, Yvonne-Maria, Y-Maria or simply Maria in this book, please. Thanks!

Spellings of Greek words may also vary. I'm not even going to explain why here, just stick with it, ok? Thanks again.

This book sort of follows on from the first two "*Ramblings from Rhodes*," But only sort of. So if you haven't read *Feta Compli!* or *Moussaka to My Ears*, it shouldn't mean that you don't enjoy this one. That's assuming you do, of course, enjoy it. But on the other hand, I'd probably be a little better off if you'd purchased those two already. Got the idea? A nod's as good as a wink, eh? Thanks, a third time.

The majority of the characters appearing in this book are real. Some are amalgams of one or two and some names haven't been changed, but most have. Just in case.

GROVELLING DEPARTMENT...

I am very indebted to Nigel Sparks, from Somerset, England, for supplying the wonderful photograph of a Greek table, replete with a very appropriate dish of Tzatziki, for the front cover, plus one or two other pictures I've used inside.

I had writer's diarrhoea in every area except that of thinking up a name for this third volume of *Ramblings*, so I also must thank Colin Anderson, from Bristol, England, for coming up with the title.

JM. Oct 2010

By the same author:

FETA COMPLI!
ISBN No. 978-1-4092-4626-8

MOUSSAKA TO MY EARS
ISBN No. 978-1-4092-6732-4

The author's website:
http://honorarygreek.blogspot.com

All of John Manuel's books
are available from his website,
the publisher's website (www.lulu.com)
and from Amazon

CONTENTS

1 - *A Misnomer*

"It's a bit of a misnomer that really, isn't it." Said Gary, as he and his "men" (if a gang of two qualifies for such an epithet) were sitting in the shade sipping their tea and dunking their biscuits. They were taking a break whilst tackling one of the myriad jobs (large and small) that needed completion on our new home in Rhodes during the first year or more after our arrival here. The tea and biscuits were courtesy of my wife and I. It was costing us a small fortune, considering the amount of both which they'd consume during a day's "work."

We would make them tea on a regular basis as Gary (quite rightly really) forbade his "men" from drinking beer whilst they worked. Slippery slope and all that malarkey I suppose. It all seems such a long time ago as I sit typing this just one month shy of our fourth anniversary of living in Rhodes. It's July and hovering around the 38°C (100°F) mark outside as Yvonne-Maria and I hide in a shuttered-up house waiting for the cooler evening hours, when temperatures will drop to a refreshing 29-30! Each year at about this time we vow to return to Britain for maybe the whole of the month of August to escape the temperatures, the humidity and the hordes. Not that we have managed to do it as yet.

The humidity is only ever a problem for us during the hottest two summer months and then not all of the time.

There are days when you can throw open the front curtains and stare out at a crisp blue horizon where the deeper turquoise of the sea contrasts sharply with the slightly paler azure of the sky. It's on these days when you understand why so many who have visited Greece remark on the uniqueness of the light here. There is no scientific explanation for it, it's just a fact. The light on a Greek island during a summer's day, when the humidity (the *"ygrasi'a"* to a Greek) is low, is simply stunning. Everything seems to compete to throw its own colour or hue at your eager eyes and you want to reach either for a camera or a paintbrush; or better still, a cool beer, so it's just as well I wasn't working for Gary when he was building houses really.

Gary told us, not long after our initial arrival, that, to use his words here, "The climate here is wonderful. In fact there are only really two shitty months…" to which we rather naturally thought he was going to add "December and January," or maybe "January and February," when he continued, (to the accompaniment of the sight of our eyebrows raising in unison), "…July and August." After now having spent almost four complete summers here we can understand why he made that statement. If you come to Greece for a vacation it's not going to be a problem, as long - that is - as you have air-conditioning in your accommodation. You can spend all day either in a pool or in the sea. But if you live here, and even worse if you live and work here, those two months can be simply impossible to enjoy. It's too hot to do anything strenuous as soon as the sun crests the Eastern horizon, which is around 6.00am, and it remains so until maybe a half an hour before sunset, which is around 8.30pm at this time of year. We now completely understand the need of Gary and his men for so many tea breaks; plus the reason why they'd be working outside our bedroom window well before we awoke and would be packing up for the day at around 2.00pm, when the hottest couple of hours are just coming upon us.

Fortunately, even though the world financial crisis has virtually robbed us of our entire means of income in the past year or so, we are managing to get by financially by finding odd bits of gardening work, decorating and even a bit of general maintenance for other Brits who've bought property over here. Plus, this summer I have found work doing airport transfers for one of the British tour operators. This job involves me leaving home very late on a Wednesday evening and getting home around dawn. Then there's the general gardening and property upkeep we do for John and Wendy, our landlords, which is also a big help at present. All in all, we aren't in the trap that a lot of ex-pat British have succumbed to, that of working seven days a week for the summer season. We always said that if we got into such a situation we'd seriously contemplate going back to the UK and reverting to coming here for a couple of weeks for our holidays each year and being able to enjoy the place, much as we did for decades before making the move. Writing books and receiving enthusiastic reviews from one's readers doesn't make you rich, sadly.

When the humidity is low it's a lot easier coping with the temperatures during the summer months. Low humidity means your sweat (or, if you're a lady, your perspiration) immediately evaporates from your skin, thus not only cooling you, but leaving any clothing you may still be wearing quite dry. It's a common fallacy that when the humidity is low you don't sweat as much. Your body will sweat according to temperature and temperature alone. But when the humidity is high the sweat can't evaporate as quickly and so remains on your skin, thus making you feel clammy and soaking your clothes.

Today is such a day. I can feel the liquid erupting from the pores under my armpits as I type and running in rivers down each side of my body. Too much information? Sorry, but it helps to talk about it. There's nothing for it but to go outside and use our newly-constructed outdoor shower.

As I mentioned in "*Moussaka to My Ears*," unlike many foreigners, Greeks who build new houses here never install swimming pools. They frequently do, however, install a showerhead in the garden somewhere, so you can have a quick "dampen down and reduction of temperature" in order to cope with the heat of the day. We almost bought a free-standing garden showerhead a couple of summers ago, but decided we couldn't afford it at the time. However, a couple of days ago I was using the hosepipe to water some plants that aren't on our irrigation system and I had a brain wave. We have a wooden carport just a few feet from the side of the house and just one screw strategically inserted in a beam would be enough to retain the hosepipe gun at just the correct angle for drenching an overheated human. I excitedly sought out my trusty toolbox and set to work. Soon, after a few minor adjustments we had an outdoor shower. Since then Yvonne and I have been casting caution to the scorching breeze, throwing off our few clothes on a regular basis when at home and enjoying a good cooling off extremely frequently. We're almost now looking for excuses to go outside and enjoy the sensation of cool water running all over us. Bliss!!

So, to return to Gary's statement, which I referred to

earlier, "It's a bit of a misnomer that really." This was in reference to the fact that we were now, come the first of November 2005, just a few months after having arrived here in our trusty Mitsubishi L300 van, the proud owners of a five-year old Suzuki Swift. We'd thus far been doing all our trips up and down the island in the van, which would frequently attract the attention of the Greek Police. A vehicle with British licence plates is always going to get a good staring at from any roadside police officers. But a commercial vehicle, especially one that doesn't look like it's simply being used by a few intrepid tourists who'd be mad enough to drive to Greece from the UK, well that's sure as there were scalpel marks on Michael Jackson's face going to get stopped.

The truth is there are far too many British registered vehicles roaming the roads of Rhodes. The regulations state that a vehicle from another European Union country may remain on Greek soil (well, asphalt - if it's lucky) for up to six months before leaving again. Either that or it must be registered with Greek plates, which costs a small fortune for older vehicles. For example, it would have cost us three times what the van was worth to register it with Greek plates, so we had to either park it up and use it as a shed, or find someone who wanted to buy it. The fact that we managed to do the latter resulted in great rejoicing on our part! And the cost is only the easy part of it, imagine the bureaucracy involved in registering a British van here, when even a Greek can't just go and buy a commercial vehicle without papers to show that he's in the kind of business that necessitates the use of such a vehicle in the pursuit of his livelihood.

There are loads of ex-pat Brits here, though, who still run around in their British registered cars. The authorities had taken a relaxed attitude to it in times past, but, with the increase during the "noughties" of British people moving out here, they decided it was time to make a stand. Despite the difficulties it was going to create if we'd kept our van, I'm glad they did. After all, it's great if you can flout the law and tootle around from home to beach to taverna to town with no road tax, no vehicle roadworthiness certificate and no insurance. Great - that is - until you have an accident. Plus, if you're the *legal* driver and one of these British-plated cars hits you, you're going to be well pleased aren't you?

Accidents are not all that rare here either. The reason for this is evident to anyone who uses the roads, however briefly. Frequently you'll drive past a wreck that I reckon the Police have instructed to be left where it is for a while as a salutary warning to all the Michael Schumachers that zip around the Rhodean roads.

So now the Police, who are terminally bored much of the time anyway, can often be seen parked beside the road, usually near a junction, waiting to flag down some poor harassed motorist and do a spot check. When we still had the van we were stopped four times in three months. I'm very glad we had all our papers in order or I'd be an expert on Greek prison food by now. The usual routine was:

We're travelling along the "Rodo-Lindos" highway, maybe passing the main junction with the road into Arhangelos. Just before the junction there's the familiar Greek cop, standing by his little white Citroen Xzara with his whistle in his mouth (you seldom see one outdoors without it) and he's pointing his finger at YOU. His other hand now gestures for you to pull over onto the shoulder. He approaches your window and asks to see your "diploma", which to us Brits is our Driving Licence. That's all in order, though he makes sure he's giving you his sternest "*don't mess with me sonny*" look (even though he's probably half my age!) over his ever-present shades while perusing it. He hands it back to you and then wants to see proof of insurance. In my case (phew!!) I had the "green card", which is actually not a card at all, but a sheet of green paper. Never mind, it proves my insurance is valid for another couple of months yet. Looking rather disappointed, he kicks the tyres and asks what we're doing on his island and where we're going. Realising that he hasn't caught a villain (in the shape of an ex-pat British vehicle that's been here more than the permitted six months), he assures us he's just doing a seatbelt check and waves us on our way.

That's the thing here in Greece. You have to have proof of insurance about your person while driving at all times. You also have to have the vehicle's registration document (if it's Greek registered) with you. So I keep a photocopy of mine at home in case my little Swift is ever stolen. Fat chance of that really, but there's a first time for everything.

While Gary and his men have been busy rearranging the terracotta tiles on our future roof for the umpteenth time (and literally begging to get malignant melanoma as they never use sun protection) to get the various shades to look right together, I've been squatting close by, while carefully using a scalpel to remove the vinyl decals advertising "G.A.M. Car Hire" from my newly acquired Suzuki Swift's doors. I am at the rear tailgate just making "Friendly Service" read "endly Serv" when Yvonne presents Gary and the men with another cuppa. It's now that Gary looks across at me, my tongue busily caressing my top lip as I achieve "endly S" without marking the paintwork, he dunks another rich tea and says, "It's a bit of a misnomer that really, isn't it."

Now, this is still at the stage in our relationship when I

don't get his attempts at humour. So I bristle, but continue on, achieving "end" before he proceeds to further enlighten me as to what he's getting at.

"I mean, 'SWIFT' is one word you wouldn't use to describe one of those little blighters, would you."

"Friendly Service" now consigned to the plastic bag full of vinyl shavings, I reach for my trusty bottle of car wax to attempt to remove the "G.A.M. Car Hire" and "Friendly Service" shaped shiny bits that remain on the doors and tailgate, when he asks, "You didn't buy that from a car hire bloke did you?"

Duh?

Now I really bristle, as he's obviously about to attempt to offer some advice, belatedly. "Only I could have told you never to buy a car from a car hire place. They're all crooks and you'll buy a 'shed' as sure as eggs is eggs." I'm still deciding what to say in reply when he continues, "Best way to buy a used car here is: go to town, buy the local paper and pick one up through the small ads. You stand a better chance of getting something half-decent."

Now, to be even-handed here, his advice about car hire vehicles is probably generally correct. But he is unaware of the fact that George (the "G" in G.A.M.") knows John and Wendy, our friends and landlords, and has been renting vehicles to them for a couple of seasons already. George is the gentlest man you could ever meet and not at all like most fiery Greeks. Plus he had already kitted out – at his own expense - one of his small four-wheel-drive vehicles with a tow-bar so that John can take his jet-RIB down to the sea whenever he's here. In short, George has a vested interest in looking after both John and Wendy and ourselves, as he's well aware of the ongoing business he'll be getting whenever John and Wendy, or any of our mutual friends, are over here for a visit. George would know that to sell us a "shed" would lose him a great deal of repeat business. John had asked him to sort out a modest car for Yvonne and I before we even arrived here and George had promised that, when he had a good one, that is one with a sound engine, he'd let us know. He even let us have it for a weekend before we decided whether to buy it so we could be sure it was what we wanted. I'd "swiftly" taken it to my friend and motor mechanic Adonis, who'd given it the once-over before we'd gone back to George and shaken hands on it.

So all in all, I don't need this type of advice from a well-meaning Gary. Plus, had this conversation been taking place about three years later, I'd be able to counter with a witty put-down that would see Gary grin from ear to ear, as he loves a good verbal tussle. So I settle for a "We'll see won't we." And polish away slightly more vigorously.

What's odd really, is the fact that Gary is a petrol-head. He can work wonders with things mechanical. Yet if you'd seen the "sheds" he turns up in for work you'd be left wondering, nay, recalling the expression, "physician, heal thyself."

The funny thing is, four years on, Gary's been through a number of "sheds" or "lemons" and changed gearboxes, steering racks and various other mechanical stuff on them, even re-sprayed one or two (he's very good at that, it must be said), and we're still running round in our little Swift. Gary's even done a service on it a couple of times for us and the last time he did so said to me as he dropped the keys into my hand, "It's a good little runner that. Goes pretty well for a one litre. Engine's sweet as a nut."

I didn't remind him of his previous pearls of wisdom. I just accepted the compliment gratefully!

Tzatziki for You to Say

2 - Livestock

I have acquired a whole new respect, nay affection, for ants. It's strange isn't it? I mean, in the UK it's common to dash into the kitchen for a kettle of hot water, fiendish frown on one's brow, as one races to exterminate as many of the little blighters as one can, having discovered the location of the dreaded ants' nest in the garden. Since moving over here, I've changed. I'll explain.

Our *avli* (terrace) is paved with ceramic tiles and contains several tables and even more chairs. A couple of potted plants now soften its ambience, as we decided that most *avlis* look much more "warm" or "homely" with a plant or three strategically placed by a pillar or near an arch. All through the year we regularly take lunch on the *avli*, a procedure that invariably results in bits of food dropping on to the tiles around our feet. Also, there are frequently dead insects of varying descriptions (or those in the throes of dying) to be seen lying around.

It was while eating breakfast out there one morning that my eye was drawn to a spot somewhere near my left foot. I had caught a small movement in my peripheral vision and wanted to check it out. Easing another spoonful of yogurt-and-banana-covered muesli into my mouth, I glanced downward to see a team of tiny ants, all working in concert to transport a dead fly away from the ceramic tiles of the terrace and off to the flower bed out front. My curiosity aroused, I gave this little logistic operation my full attention, only to elicit another comment from Yvonne to the effect that I never listen to her when she's telling me something. It's strange isn't it, how one's visual attention can be drawn to something so intensely as to make one's ears cease to function. Happens with me all the time. Sorry, did you say something there?

"How do I know what she said?" You may ask. Simple: because she eventually prodded my arm to ensure I was in "audio reception" mode before castigating me and repeating her comment.

The distance from the area around my feet to the edge of the terrace was probably eight feet. Yet by the time I'd finished my breakfast the little team of engineers had accomplished their task and our *avli* was free of one more piece of organic debris. Since that time we've both frequently watched with great admiration as these little six-legged wonders perform their task of cleaning our terrace of old breadcrumbs, dead insects, water melon pips and all sorts of other odd stuff that litters it up. They perform this task at great risk to their own personal safety too. I mean we walk in and out without regard to the location(s) of their little ant "scouts" who wander systematically over the tiles in their endless search for something to remove. How many we must have walked on unwittingly doesn't bear thinking about.

So, as stated earlier, I've acquired a whole new respect for ants. Come to think of it, if it's got six legs it's OK with me, generally. There's a kind of wasp we get here in the high summer that looks really mean. And I mean "*mean.*" It's as big as the last section of your middle finger and a sort of dark reddish-brown in colour. The joint between its thorax and abdomen is so small as to be the envy of every anorexic would-be model. The abdomen has a thick yellow stripe around it, which just adds to the sense of menace it exudes. Yet by and large it's not aggressive. In fact during the high summer, when there has been no rain for weeks, they will come from nowhere at the first sniff of water. Whenever we are using our exotic outdoor shower (well, our hose pipe rigged up just high enough and with the gun set to "spray" so we can cool off when we're sitting outdoors in the shade) they'll turn up, probably by the half a dozen or so, to fly through the spray around us and to perch on the periphery of the wet area on the ground to suck up the liquid of life. Often we'll accidentally swipe one with a hand as we go about the business of showering, but they never become aggressive, they just carry on as though we weren't there.

We don't mind these creatures at all, though I still haven't found out what they're called, even after e-mailing a couple of web sites that purport to be able to answer such questions. But we get a bit fed up when we have guests and these little flying neighbours arrive for a bit of a mooch around. Our guests usually start flailing their arms about and standing up, often with the effect of knocking food and drinks hither and thither as the table gets a hefty rocking in the process. We continue to sip our ouzos, wine or fruit juice through our straws and pretend not to notice the wasps, but the visitors still feel they need to swipe at them for all they're worth in a (usually vain) attempt to consign them to oblivion. I actually do get quite upset if someone succeeds in bringing one down. It's quite sad seeing it on the terrace tiles, wiggling its legs in its death throws as our guest proceeds to assume their original sitting position with an air of "There, I saved you from this dangerous beast" about them. A lot of ex-pats call them hornets just to emphasise their suspicion that these creatures are malevolent, but they're actually a kind of wasp. Well, I think so and who's writing this stuff anyway?

Still, at least it gives the ants some work on the nightshift. Whenever we do see such a body, it's usually gone by the morning as the ants often carry out their cleaning routine during the night time hours.

Now, if something has just that extra couple of legs, you know, adding up to *eight*, that's a slightly different story. I try very hard not to dislike spiders. I really do. But it's very hard to be that way here. I'll illustrate.

There's one particular type here in Rhodes which gets rather large, in fact large enough to do a passable job of covering the palm of your hand when its all grown up. Its legs are often striped too, making it look quite the formidable foe. When it runs, it goes like the proverbial clappers and, if you're unlucky enough to encounter one in your living room during the evening, it'll be all you can do to keep up with it if you want to either capture it or, dare I say, swot the fiend. When it's at rest it lays its legs out to the sides, flat and close together, almost like a bird's wings when outstretched; just ever so slightly "fanned". You wouldn't even think it was the same type as that I've just described, until you actually see it start to move, when its legs assume the classic horror-film stance, arched, jointed, ready-to-run.

I am watching TV late at night. It's the small hours. It's another of those nights when I wake up after midnight and can't sleep for so long that I eventually get up and do something. Sometimes I'll switch on the Mac to write, other times – if there is moonlight - I'll take a stroll round the garden or, as in this case, watch some American movie or other, with Greek subtitles, on the TV. Suddenly I'm aware of the fact that there's movement on the screen and it's not part of the picture. I recover from the initial shock and immediately do the thing you have to do in such circumstances, switch on as many lights as I can so as to get a good "visual" of the situation.

Easing my way to the wall switch, eyes never leaving the object of my dismay, I throw light on the problem. It's one of the afore-described monstrosities, actually sitting on the TV screen. Now, I know it must be down to conditioning. Something must have happened to me when I was younger. Maybe all those awful horror books I used to read when I was in school, I don't know. Perhaps even the thought of Frodo Baggins and his duel with Shelob in "The Lord of the Rings," I can't put my finger on it.

No, literally, I can't! For all the fact that I don't want to see one of God's creatures become a smudge on my wall, not to say the bottom of my slipper or piece of tissue, I am not one of those men who can just pick up one of these adversaries with my bare hands. The really spindly ones I can usually manage, but the formidable ones with the thick legs and chunky bodies, not negotiable I'm afraid.

So now, with all the lights on and my eyes smarting from the sudden intensity of the brightness, I proceed to plan my strategy. There's no way I can safely go back to bed with this monster on the loose in the lounge, just feet from the bedroom door, which has a gap under it.

I retreat to the kitchen area, still in sight of the TV in our mercifully open-plan home. I am able to keep my eyes on "Shelob" as I do so. Just for a fleeting instant I take my eyes off my foe to open a kitchen cupboard and reach for as large a glass tumbler as I can find. Turning back to check on the adversary's position I'm horrified to find it's moved. Now what? I decide to continue with Plan A and grab a piece of copier paper from the office, fold it into two for added rigidity, and tentatively approach the TV.

"Where the devil are you?" I mutter almost aloud. "Come on out you swine and face the music like a man!" Well, like a male spider anyway. I don't under any circumstances want to wake Yvonne-Maria because what I don't need at this moment is a naked hysterical woman screaming, "GET IT! KILL IT! DON'T BE SO SLOW! STOP BEING A WET COWARD AND FIND IT! GET RID OF IT, etc…" You get the general idea.

I gingerly tap the TV set and, as I do so, my enemy zips out from under the set at lightning speed, down the front of the TV cabinet, across a metre of so of floor and up the white (thank goodness) wall to the CD racks that are mounted a few feet from the floor. I almost jump out of my skin, but manage not to drop the glass on the ceramic tiled floor. I now stare at the beast, which is virtually at eye level, as I'm crouched on my heels, glass in one hand, folded sheet of paper in the other, sweat breaking out all over my body, but especially under my arms. In this current position there's no way I could use the glass as the crafty monster is right up in the corner where the wall meets the light oak colour of the CD rack.

Now what? I have to get him to move, so I can get an opportunity to swiftly pop the glass over him, before sliding the piece of paper under it to trap him, so I can then dash out into the night and throw him out onto the flower bed. I wave a hand about a foot away from him to see if he'll be freaked into moving. No luck. The sweat is now running down my two sides. At least I'm not wearing anything on top, so I'm not soaking another one of my t-shirts.

Without warning, the adversary decides to dash off again. This time it runs horizontally along the wall, right across the frame and glass panes of the closed window in this particular wall, and towards the front door. I hover above it with the glass, barely able to keep up, it's running so fast, and realise to my horror that even this glass isn't big enough to trap this gargantuan foe and I have to think of another solution in double-quick time.

All this takes place in milliseconds, but I realise that the trajectory of my adversary takes it right to the front door, almost halfway between the floor and the top of the frame. I dash to the door, grab the handle and pull it open wide, thinking all the while: "I'd rather cop a couple of mosquito bites than leave this baby on the loose in my home!" Almost on cue the eight-legged terror runs right round the doorframe, out of the house and on to the outside wall. Quick as a flash I close the door, being careful not to do it too vigorously so as not to wake my beloved. I then turn and fall back against the door, heaving a massive sigh of relief as I mentally resolve that this night I most certainly won't be going out for a moonlight stroll. There's no way that door is going to be opened again until sweet, lovely, broad daylight has returned.

All I have to do now is unstick my bare back from the uPVC surface of the door and fetch a damp cloth to wipe the back-shaped perspiration patch from its surface. This night I think I'm going back to bed. I'll stick Eric Clapton & J.J. Cale's "Road to Escondido" on the iPod in an attempt to get my dreams away from giant arachnids devouring me from above and try and drop off until morning.

On more than one occasion, during the day, we've discovered one of the formidable spider types, evidently female, lurking under the rug that we usually place on the tiles outside our French windows. We've discovered to our horror, on lifting the rug to shake it, that it was indeed a female when we've tried to brush her away from the proximity of our doorway, only for her to begin haemorrhaging babies by the thousand (or so it appeared) from her abdomen! Suddenly the ceramic tiles outside the French windows would be alive with tiny eight-legged offspring running in all directions.

Aware of the fact that every single one of them had the potential to grow into one of those frightening, palm-of-the-hand-sized adults that can outrun your vigorous attempts to swot it, we'd grab a brush and sweep for all we were worth in an attempt to get the newborns as far from our building's egress as possible. The thought of innumerable potential night-frights, each no bigger than a couple of pin-heads as of yet, making their way into the house and secretly growing up behind the sofa brought scenes from the movie "arachnophobia" vividly to mind.

One of the hazards of living in the Mediterranean climate is that, when you go out for the evening, if the winds are light there's a good chance that on your return there'll be a regular cornucopia of insect life infesting the area around the wall-lamp, not to mention all sorts of flying bodies zipping around and around in the spherical meter or so of air around it too. Of course there will also be a few geckos hanging around to pick up their evening meal, plus we've returned home before now to see a brown snake, maybe a couple of feet long, slithering up the wall beside the window so it could also drop in at the free takeaway.

My wife's usual reaction is one of aversion, especially to the snakes, although they usually beat a retreat if humans show up. She also used to utter expressions of disdain at the quite beautiful Mediterranean toads, which also frequently put in an appearance on the terrace during the evening, attracted, as are the snakes and geckos, by the prospect of a tasty morsel or two. I suppose if the truth were known that the toads may well also serve as a meal for the snakes, but thankfully we've never witnessed this and hope we don't. My wife used to say "uuuueeeaaarll" on seeing a toad. All that changed though in just one evening.

We returned home at an hour approaching midnight and, as I drove the car into the carport, the headlights revealed a nice fat toad, about the size that would fit snugly into your hand, positioned right up close to the house wall and sideways on to it. The usual expression came from Yvonne's lips until I suggested she watch what was very likely to happen imminently. I'd spotted a substantially sized spider just inches away from the toad and walking totally unwittingly along the tiles, right adjacent to the wall, toward the said toad. Much as I had hoped, the spider was yet a few inches from the toad when the toad's tongue flew out, lapped up the eight-legged fiend and whipped it back into its mouth all within the proverbial batting of an eyelid.

Oddly enough, ever since that occasion Yvonne-Maria has loved the toads. We've even nicknamed them "Tassos" (all of them, regardless of which sex they may be), or, if they're small, "Tassaki." Whenever she sees one out on the *avli* of an evening she goes into paroxysms of delight and talks to them as though they were our pets, even expressing the wish that they were.

Some time back we were sipping cool drinks with Brenda, our friend in the village of Pilona, when we got around to discussing the "wildlife" problems heretofore discussed. She said she also found it difficult on some occasions, when returning home from a night out and with no man to brave the situation confronting her, to get into her house via the front door if she'd left the light above the door on for the evening.

"I have to duck and go for the door with the key already in hand in the hope that I'll get it into the keyhole quickly before I end up with various species of 'livestock' attached to me!" she said. At our place we have sort of beaten this particular problem now. Fortunately for us, we have two sets of lights recessed into the ceiling under our front portico. We can mercifully leave the farther lights on, whilst those right above the front door are switched off, meaning that the livestock usually gathers sufficiently far enough away from the front door to allow us to get in without a herd of diverse creatures following us.

Of course, if you're keeping your windows open wide during a long hot Greek summer evening, you can usually keep the mosquitoes at bay with the ubiquitous "mozzie screen" that every window here sports. For a long time, though, I was getting woken up during the night in summer with an urgent need to scratch some part of my exposed body, since we often sleep on top of the bed in the high summer months. I'd check the place where I needed to scratch, only to find a miniature version of that huge rock in the middle of Australia, it used to be called Ayers Rock, but I believe it's now known by its Aboriginal name, Uluru. Sometimes in the hot summer nights I find up to half a dozen or so of these raised itchy nightmares on various parts of my body, some as big as your thumbnail – and do they itch!

For a long time we couldn't work out what was causing these extremely irritating "Ulurus," but we've now decided that the culprits are what we now call the "flying full-stops." I guess if you're American you'd call them "Flying periods," but in the UK that conjures up an altogether unpleasant mental picture, trust me. These nasty little so and sos are extremely difficult to stop because they are so small they sail right through the mosquito screen with total disdain and head straight for a nice exposed bit of flesh, whereupon they alight, bite and take once more to flight. Just typing about them on this much cooler late October night is giving me the itches and I'm compelled to scratch my neck, posterior and arms. They have the tendency to hover around you if you're sitting outside at dusk and you just see this tiny black speck, just like a full-stop, which will often hover irritatingly close to your face, yet they prove very difficult to swat. I don't like using chemicals, but each season I crumble and give in by purchasing a bottle of insect repellent which I liberally spray all over any of my flesh that may be exposed during an evening or night. They still manage to get me on a regular basis, but that's where my trusty Lane's Tea Tree & Witch Hazel Cream comes into its own again. If you read the chapter in *Moussaka to My Ears* about the time my wife called me the "Elephant Man," owing to an allergy to a certain caterpillar which infested the surrounding countryside almost to plague proportions a couple of Februarys back, you'll remember that the only source of relief I was able to find was this miraculous cream. So I always keep several tubes of it in various locations around the house and frequently during summer nights find myself up in the small hours reaching for the nearest tube, so I can smear it over an "Uluru" that's appeared while I tried vainly to sleep. In fact these days, whenever we pay a visit to the UK, top of my priority list is the purchase of three or four tubes of the stuff. Don't know where I'd be without it, to be frank.

Having spent a number of vacations on the nearby island of Symi, we can vouch for the fact that the Symi spiders are really formidable. I mean, *really*. These chaps aren't spiders in the normal sense of the word, they're beasts. I used to know someone in South Wales who had a pet tarantula. He kept it in a rectangular glass fish-tank (without the water, obviously!) and fed it live grasshoppers. The tank had a piece of glass as its top on which he would place a house brick because otherwise the beast was able to move the glass on its own! I have to say that the Symi spider does a passable impression of a tarantula. Ask my friends James and Neil who live on Symi and run a business about two thirds of the way up the Kali Strata (about 450 stone steps than take the intrepid walker from a small street behind Symi Harbour up to Chorio, the village on top of the hill). They even have a couple of photos of these mutant monsters on their website, try going to this URL, but be warned!!

http://www.symidream.com/images/spider.jpg

Or here's one taken indoors…

http://www.symidream.com/images/symi%20spider.jpg

There, I told you. You'd have been better off just leaving those links where they were on this page wouldn't you. Don't go blaming me if you have nightmares now. The Symi spider surely is nothing short of tarantula-like both in size and shape. Apparently they're quite harmless, but Yvonne-Maria and I have come across them on several occasions during warm Symi evenings, as they add to their legendary menace by being nocturnal, of course.

We've been walking back to our accommodation through the dimly lit back streets, most no wider than a small car with its mirrors folded in, only to encounter the dreaded SS calmly strolling right across the alley on the smooth flags in front of us. We simply stop and wait for it to complete its journey before continuing ours. It's the only way. Once we stayed in a small studio toward the rear of Symi Harbour, where the access was up a fairly steep stone staircase from between two buildings at street level. We came back from a splendid evening spent at a local taverna, followed by a nightcap at our favourite waterfront bar, pleasantly lubricated by a warming Metaxa. On turning from the street to ascend the more dimly lit and menacingly dark stone steps, of which there were probably twenty or so, we saw to our horror that, sitting squarely in the middle step of a group of three or four, was the thing we most feared, the Symi Spider.

After several minutes of wondering how we were going to get up the steps to our rooms, we decided, since our adversary had made no attempt to move, that the only way to get past it was to jump for it, hopefully completely missing the step on which it rested. We just had to hope that neither of us missed our footing, the outcome of which was beyond contemplation. I went first and made it – to my great relief - to the second step above the arachnid in question. My spirited though slightly less confident wife took some time before finally mustering up the courage to make her jump, narrowly escaping a fall as I grabbed her hand and pulled her to safety.

On still another occasion, whilst enjoying a splendid meal at the taverna we like best in the whole of Symi Harbour, Taverna O Meraklis, run by Sotiri and his wife, who we've now known since 1993, one of these huge beasts came trolling across the shiny stone flags and proceeded to trot along beneath the tables and chairs of the taverna, which of course were all laid out on the narrow street in front of the taverna building. One of the female diners spotted the invader and promptly leapt to her feet, sending an assortment of tzatziki, salad, Retsina and "big beans" flying in several directions. Panic erupted as more diners caught their first glimpse of Symi's hidden terror. Tables and chairs tumbling all around us, we all stood up as Sotiri exited the building with what looked like a coal shovel, found the offending hand-sized invader and brought the said shovel mercilessly down hard on top of it.

The weird thing about the Symi Spider is the fact that, if you swot one, it goes to "nothing." It is evidently full of very little actual substance while alive. Once swotted, you stare at its remains and wonder what the fuss was all about. If you, like me, have a problem with any "livestock" which sports a leg number of eight, you most certainly couldn't get within feet of one of these, leave alone pick one up - while they're alive; but once dead they seem quite pitiful and you find yourself wondering why you were quite so terrified by it.

One year, whilst we were sitting very late one evening in Hari's bar (now re-located), right at the rear of the harbour, enjoying a good chilling session with a couple from Britain who we'd met several times on vacation on Symi, a Symi spider put in an appearance. Hari, who ran the bar, had his cousin "Mad" Mihali working for him as his "get 'em in" man. Mihalis certainly lived up to his nickname. He almost broke my spine once trying to show me how he cures back problems. He was, however, a great person to spend an hour or two with over a late evening drink.

Carol and Colin were the friends from Britain. With Carol and Yvonne-Maria now in hysteria mode and standing stiletto-heeled on the comfy cushions in the cane chairs as they spotted the invader trotting through the bar beneath them, Mad Mihalis sprang into action. I thought he was going to end this creature's days. No way. Mihalis swept the thing up in his ample hand, although even then leaving spider extremities still visible all around his closed fist, ran a few metres away and released the monster at what he considered a safe distance. The girls remained nervous for the rest of the evening, not happy that such a threat still remained in close proximity, even though the fiend never had the nerve to put in another appearance that night.

Another regular visitor to our garden is the locust. No, we don't get them in Egyptian proportions, thank goodness. But one is enough to cause major damage to our fig tree's leaves. Last year I discovered that the game little tree (which despite still being only a couple of feet high, already produces a respectable number of delicious dusty purple figs every summer, usually in late August and September) was having its leaves eaten away at a rate of knots. Closer examination revealed that a locust had taken to sitting quietly on the main trunk and taking its meals as and when it felt hungry, it's sole diet being our fig tree's leaves. Despite numerous attempts to make it fly away, it would soon return and continue its assault on our poor tree. Finally in desperation my normally even-tempered wife took her sweeping brush and pulverised the offender. Woe betide any of its relatives who show themselves in our garden since then. If my dearly-beloved sees one it doesn't usually survive; especially since she's also recently found them on our pride and joy hibiscus plants, to which she regularly gives the "Prince Charles" treatment, talking to them and calling them "my babies!" in much the same way that she talks to the toads.

One good thing about slaughtering locusts though, is the fact that we only have to wait a short while after placing the offender's carcass on our ceramic tiles near the house, to see a formidable army of ants put in an appearance. First the scouts make an inspection, then, within a quarter of an hour or so, I can spend ages squatting nearby and watching as they perform their engineering feat par excellence and gradually drag the body away. They even have a couple of clean-up boys detailed to make an inspection afterwards and clear away any odd bits that may have fallen off the corpse.

I tell you, I've acquired a whole new respect for ants since moving here.

"My hero!"
"Mad" Mihalis gets rewarded for actually picking up
a Symi spider

3 – *That Sinking Feeling*

John's got a "jet-RIB." No, I didn't know what a "jet-RIB" was either. Basically, it's a jet-ski with a fibreglass hull all around it, above which is an inflatable tube-type-thing, making it look somewhat like one of those things you see people going white-water rafting in, only smaller. It goes like a rocket. In fact it's quick enough to tow a water-skier. The "RIB" bit stands for, apparently, "rigid inflatable boat". Obvious when someone tells you, eh? But I couldn't work it out either.

Two people can ride this craft like they would a jet ski. Plus there is room in the area around the jet-ski part, in the bit that's "inflatable" that is, for a couple more passengers, but it's much more fun with just the two aboard. John used to keep it in Swansea marina, but was always disappointed by how seldom the temperamental British weather would allow him to go out with it and "play". So, when we made the move out here to Rhodes in August 2005, John decided that, not only would he and Wendy make the drive out here with us in tandem, but that he'd take the opportunity to tow his jet-RIB all the way across Europe too. He kitted out a Renault Espace with a tow bar and so, Espace plus jet-RIB in tow, plus

Mitsubishi L300 van for my beloved and I, we set off on the morning of August 19th for the four-day trek which ended with us driving up a dust-track to our new home on Rhodes on the morning of Tuesday August 23rd.

I really ought to have remembered that whenever John took me out on the "RIB," there'd be problems. One time, back in Oxwich Bay, a beauty spot on the Gower peninsula in South Wales, he'd taken it out with me on the back for a bit of "wave crashing". That's what I call it when he gets out of the bay into the less sheltered ocean waters and drives it at right angles to the direction of the waves so we can crash down (not your backbone's very favourite pastime!) between them for fun. Obviously some new understanding of the word "fun" that I wasn't previously aware of.

To be fair, I was actually enjoying having my spine pulverised when, glancing forward over John's shoulder, my hands losing their circulation as they held on grimly for dear life through the grab-straps attached to the inflatable on either side of me, I spotted the fuel gauge. It read empty.

Now I'm not normally the sort to panic. But I decided to refer John to this fact, just in case he'd forgotten to fuel up, as we were possibly a half a mile or so from the safety of the bay at this point in quite choppy seas.

"The fuel gauge reads EMPTY. Is that OK?" I asked, trying to sound cool.

"It doesn't work. Don't worry, there's plenty of fuel in there. There should be anyway." Said John, ever in control of the situation.

I didn't intend to feel alarmed, but at this very juncture John decided to turn around and head back toward the bay.

I felt alarmed.

No sooner had we rounded the headland that juts out into

the sea to the west of Oxwich Bay, thus sheltering it from the prevailing winds, than the engine began to splutter.

"We running out of petrol?" I asked. Once again, trying my hardest to sound casual.

"We can't be. I'm sure there's plenty in the tank." This time John's attempt at reassuring me was even less successful. My ears told me a different story. Two hundred yards out from the beach, with the tide about halfway out and receding, the engine died completely. John immediately set about cranking the starter motor. "Could be a problem with dirt in the fuel line." He proffered, confidence evidently draining from him by the second. The beach looked tantalisingly close, though our progress toward it had now ceased. In fact, with the direction the tide was going, we were in danger of being carried back out to sea.

After a few more seconds, which seemed to me like hours, John conceded, "Can't understand this, but looks like we're out of fuel after all." Without a word needing to be said, we both leapt from the central seats to the inflatable sides and began "rowing" with our hands for all we were worth, John trying to keep one of his on the RIB's handlebars to keep the "tiller" pointing in the right direction. That's always assuming jet-RIBs have a tiller. I don't know. When we'd just about run out of puff, I leapt over the side and, mercifully, found we'd managed to get far enough into the bay toward the beach to be in only two feet of water. Oxwich bay is very safe for bathers as it's very shallow and sandy for a couple of hundred metres out from the beach, especially at high tide. John threw me the anchor rope and I walked the boat in toward the beach, where we eventually dropped the anchor and waded ashore, only to collapse on our backs on the sand of the beach and privately express thanks that we weren't at that very moment being swept out along the channel to the open Atlantic, just a few miles to the west.

So, as I said, I really ought to have remembered that whenever John took me out on the "RIB," there'd be problems! But when it's a hot September day at Glystra Beach, a sheltered sandy bay just a mile or two from the house here on Rhodes, you can't help thinking that the correct response to John's "Fancy a go on the jet RIB then?" should be a "Yea, why not?"

With me having responded as detailed above, we've hooked up the trailer to the 4x4 and within ten minutes the jet RIB is sliding into the brine, the wives are finding their places in their current novels, after settling themselves on the sun beds under a parasol, and we're all set for a session of zipping over the water, the warm Greek air caressing our bodies as we go about the serious business of enjoying life.

One of the "toys" John has purchased in order to add to the whole jet RIB experience is what's called an "Airhead." It's about the same diameter as one of those rubber tubes you see boats towing all over the place, with their incumbent's bums skimming the water through the hole in the middle, but it hasn't got a hole as it's not a "tube" at all. Instead it has a central raised area toward what could be called the front, either side of which is a grab handle. The raised bit in the middle assumes the position that a motorbike's fuel tank would do, with the grab handles standing in for the bike's handlebars. There are non-slip pads for your knees toward the rear of the thing, so you leap on, assume a kneeling position, then lean forward to take firm hold of the straps in readiness for John's attempts at throwing you off as he does "sixpenny" turns and all kinds of other heinous manoeuvres in his gleeful attempts to see you hit the brine. The secret is to ride it like you would a motorbike. Fine if you've ever done so. Probably a sure way of proving whether your suntan cream's waterproof if not. As John does his tight turns the Airhead at the end of the rope has a tendency to lean outwards, responding to the laws of inertia, so you have to compensate by leaning into the turn, exactly as you would on a motorbike. As I've owned several bikes in the past I soon got the hang of it and can proudly boast that I'm the only person John hasn't succeeded in dunking in the Mediterranean, at least not so far. Mind you, I spent the whole of the next day looking like John Wayne while still in his saddle, only minus the horse, as my thigh muscles burned so badly!

As it turns out this particular day, he isn't going to need the airhead to get me immersed. Following his vain attempt to dunk me, we disconnect the line to the Airhead and set off, the two of us, in the RIB for a rocky bit of coast where we'll maybe don snorkels and fall over the side for a mooch around. But then, maybe we won't. John finds a quiet spot a little away from some rocks, where we can peer down through the turquoise water to a bottom that's maybe thirty feet down and watch the fish ambling around their feeding grounds. He kills the engine for a bit of chilling time. We sit on the inflatable either side of the seats and, dangling hands over the side, start to put the world to rights. We talk about various things as we gently drift for maybe twenty minutes or so, when I decide that my feet are much wetter than I'd assume they ought to be. Looking down I see that the hull is in several inches of water and it seems to be getting deeper at an alarming rate. Once again, I assume my best "I'm sure I'm being silly here, but…" sort of voice and ask:

"Ought there to be so much water inside the boat then?"

John looks at his own feet and, cool as the proverbial cucumber, looks up and says,

"No. We're sinking."

"We're sinking," I repeat. Hoping that he's having a laugh. "Like, *actually* sinking?"

"Well, the boat can't sink entirely, but we are taking in water, so we might have a problem."

At this John leaps to the driving position, applies his thumb to the starter button and presses it.

You know how sometimes something happens, or doesn't, as the case may be, and your brain says, "This isn't really happening. I'm momentarily having a lapse of reason (what a good title for a Pink Floyd album, eh?). I'll blink and it'll be OK." Well, this is one of those moments. I'm sure I'll blink, look down and see just a few cupfuls of water swishing around and John will start the engine and we'll zoom off across the impossibly flat sea.

Umm, no. The water isn't only still there, it's now several inches deeper and it's quite apparent that the boat is sitting far too low in the water. John flips the catches that hold the seat in place, and then hinges the seat up to reveal the engine compartment. The engine is taking a bath in the salt water of the Med. All electrics quite obviously now shorted out. Battery flat, plus very wet too.

John assures me that we're in no immediate danger. Then he tries to make sense of what's happened here.

Now I don't know about you, but a landlubber like me has no idea about "bungs" and things. That's always assuming that "bung" is the correct term to describe the little black rubber things that apparently a lot of fibreglass boats have at their stern just below the water line. They rather resemble the drain lug, which a car engine has in its sump for letting the old oil run out before replacing it by pouring in the new, only they're made of rubber. The idea is that when you winch the craft out of the water and onto its trailer, you can undo the said "bungs," to let out the usually modest amount of seawater that's managed to get into the hull while you've been at sea. Of course, you're then supposed to put them back in, as they're liable to have the reverse effect when the boat's in the water if they're not in place.

"I think I forgot to put the bungs back in last time I took the RIB out of the water." says John, still managing to sound relaxed. Like, Oh, that's all it is then. "It didn't matter when we were making headway," he continues, "as the inertia of the craft kept water from going in through the holes, but once we became stationary in the water, it just flowed in."

"Umm, what are we gonna do then?" I ask.

"Well," says John, "as I said, we won't sink, it's impossible, what with the inflatables, but we'll have to get back to shore somehow and get the RIB out of the water. Then she'll need a good drying out."

"Nothing to it then, eh? " I add, rather too ironically if the truth be told. I go on to ask, "How are we going to do it?" Rather wishing I hadn't, as I already know what the solution is going to be.

"Well, you've got your mask, do you think you could drop over the side, grab the rear and swim it to the shore?"

There is a shingle beach maybe 50 yards away, between us and which is a stretch of water under which lay not a few huge rocks, some very near to the surface. The beach is around the headland from Glystra, where our wives are blithely enjoying their chinwag, hands resting on the open pages of their novels, like they really intend to do any reading while their boys are away playing with their toys and they have the opportunity to share some juicy girl-talk. So it's not going to be easy to let them know where we are and why we've been away for so long. Also, it looks like there is a patch of this beach that's under the auspices of a hotel, since the usually close-knit bunch of thatched umbrellas is in evidence, under which are to be seen the usual collection of lobsters in their sun cream, shades and bathing costumes. There's a small bar toward the rear of the beach too, so maybe once someone spots us struggling toward the shore they'll take pity on us and come to our aid.

I drop over the side, mask on face, and place my hands on the stern. I begin kicking with my legs, á là breaststroke. John assumes the position of lookout at the bow and starts to warn me of approaching rocks, some of which are so near the surface they'd easily take the skin off my knees.

"Left a bit." He opines. I duly adjust my leg kicks to accomplish the change of course.

"Right a bit...

"You're OK for a while now."

I can hardly speak as my head is below the water for 90% of the time sending alarm signals to my brain regarding how near my legs are getting to some very nasty looking rocks, but on hearing this I make a gargantuan effort to raise it enough so my mouth clears the brine and attempt a shout, "I THINK [glug], I THINK I'LL BE THE [glug, glug] JUDGE OF THAT!" I feebly call. I can't see if he's smiling or not.

After what seems like a week I feel the bow touch the steep ledge of shingle where the beach enters the water and, as John jumps overboard holding the anchor rope, I release my grip on the stern and swim the few feet to the shore. My arms feel like that Charles Atlas bloke's arms must have felt after a session of holding that globe aloft for a while. My legs feel like jelly. Not just jelly, but jelly that's not yet set. In short, I've expended myself and now we're faced with the task of trying to beach the boat.

When you're in the water these jet Ribs seems so light. You try getting one out of the water without the benefit of the winch and trailer. We pass a very un-enjoyable ten minutes or so pushing and tugging, as first the bow, then the stern returns to the water as we succeed in getting the other end a little way up the shingly slope.

"Ah, look!" I exclaim, as my eye has wandered along the fifty meters or so of beach to the first of the sun umbrellas and I notice a couple who have begun to stroll along the beach in our general direction. John picks up on my body language and we both exert ourselves even harder in an attempt to elicit a bit of human kindness from the pair. Just when we're going to let out something like... "Thanks! It only needs a bit more muscle and a couple more hands to get it that couple of feet further up the slope," the couple deliberately move a little further from the water line so as to give us a wide berth and continue their stroll right pass the struggling duo.

We catch a snippet or two of their conversation. Not British. Probably Germans we think, but we aren't sure enough to start cursing another nation without good reason. Almost unbelievably they stroll a couple of hundred yards past us, do a u-turn and stroll back, passing us for a second time without so much as a "You've got a hard job on your hands there, chaps!" passing their lips. They studiously avoid making eye contact with either of us and we want desperately to shout and swear at them, but think better of it. What would it accomplish? Actually...

Now I have to say that I'm frequently ashamed to be British when on holiday, the primary reason being the way an unfortunately large percentage of British tourists behave. I'm disgusted at how a lot of the younger generation comport themselves at some of the "party" resorts, like, for example, Faliraki. Yes, I do realise that qualifies me for the "Old Fart's Club." Good!

I also wonder at the mentality of many a British tourist who gets genuinely put out by the fact that he or she can't find HP sauce in a Greek taverna. I vividly recall meeting a British couple of dubious intellect on a superb sandy beach in Kefallonia who once who told me: "We won't be coming back to Kefallonia, oh no." To which I responded with a "Why's that then?"

"Well, ...*there's nothing 'ere is there,*" was the stunningly perspicacious response. "*Nothing*" here? What exactly would have qualified as "*something*" they didn't elaborate on. But I'm willing to bet it would have included amusement arcades, Irish themed bars, British beer and fish and chips; perhaps an "end-of-the pier saucy show" thrown in for good measure. The fact that they stood on a beautifully unspoilt Greek beach, with the crystal clear waters of the Med a few feet away and a perfectly adequate cantina nearby to offer a Greek salad and cold beer for lunch, the cicadas rasping away in the olive groves a little way up the slope behind the beach and the prospect of a warm evening of Greek hospitality in any one of loads of tavernas down the road in Argostoli had evidently qualified as, "*nothing.*"

But there are occasions when the British make me proud. John and I, both disgusted at the evident effort to avoid being of any assistance to us of the couple who'd just walked by, twice, agreed that, if the hotel with its sun beds and umbrellas just along the beach had been filled with British tourists, a clutch of "blokes" would have been with us in minutes, spitting in their palms and saying, *"Got a problem lads? No worries, we'll give you an extra shove."* Whether this may have been simply to impress their female companions or not wouldn't have made any difference. British blokes would be there in a shot to help out, chest medallions swinging over their bronzed hairy chests. Sometimes a British bloke comes through.

The problem here is, though, there don't appear to be any British on this particular beach. Never mind, John has a waterproof pouch for his cell phone, so he can use it when out on his boat in case of emergencies. The only snag is, he's left it on the beach at Glystra with Wendy. After a couple more minutes of chewing over the alternatives, it's decided that I should walk back to Glystra and get Wendy to call "Gary," who built our house, as he's sure to be able to help us out, him being a petrol-head and all that.

So a few minutes later, there I am striding purposefully along the beach toward the rocky promontory that cuts off this beach from the one at Glystra (where the women lay blissfully unaware of our plight), my feet hurting as they're crammed into Johns' rubber sea shoes which are several sizes too small for me. I scramble up twenty feet or so of rocks to the top of the promontory and stride hesitantly into the undergrowth in the direction of the dunes that sweep down onto Glystra.

Why is it that all the undergrowth in Greece is designed to slash your skin to ribbons? Have you ever noticed that? Whenever Yvonne and I go walking during winter time we wear denim jeans and heavy walking boots to avoid returning home an hour or two later with blood running down our thighs and calves, as we often strike out away from the lane to get a different perspective of a view, or to reach some spot we've never stood at before to take in the natural beauty all around us.

When you're setting out with the full knowledge that you'll be tackling the Greek "bush" you know what to wear in preparation. When you're faced with the need to make your way through the same type of scrub with only a T-shirt and your swimming trunks for protection (not to mention a pair of rubber boating shoes that are too small for your bare feet anyway!), you tend to tread very warily. It's not just the vicious plants either. On more than one occasion I've almost walked straight into a spider hanging in its two-foot-wide web, looking for all the world like a huge crab that ought to be somewhere just below the water line.

After mercifully sustaining only a few small scratches I exit the undergrowth and come into sight of Glystra, where I spot the women, who are looking at their watches and then out to sea as though they really are wondering where their men are. They don't spot me until I'm close enough to offer to rub some more sun cream on them as they seem only to be able to look toward the sea, evidently still expecting that we'll return that way. This irritates me as I've just trudged all along the beach, past loads of tourists who were all wondering why this weird bloke has trotted past waving his arms and whistling at nothing in particular that they could see, since the objects of my gesticulating were totally unaware that I was there.

"Where've you two been? Where's John (the other John that is. Of course – you knew that didn't you)? where's the boat?" They ask. I explain, to the inevitable "Trust you two. Should have known you'd get into bother..." and so on. Amazing how these aren't the moments when you feel like saying "Darling, I love you" isn't it? We fish John's mobile phone out of his bag and call Gary, who, in between guffaws of laughter, promises to get down to the beach where the boat is as soon as he can.

I stand looking at the women. They stare back at me. They've realised before I have that John won't know what's happening unless I make the return trip on foot, to tell him that Gary will be along as soon as he can.

For the second time that day I get that sinking feeling.

Tzatziki for You to Say

4 – Hares And Hosepipes

Our garden is finally taking shape. The perimeter fence having been completed some eighteen months or so after we moved in, the front gates having finally been lifted into position and dropped on to their hinges, we are beginning to feel that we may finally risk planting something that may stand a chance of growing to maturity before being eaten either by pigs or goats. Hey, we may even eat some of it!

Of course, there are loads of Greeks who don't have complete fences around their properties. But then, loads of Greeks have dogs tied up and left to their own devices for 90% of the time. Goats approach, dog barks, goats retreat, end of story. Just about all the Greek friends we've made so far never relent in their efforts to get us to have a dog from them. This is largely because they wouldn't dream of getting their animals neutered. That would, heaven forbid, cost money! So we can hardly pass the time of day with any number of people without them insisting that we take one (or more) of their new litter of puppies. They don't understand at all when we say that we wouldn't want a dog for several reasons. One, it could get poisoned, as happens all too often, as you'll know if you read the chapter in "*Moussaka to My Ears*" about Lady, the dog that our neighbours Mac and Jane adopted, only to have their hearts broken when she died an agonising death through the wanton use of poison in the country tracks around here. Two, a dog is a tie that would mean we'd be putting upon others to care for it if we were to be away for any length of time, like, for example, during a visit to the UK. Three, we don't want a dog!

"We don't want a dog" doesn't compute at all to a rural Greek. Not, of course, that they have them as pets like us crazy Brits. No, but a dog is an essential tool in the area of vegetable security, not to mention the "home" kind too. Have dog will eat. Simple. There's no legitimate argument against such logic says our friend Mihalis.

We've begun our vegetable growing careers with a recommendation from Mihalis, who was born and raised in Kalathos and has grown vegetables and tended livestock since he was running around in nappies, so that's upward of four and going on five decades. Well, it's slightly more than a recommendation really. Mihalis had dropped a plastic carrier bag in the car when we saw him one evening. In it we found a lot of pink beans with black spots on them.

"So, I just push them in and wait for them to grow?" I ask, really rather hopefully if the truth be told.

"No, no." replies Mihalis, a serious expression on his face indicating that the planting and raising of vegetables is anything but something to be taken frivolously. After all, these simple British folk have finally realised that you can't eat flowers and set aside a rather too small area of their garden for his liking as the place to grow sensible stuff; you know, stuff you can eat and not just shove your nose into so you can go: "Aaaah, smell that. Isn't it wonderful?" ...just as a bee flies up your nose. Mihalis explains what you must do in order to grow these beans successfully.

"First you make dish. You understand?" At this stage in my Greek-learning process (circa summer 2007) he makes attempts to explain to me in his very poor English.

I'm mystified. "I make *dish?*" I ask, wondering if he also expects me to install a potter's wheel somewhere.

"Yeees. You take, …what you say? This thing…" he's now miming some kind of garden tool with his hands that I eventually come to understand is a trowel. Well, perhaps. "You take this and you arrange the *ho'ma* like dish." I eventually (after he's already torn out some of his rapidly receding hair, which he can ill-afford to lose) get the point. I must scoop the soil (the *ho'ma*) so as to create a breakfast-cereal-sized "bowl" at regular intervals along what will eventually become my "row" of beans. These "dishes" will be the receptacles, which we'll fill with water on a daily basis while waiting for the beans to grow.

"Now," he continues, "you have *molee'vi*, and you push four times, like the clock." From this I gather that I must use a pencil to push four small holes into the edges of the "dishes" at the four "compass points" so to speak. Into these holes I am to drop an individual bean, then scoop the soil to cover the hole into which the bean has been dropped.

"You must water every day, every day." Since these beans are usually planted during August, that's a given really.

"Doesn't sound too difficult." I opine.

"No finish. I no finish!" Exclaims Mihalis, with the utmost earnestness. "When you have green about this high…" Here he gestures with his hands to show me that he means that once the young shoots reach about four or five inches in height, "you choose the best and pull out the two most small, most *adee'nato'*. So you have two good plants you let grow from here." Ah, so we're not growing four plants per "dish," as it were. We're going to select the strongest two and tear out the two weakest out from each "dish" and leave the best two to continue growing. This is starting to get a bit too involved for me by this stage. I decide to be patient and let Mihalis complete my horticultural lesson. He goes on:

"When you have nice plant like so," now I grasp from his hand movements that he means when the plants are about football sized, "...you see long, how you call it? ...Like this." Once again I have to work out what he's saying. At this stage the plants will be sending out long shoots that will be looking for something to climb up. I try to be intuitive here and suggest that I shove in some bamboo sticks.

He disapproves. "No, no! You cut just above two leaves. So the plant goes stronger." Then you will have flowers. Then you will have beans. But you keep cutting the...the..." he's lost for his English words again...

"Shoots?" I suggest,

"Yes, shoots. Shoots? That what you do with an *oploh*? [gun]." I explain as best I can what a 'shoot' is when one is talking botanically.

So, I think I've got the idea. I am to make a row of "dishes" in my vegetable patch, use a pencil to make four holes around the perimeter of each and drop in my beans. Then I cover the holes and begin watering.

Fortunately we have an irrigation system, which, owing to the rapidly developing state of our garden, I'm fast becoming adept at adjusting and expanding. The pipes and fittings are on sale locally at most DIY stores and I regularly turn up at Pandeli's store in Gennadi and trundle home with a plastic bag full of assorted elbows, T's, ends and isolation taps which I, using my newly acquired specialist tools for cutting pipe and making holes into which the watering nozzles are "popped," fit to the ever expanding system of black pipes which lay all around the garden. You won't find a house with a garden of any decent size in southern Greece without a watering system. The climate being what it is, you'd be watering every waking hour without such a system. John had the foresight to pay for a computer controlled timer which services both his and Wendy's side and ours too, so I just had to begin running the pipework as and where it was needed as we planned and laid out our new beds, one at a time.

I follow Mihali's instructions to the letter. I dutifully select and remove the weakest two of the four shoots as they grow and continue watching as the remaining plants grow on at a rate of knots. I think (but no doubt an expert will correct me) that these are what we'd call "French" beans. The rapidity with which they grow is amazing. It's only a couple of weeks before we're sipping our gin and tonics one warm evening, looking across at our fledgling vegetable patch feeling very proud of ourselves, as we study all the football-sized plants, lush with huge green leaves and bursting with promise of the beans soon to develop on their stalks, now made more robust by my diligent pruning of the long shoots that the plants keep sending out.

"This vegetable growing lark's not all that difficult really. The flowers are gonna be out soon." I smugly remark to my good lady as we enjoy the evening warmth. Just for a couple of hours on an August evening it's relatively safe to sit out in the sun. Something you'd have to be a mad dog or an Englishman to do during the daytime hours.

"Well," says Yvonne-Maria, "I must say those beans do look good. I still can't believe that the goats won't get them, or the pigs! It's still a bit of a novelty having a complete perimeter fence so I'm still a bit nervous about this."

"I'm only now beginning to think we can relax. It's been a couple of weeks since we planted them after all." I'm still feeling too smug for my own good.

The next morning, …disaster. I take a pre-breakfast walk out to inspect the beans and see whether the flowers have begun to open to find that several of the fresh, healthy young plants have been eaten down to within an inch of the soil. I'm perplexed to the most perplexible extent to which one can be perplexed, and then some. We have a complete perimeter fence. We have huge iron gates, both of which we keep closed all the time. We only open them when we're going in or out and we never leave them open at any other time.

Yvonne joins me and expresses herself as only a woman can. "Told you I wasn't sure about this. I bet it's a hedgehog or something." I exercise an immense amount of self-control and say nothing. Inside I'm screaming "YOU COULDN'T HAVE KNOWN ANY MORE THAN ME THAT SOMETHING WOULD GET IN HERE NOW THAT WE HAVE A COMPLETE FENCE!!! IT'S NOT MY FAULT!!"

I count to twenty and then calmly say, "I'll get to the bottom of it. It's only plants after all. We'll sort it, alright?" She walks inside tutting at my rashness.

I don't sleep all that well and I'm frequently up and about during the night. This particular evening I'm glad of my insomnia and, throwing on a pair of shorts, I venture outside at about 2.00am. I creep over to the vegetable patch and take a look, hoping to catch the culprit in the act.

Nothing.

This happens a few times and all the while more bean plants are being consumed, much to our chagrin. Another day passes with the two of us skirting round the subject of our fast-disappearing bean plants and we take our seats out on the terrace at around 8.30pm to sip our gins and tonic and put the world to rights as the sun heads speedily towards the Western horizon. After a half an hour or so it starts to get dark. Our conversation is brought to a halt when the front gates, not thirty feet in front of us, rattle as though someone's trying to get in and can't find the latch. We're both drawn to look towards them and there, sitting on the block paviours of the drive, INSIDE the gates, is a hare, licking its front paws in anticipation of its coming nocturnal repas, cool as a cucumber.

For the first few moments we're both stunned at its sheer brazenness. We'd been feeling falsely secure over the fact that the gates and fence were now intact, but the gates are constructed with vertical metal bars, spaced approximately 4 or 5 inches apart. There's no way a pig or a goat can get through, but old Hartley here (a name our neighbours Mac and Jane give him, since they have his mates around at their place, a fact which we discover when we compare notes over coffee) just treats them like the turnstile as he enters his favourite fast food joint.

Some fifteen minutes later, both of us are exhausted after a mad chase around the garden before our unwelcome guest finally rattled the gates on his way out, we flop back into our chairs to finish our drinks and discuss how we're going to make the front gates "hare-proof." There's nothing that can be done this night, as all the shops are shut we have nothing large enough to protect both front gates, since the two of them span some fifteen feet from post to post. Then I remember I do have a roll of thin wire around the back, which I'd been using for some other project. I'm soon busily running this wire in and out of the gates at various angles to form a barrier that I hope will keep the culprit from being able to push its way through.

It's pitch dark when I finish and finally put my pliers and wire cutters away. We decide that there's nothing for it but to retire for the night and wait until morning to see if my extra wiring has done the trick.

As is often the case, I get up some time after midnight, after once again laying wide awake in my bed for long enough. I've listened to a couple of laid back albums on my iPod (maybe "Wish You Were Here" or something by John Martyn) and I'm no nearer to falling asleep than when I turned off my bedside lamp. I grab my shorts, gently creep from the bedroom to the sound of Yvonne's rhythmic breathing, and venture into the starlit night. I decide to creep quietly toward the vegetable patch, just in case my protective measures have failed.

They have.

There, not ten feet away, as I shine my torch toward the ever-diminishing bean plants, sits the enemy, chomping away as his retinas reflect the torchlight back at me in bright magenta. He makes no attempt to run, the cocky blighter. I'm frustrated that my wires didn't do the trick and continue to sit there, eye to eye with the adversary, while I try and think of something that'll put him off coming to this particular "restaurant." Ah! I've got it.

I gently retreat to the side of the carport and grab the hosepipe. I unwind it as quietly as I can and gently return to my spot on the drive just feet from the long-eared intruder. I've ensured that the tap on the wall is on, and set the nozzle on the pipe to maximum pressure, whilst also ensuring that the jet will be concentrated and not a spray. I've got to time this right. I've got to press the trigger on the hose gun just perfectly to get the element of surprise working in my favour. In short, I've got to hit the little devil with the water jet before he knows it's coming.

I hold my breath. I see he's still sitting there. He's evidently far too confident for his own good. Well, I'll show you, you thieving…

POW! I let rip with the water jet and hit him before he's even aware that I have a weapon! In milliseconds he bounds away over the low fence into the orchard and out of sight. I have no idea where he goes, but I decide to sit it out for a while to see if he's cheeky enough to make another entrance. After fifteen minutes, during which I'm able to gaze in wonder at the Milky Way spanning the sky above me and counting several shootings stars in the process, I decide he must be giving it up for a bad job for tonight.

I return to the bedroom and try to slip back under the cotton sheet without waking Yvonne. I'm nowhere near confident that I've done the trick more than temporarily, but this time I sleep until dawn.

Next day I'm off down to the builders' merchant in Gennadi where I purchase a roll of rigid wire meshing, which I soon ensure is tied securely all along the lower two feet or so of the garden gates. It has the added benefit of making it appear that we have a dog, which needs keeping in, rather than a hare, which needs keeping out.

It's a week or so later and I'm talking to Mihalis, who's just enquired about the growth of our beans. I bemoan the fact that we've been battling the long-eared intruder. Mihalis holds up his hand and makes the unmistakable movements that suggest I simply get out a gun and shoot the furry fiend. "You must shoots him, yes?" He chuckles, evidently with a symbolic nod back to our conversation about the other kind of shoots. "Then he goes in the pot, very tasty."

"Yes, but, a) we don't own a gun Mihali, and b) we're vegetarians. We don't eat anything that used to have a face."

"You know what you need." He replies, now looking me right in the eye as I think I know what's coming next. "I have new litter of puppies. I bring you one."

Hartley, fur all wet, retreats. This was taken at night, which is why it's hard to make him out.

Tzatziki for You to Say

5 – Live the Nightmare

"We can't sell." Say the couple we're talking to one hot afternoon in Lardos village.

"Why ever not? It's your house. You paid cash for it. Surely you can do what you like with it," is our response. After all, we're from Britain. That's how things are over there.

"We don't have any paperwork," they say …and they proceed to explain that indeed they don't. They've had the house for three years (and counting) and still have no proof on paper that it belongs to them. Why not? Because whenever they ask the builder, he says, "Talk to your lawyer." So they talk to their lawyer and he tells them "The civil engineer has all the files. It'll be with him. He was responsible for getting the property signed off as finished and ready for residential use."

They phone the civil engineer and he tells them, "No I don't keep the files. Perhaps your accountant has them."

You know where this is going don't you. It reminds me of the old song, *"There's a Hole in My Bucket."* That song begins with the poor guy bemoaning to his wife Liza that his bucket has a hole in it. So she says, "Fix it." He asks what she'd suggest he do and the song continues until she says he'll need a little water to wet his sharpening stone. He has no water, so he says, "In what shall I fetch it, dear Liza?' Her reply is, of course, "in a bucket dear Henry." To which he begins again with "There's a hole in my bucket," and off they could go again, had it not been for the fact that the record fades at that point.

Going round in circles is something which many who've moved over here to "live the dream" have become very good at. And that's just the lucky ones. The rest have lost thousands when their "butter wouldn't melt…" builder had asked them to lend him a sum for a short period, due to cash flow problems, or for an advance because he'd assured them it would get their property finished that bit quicker, only to find he disappeared from the face of the earth, no doubt a few hundred thousand the richer, whilst some of his poor unfortunate purchasers end up without two brass farthings instead of being able to live in retirement with some creature comforts, and still others end up without a home, as their particular house is still just a bunch of concrete pillars with a slab atop them. Oh, and, of course, a forest of iron reinforcing-bars sticking out the top.

Don't get me wrong here; Rhodes is a beautiful place to live. On a daily interpersonal basis, the people are warm and friendly. The climate is very sunny, with the winters resembling a British summer, only more reliable! It rains now and then; on occasions with such force that you begin to think you could do with a very large wooden vessel with a whole bunch of paired-up animals inside. The thunderstorms need to be experienced to be believed, yet the clouds never remain for long and before you know it you're in your t-shirt supping at a frappe in the hot sunshine, and that's in January! The worst month is August, when it's just too hot to do anything apart from keep your blinds closed, swim whenever possible and stay in the shade drinking copious quantities of water. Mind you, the evenings are blissful; sitting out until past midnight under a deep starry sky, with the Milky Way clearly discernible on a nightly basis, as you sip a brandy and exchange the wisdom with which we're all blessed after a hearty meal with friends and just enough alcohol to make you feel mellow and magnanimous to all and sundry.

But, having lived here for over four years now it has become very apparent that most British people's experiences of purchasing property out here is - and believe me I do not exaggerate - a complete nightmare. Stories of major structural problems with new builds and builders who cut off the power and or water supply to their hapless buyers over disputes about who was supposed to pay how much for the bathroom tiles abound. As I've already said above, I don't exaggerate when I say that almost every person or couple we talk to comes out with things like, "Our electricity supply is 'piggybacked' off the house next door because we can't get our meter fitted for the foreseeable future." Or "The builder was supposed to have given us a four-foot wall all around the perimeter, but it's only two feet high and the goats are always getting in and eating our garden plants. Every time we call him he doesn't answer the phone. If we are fortunate enough to be able to leave a message, he never returns our call."

A single woman we know, in her sixties and living in a village not far from our home, told us just this week of the occasion when she was told by her builder that she owed him six thousand Euros for the tiles in her house. As you'll appreciate, a house in Greece has a lot of tiles. These days they don't tend to lay crushed marble floors any more, opting instead for a concrete "screed" over which are laid ceramic tiles. The fact is that every floor in the house and any terraces around the outside all sport ceramic tiles, plus the bathroom walls and kitchen work areas are all tiled, so the cost of tiling in a new house can be quite considerable. Our friend had paperwork and signed contracts showing who was due to pay how much for what and she had proof on paper that she did not in fact owe him the sum he asked for at all. It was more like a thousand, a sum that she'd happily have paid him had he not defaulted on several other promises. She'd told him that if he'd just come good on these things, she'd happily pay him the balance for the tiles. He shouted and swore that if she didn't pay up she'd be sorry. She suggested that he come to her house to discuss it and that they both have their lawyer present.

During the course of the meeting that ensued, this bear of a man went blue in the face yelling and swearing in Greek and broken English that she had to give him the money – in cash - or he'd do this, that or some other terrible thing. Finally our friend's lawyer banged his fist on the kitchen table and told this bully that he'd just threatened violence to a woman in the presence of two lawyers. Our friend told us she had his face spitting fire within inches of hers as he ranted. A fairly upsetting experience you'll agree, even for a big macho man, but we are talking here of a single woman trying to run her life and deal with all the situations that she comes up against entirely on her own.

Stories of major snagging issues abound here. A lovely couple moved from Scotland into a house within walking distance of where my wife and I live, so we paid them a visit to welcome them to the "neighbourhood" as it were. Guess what. They regaled us with tales of how the builder had defaulted on a whole bunch of things he'd promised to have completed before they arrived. The fence is falling down and not even finished, there is a missing air-conditioning unit in one room, plus various cracks in the external rendering that need making good. They've now been here for almost two years and have hardly seen the builder. They still haven't had an electricity bill. None of the "snags" have been put right. Another couple, who bought a house in Pefkos, found one winter's evening that the bedroom immediately upstairs from their open fireplace (what the Greeks call a "*Tzaki*") was thick with smoke. It was so dense that they couldn't breath without covering their mouths with damp cloths and feeling their way to open the window. The reason for this? The flue from the fireplace went up through the corner of this particular bedroom, but there had been no fire cement used in constructing the block flue as it rose through the room. This meant that smoke seeped out between the blocks and slowly filled the room. Had there been a young child asleep in that room, the possible outcome doesn't bear thinking about.

One housing estate, well, it's a cul-de-sac of about a dozen single story homes on the edge of the village of Lardos, now has about three quarters of its properties occupied. All the buyers are from the UK. The remainder of the homes on the site are, as yet, unfinished and have been at the "concrete skeleton" stage for years. The "road" is just dirt and potholes, which is just about negotiable in summer, but during the winter months the potholes become lakes that you'd hesitate to drive a normal family car through. The entire development had its electricity cut off by the electricity company, DEH, last year owing to the fact that the work hadn't been completed to the correct standard and was considered dangerous. It seems that no small number of houses were all receiving their power from one single domestic meter. If my information is correct, the residents were without power for five days, during which one "lucky" couple, friends of ours, managed to get by with a borrowed generator. The residents had to fight their way out of the paperwork maze together, as the builder had long since done a bunk with a few thousand Euros which he'd borrowed from several of them on a verbal "butter wouldn't melt" promise, plus from another couple who hadn't even moved in yet.

Stories such as the foregoing are many and varied. But unfortunately, they are not rare. So it's only right that someone sound the alarm for the poor unfortunate British who may still be contemplating buying here so that they can "live the dream." It's no picnic buying a property here even when things go well, but when they don't go well you're talking about years of serious stress, second thoughts, financial disaster, court appearances and who-knows-what other problems that can easily turn that dream into your worst nightmare.

So, to try and put some perspective on this, here is a list of things to bear in mind that may well help you avert experiencing the nightmare whilst yet salvaging your dream:

1. Never use the same lawyer as your builder.

2. Get some information on the person or company you may be considering buying from. There are some reputable builders to be found, but the best way to find them is to be here a while, talk to British people who've already bought and get a feel for who to avoid and who to see about your prospective property.

3. Take out a mortgage, even if you can afford to pay cash. The bank will appoint its own surveyor to monitor the build and will not release the final payment until all work

and paperwork is completed. It may cost a little more, but builders do not like arguing with banks. Shop around as many banks offer deals.

4. Never use the same accountant as your builder.

5. Try to be present during the course of the build, many cases of poor workmanship are covered over before the buyers reappear on the island.

6. Always get a full written contract with detailed specifications, ie: allowance for tiles, bathrooms, kitchens etc. I know of one instance where someone agreed to buy and found he had only bought the bricks and mortar, no fixtures and no fittings. Not even the doors and windows!

7. Check builders' merchants and find out what sanitary ware, tiles, kitchens etc. are available and then compare what your builder is offering. Many put the cheapest fittings available into their houses, but tell the buyer they've fitted the best.

8. Make sure that the electricity, water, telephone, roads (where applicable) etc. are included in the purchase price.

9. Stipulate in the contract that any extras must be notified to you in writing and that you must agree in writing before any extra work is instigated.

10. Make sure that any promises made by the builder before you agree to buy are put into the contract. Some builders will promise the earth to get a sale and then deny all knowledge of any such promises.

11. Have all documents translated into English before you sign them. Have your lawyer sign that it is a true translation.

12. Do not hand over any money until you have a legal contract to buy the land and house. If the builder is honest, he will wait. Do not be fooled by the assertion that you will lose the house if you do not pay a deposit immediately.

13. Contact the Greek Builders Federation (**http://www.greekpropertysociety.com/**) to find reliable builders etc. If your builder is a member, the Federation will ensure that your property is completed to their standards. They will also complete the build if the builder defaults.

The fact is that there are many ex-pat British people living here on Rhodes and enjoying their lifestyle in their newly adopted homeland. But many of these have had to go through all kinds of "nightmare" experiences to get to that point. If you follow the suggestions offered here, hopefully you can learn from others' experiences and not have your dream turned into a nightmare.

"How does he know all this?" you may ask, in the knowledge that Yvonne-Maria and I are, in fact, renting our home. The answer is simple. Our landlords are very close friends of some two decades and we've been through their nightmare every step of the way, plus some of the friends that we've made since moving out here have been only too pleased to regale us with their problems and proffer advice for others who may be just about to "live the nightmare."

The most common problem that buyers have here is that of getting their domestic electricity supply connected. An expression that you hear in most conversations is "They haven't paid the IKA." This is a tax that is due to be paid on the completion of each of several stages of a new build. Sadly, a huge number of Greeks who own land have seen the potential of developing it and thus have become "builders" virtually overnight. They get planning permission to build a few villas, sell the plots "off plan" to unsuspecting foreigners who think that purchasing a property over here will mean they get the same safeguards as back home, which they don't.

They agree a price, but the builder doesn't bother to acquaint them with such details as the fact that he must pay the IKA (which ought to be included in the purchase price) at various stages during the build. Come the time for the building's completion and the builder decides that he'll be able to further line his already-bulging back pocket if he just delays the final IKA payment while he deftly (in his eyes) uses the cash to begin yet another build, solid in the hope that he'll have sold this new one well in time to pay the tax by the time the purchasers of the property in question need to move in.

The buyers are told that the property is ready and so in they move, on the promise that - although there are still a few finishing touches to be done - these will soon be brought to a completion 'around' the new residents, with minimal inconvenience. Our hapless purchasers have never heard of such things as "builder's supply" with regard to the electricity meter. For a house (even assuming it's lucky enough to have had its own meter installed, since there are too many homes for comfort still "piggybacking" off of their nearest neighbour's meter) to have its electricity supply "signed over" from "Builder's Supply" to "Domestic Tariff" there are a number of documents required by DEH, the electricity company. These include proof that the final IKA payment has been made. Since the builder hasn't paid this, preferring, as he has, to use the money to start another project so that he can theoretically make even more money, the electricity company assume that the property hasn't yet been occupied by the purchasers.

Nothing seems untoward for a year or two. Then a couple of electricity company employees turn up outside the house and either disconnect or remove the meter altogether, since there is a finite limit to the length of time a new house can continue on "Builder's Supply." This time period now exceeded, off goes the power, regardless of whether the bills (which the householder may even have been receiving regularly) have been paid. This is when the householders panic, shout at the person behind the desk in the DEH office, only to be told that they owe thousands in unpaid IKA. Of course, our poor householders shout back that they've paid it all, in fact some two years previously. That's when it dawns on them that the seller hadn't in fact paid it at all and their next step is to get a good lawyer on the case in the often vain attempt to catch up with the builder and find out where the cash went.

The cash, of course is now in concrete and reinforcing bars at the site of another villa which the builder failed to sell since the property market slumped when the Euro grew in strength against the UK Pound Sterling (thus making it much more expensive for British people to purchase in the Euro zone) and the worldwide financial crisis arrived on a Greek island. The expression "caught a cold" springs to mind immediately.

The problem is, the builder still has his huge 4x4 and detached house in its huge grounds. He probably has five British couples baying for his blood, but they can't get near him. It's amazing how elusive a Greek businessman can be when he wants to be. I know personally of more than one couple who, in desperation, paid the IKA which was owing on their home for a second time, even though they'd already paid it to the builder once, simply so they could keep their electricity supply and maybe get it finally signed over to "Domestic Tariff." Their reasoning does have some merit, since they still owe the builder a final payment which hasn't yet been paid, because he hasn't finished the final touches, or the snagging jobs which the contract stipulates he must do. They simply tell us that they'll pay him if and when he fulfils his contractual obligations, but minus the IKA, which they'd now had to shell out for a second time.

By now you're probably getting a numb brain, so I guess it's time to lighten up! But I write all the above because my wife and I are *soooo* grateful that we didn't buy. To rent seems by far the easier option. If you so wish, you can leave without having to wait for the sale of your current property, which is always assuming it's legally fit for sale, which many aren't. You can easily afford your rent if you've been wise with the capital you made from the sale of your property in the UK. A bit of casual work here and there helps too.

I can honestly say, hand on heart, that I can't think of anyone in our immediate circle of friends, and that's a pretty big circle after more than four years living here, who hasn't experienced the kind of problems I've detailed above. Many are still in the middle of unpleasant legal battles with their builders. Many are wondering if they'll ever get just their electricity supply sorted out, leave alone all kinds of other issues. Having moved out here to "live the dream" and enjoy a sunnier and warmer climate, the outdoor lifestyle, the taverna-and-café culture, they find their stress levels going through the roof as they spend far too much time travelling to

Rhodes town to sit in the offices of lawyers whom they have to trust, even though they can't understand the forms they often have to sign, not to mention the conversations that go on in front of them while they sit mute in leatherette chairs, gazing out the office window and wondering if the people across the desk from them are saying "We can take these two for a few quid. They're loaded."

A Greek island has a lot to recommend it, like reliable summers, warm winters and the prospect of living out of doors for most of the year, gorgeous waterfront tavernas serving delicious traditional Greek food and cafés serving iced coffees around harbours where the boats "bob" in the expected manner.

So many Brits who've contemplated making the move have dreamed of evenings sipping brandy late into the warm starlit night, while chatting with a few friends about "how many swims they've had this summer." The fact is that a lot of people who have made the move are very glad they did so. But it's also a fact that many have finally moved back, preferring on balance to spend a couple of weeks at a time over here, simply enjoying all the positive aspects of what a Greek island offers, rather than continuing to endure the nightmare that purchasing a property here had proved to be.

Just this week we had a phone call from a couple we know who live down toward Gennadi. They moved out here in 2002 and, after finally getting into their new house six months after the original completion date, lived through their first winter without mains electricity. The builder magnanimously lent them a small generator, which just managed to power the washing machine and a few lights, but they couldn't cook or watch TV at the same time. It was six months after they moved before they finally got connected. They have been here eight years and thought that all the legalities had been taken care of and all the IKA paid and all the correct paperwork given over to their possession. They are the type of people who never get into unmanageable debt, always pay their bills promptly and are deeply suspicious of credit cards. In 2006 they received an official-looking letter, which of course they couldn't read as it was in Greek. But it looked like something that ought to be attended to. So what did they do? They took it and showed it to the builder, asking him if it was anything important. "Noooo! Of course not." He'd replied, "You can forget that, it's nothing".

Now, at the time of this chapter's writing, which is February 2010, they've just had a visit from the Municipal Police who wanted to arrest the wife. The property is in her name and so it was her they wanted to apprehend. She's been dealing with major health problems for many years and is on constant medication. Her husband, who's now 72, does virtually everything for her. Stress is something they don't need. Her husband was out when the Police knocked and, since she was in her nightdress on the sofa, she hadn't answered the door. So they'd gone nextdoor, left an envelope explaining what this was all about and told the neighbour to tell our friends they'd better get themselves down to the local Town Hall pretty sharp-ish, as they had to answer for something about which they'd been seriously remiss.

It turns out that four years earlier, in April of 2006, there had been a court case to discuss something like €17,000 worth of unpaid IKA on their property, tax which apparently had been put in their name, even though they had paid all the due IKA (as part of the purchase price) to the builder in 2002. The letter that they'd shown the builder back around the time of the hearing had been a summons to attend court. Now, you know what the builder had told them about that letter don't you. In her absence, our friend had been found guilty and sentenced to two prison terms totting up to 11-15 months, plus fines which had been accumulating, since they were unpaid for four years. Quite why no one had come after them in the meantime is a mystery, yet now it was crunch time. The husband called us because he knew we'd be able to translate the documents which the Police had left with their neighbour for them, documents which detailed the outcome of the case and the fact that they were required to present themselves to the authorities in order to be "dealt with", as it were.

How do such things happen in a "civilised" country? You tell me. I recommended they call the British Vice Consulate right away, since they were the innocent parties in all this and needed guidance as to how to go about proving it, without it sending our sick friend to an early grave through the stress of it all.

In "*Moussaka to My Ears*" I wrote in chapter 2 about "The Wall," not the Pink Floyd album, but the emotional hurdle that many come up against after having lived here for a year or two. A lot of people haven't accounted for how much they're going to miss their former friends and family. A lot of people hadn't expected to come across an ex-pat community rife with backbiting and petty squabbling such as they gradually found themselves embroiled in. These and other factors simply go to show that there's nowhere on the planet where life is totally problem free. You have to be realistic about it. Living on a Greek island has great appeal, but you have to be able to hack it. If you can take the rough (and for many it's rough with a capital "R") with the smooth, if you can deal with your close friends of many years and loved ones in your family being a couple of thousand miles away, you stand a chance of making a go of it.

If you can live without a decent-sized shopping mall being just a short drive away and the fact that you can't get the tracking adjusted on your car, after it's hit the umpteenth pothole this month, without driving 35 miles or so to Rhodes town; if you can accept that every public rubbish receptacle will have its colony of feral cats living in and around it, without taking a half a dozen of them home in a vain attempt to give them a better life, only to discover that, should you need to take one to the vet it'll also involve a day's driving, since the vets are all in the town and there aren't any to be found anywhere near your part of the island; if you can accept the fact that you're going to see stray dogs trotting along the roadside on an almost daily basis and there's nothing you're going to do which will change the way the Greeks treat animals, then maybe you'll do OK.

If you can adopt a simple lifestyle, which involves eating fruit and vegetables in their seasons, buying your bread from a local village bakery and collecting your mail from a village that's perhaps three miles away; if you can accommodate the fact that, whilst you may be able to get internet access, the connection's going to drop far too frequently for your satisfaction and sometimes remain "down" for days at a time; if you don't mind the fact that everything here, even paying a bill in the local post office, will take twice as long as it did in the UK as the person before you in the queue exchanges local news for what seems like weeks with the person behind the counter, you may just fit in.

If you don't mind the neighbours asking everything about your financial affairs and being totally mystified when you express indignation at the fact, you'll be happy.

I was hesitant at first to include such a chapter as this in a book that, by and large, I wanted to be light-hearted and entertaining. But life being what it is and the need for balance and realism persuaded me that it would be only right to put it in.

I suppose the final word in all of this is: the grass isn't always greener; a little different in colour, yes, but greener? Well, it will depend to a large extent on how well you do your homework before moving meadows.

6 – Around the Dinner Table

"I could have been Bryan Ferry's brother-in-law you know." While comparing claims to fame over a meal outside on the terrace on a warm night, the subjects flying around the table range from the totally believable to the totally loopy.

The conversation came around to this subject after someone raised the subject of Lefteris, a single man who lives in nearby Lardos village. He's somewhere in his mid forties and still unmarried. That makes him a rarity in a rural Greek community. We have quizzed him about why he hasn't ever married, to which his answers have always been a little evasive. "I love women too much to share my life with just one of them," is one of his more popular reposts. His habit of "mincing" while he walks around the central square in Lardos has set many a conversation afire with the words "Is he or isn't he?" It's really hard to be certain.

Well, it's his own business after all's said and done, but having spent an evening with him at his home one winter evening, whilst four of us huddled around his open fireplace trying desperately to persuade ourselves that it was cosy, when in fact it was just plain freezing, with all the heat going straight up the chimney, we're still not sure. But one thing we do know is that he was friends with the late Patrick Walker, who for a couple of decades was a leading astrologist with a daily column in one of Britain's leading tabloids. He died quite suddenly of salmonella poisoning at home in London at the age of 64 in 1995. Odd, he didn't see it coming.

He was, though, well known to be gay and thus, when we saw his photograph hanging on Lefteri's wall, and asked why it was there, Lefteris was quick to explain that they were firm friends. Knew each other for many years in fact. Patrick Walker loved the island of Rhodes and Yvonne-Maria and I are prompted to regale our guests with the tale of how we were once on the same aeroplane as Mr. Walker for a trip home after a couple of weeks on Symi in the early 1990's.

A few more brushes with the stars come out before, after another sip of Metaxa, I make the statement at the start of this chapter.

"YOU! Bryan Ferry's brother-in-law! How's that then? We've got to hear this one," says one of our guests, over the rim of his wine glass.

I begin the tale. In *Feta Compli!* I referred to the Greek Taverna, the Famagusta, that used to do brisk business at the bottom of the Gloucester Road in Bristol back in the early 1970's. I take my guests back a few decades:

"One particular Saturday night late in 1972, Yvonne, for a change, hadn't gone to the Famagusta with her sister, mother and various other girlfriends. But Christine (Yvonne's sister) had enjoyed a particularly interesting evening, as I was to discover the next afternoon. Since, in those days, Yvonne and Christine would rarely rise before about 2.30pm on a Sunday, especially after a late night, I'd walk the four miles or so from my parents' home on one side of Bath to their mother Lela's house on the other. I'd usually arrive around midday and chat with my future mother-in-law while she prepared Sunday lunch for her four children. I'd have a drink and sit right next to the telephone in the dining room, just across the worktop from the kitchen, while an old Greek *Laika* (traditional) music LP would play on the stereo gramophone, which was one of those that resembled a sideboard, on legs, á la G-Plan, all wood laminates and stuff.

"So I'm sitting there sipping a Coke or something when the phone rings. Since I'm virtually part of the family already I often answer their phone, especially since the girls are still under their eiderdowns dreaming of hunky Greek men, nay, hunky *rich* Greek men, the elder of the two younger brothers, Paul is out with his friends hanging around some street corner and the younger brother Philip likewise. Lela is only too glad to have me answer the phone while she grapples with the oven door and a chicken, which needs basting.

"'Hello?' I say. 'The White residence, how can I be of assistance?'

"'Is it possible to speak to Christine please?' Enquires the male voice at the other end.

"'I'm afraid she's still in bed and probably also still in the land of nod. But if you don't mind hanging on I'll nip upstairs and see if she's conscious.' To which the male voice says, sure he'll wait.

"'Who shall I say is calling?' I enquire. The reply is 'Bryan.' Not that I know he spells it with a 'y' at this moment in time, you understand.

"I trot upstairs, ease open the girls' bedroom door and spy two single beds, both with gently rising and falling duvets, indicating that their occupants are at least alive. I venture a few words, 'Either of you awake then?' No immediate response is forthcoming, so I begin to close the door when a croaky voice from Christine's bed asks, 'what?' This is decidedly a 'Can't you just leave us alone to sleep?!' kind of 'what.'

"'There's a bloke on the phone for you. Bryan someone-or-other.'

"'Tell him I'm still asleep.'

"'Who is he then?'

"'Oh, just some bloke I met at the Famagusta last night. Go away, I want to get back into this dream!'

"I go back downstairs and pass on the bad news to Bryan, who sounds disappointed, asks me to be sure and tell her he rang and hangs up. Half an hour later the two girls slither downstairs in their jim-jams and hit the fridge for something to drink. I venture a clarifying question to Christine:

"'So, who is this Bryan then? Good looking, rich, handsome, single even?'

"If you must know,' she replies, annoyance - at the fact that she evidently hadn't been able to go back to sleep and back into the dream she was enjoying - not the least bit disguised, 'It's just some bloke we met at the Famagusta last night. Funny looking bunch they were. Didn't come in until well after midnight. I think there were five or six of them and they were dressed very way out. Sequins and make-up, platform heels and stuff. Thought they were queer at first. One of them had long straight blonde hair all down his back and Bryan had a quiff, a bit like Elvis.

"Now at this stage I'm starting to get recognition signals in my brain and it's telling me, 'This can't be. No, it can't be!' I was a big Roxy Music fan and they were at the time all over the music press and TV, with their first single Virginia Plain having just been at the top of the singles chart and their first album doing the same in the album chart."

My audience around the patio table is now enraptured. Least, either that or pleasantly so mellowed by the food and drink of a Greek evening that they couldn't care less anyway. I press on with my tale:

"'You said you thought they may have been gay. What convinced you otherwise then?'

"'Well,' continues Christine, 'I don't think this Bryan guy would have been quite so interested in picking me up if he was.' By now I've run the memory banks in my brain over all the available evidence and remembered that Roxy Music had indeed been playing in Bristol the previous evening. It had to be them. Which means that Bryan was none other than Bryan Ferry!

"'So, didn't you like him? Tell me more.'

"'Yes I liked him, but not that much. I was more interested in the Greek house band really, that and having a good dance with Barbara and Aunty Ellen. Bryan said they'd found out about the Famagusta by asking a local where there was a bit of action after midnight. I didn't ask him where he was from or why he was in Bristol. Anyway, when we decided to leave to go home, at some time around half three I suppose, he asked if he could call me. So I said OK and gave him the phone number. Frankly, I didn't think he'd bother anyway.'

"'Wouldn't you be interested in seeing him again then?'

"'What's the point? He wasn't from round here and I didn't fancy him enough really.'

"'You know who they were, this bunch of "way out" guys I suppose?' I ask, now feeling totally peeved at knowing who I'd just dismissed on the phone. "Only Roxy Music, that's all!'

"'Roxy what? Never heard of them.' Was Christine's not altogether satisfactory reply.

"'They're only one of the hottest new rock bands! They've

just had a number one single and their album is top of the chart. If I'd had more money I'd have been there in the Colston Hall last night to see them!! And because you were enjoying some daft dream or other, I've just put the phone down on BRYAN FERRY! He could have been my brother-in-law!! I'm devastated!'"

I gaze around the dimly lit table to gauge the effect my claim-to-fame tale has on my guests.

"Roxy what? Bryan who?" ask various individuals who are too young for their own good.

A female guest soon moves the conversation on by bringing up a totally different subject.

"Have you noticed how many '*kali's*' they come out with sometimes?"

She has a point. Almost everyone who knows anything trivial about Greece knows that "*kalime'ra*" means literally, "good day." It's one of those ubiquitous expressions. Yet living here for any length of time you can't fail to notice that there are quite a few more "*kalis*" that have to be employed at various times during the week, month, year, millennium…

I'll illustrate. If you meet someone, maybe simply someone who serves you when you buy a loaf of bread, on a Monday morning, they'll often give you not only a "*kalime'ra*" but also a "*kali ebdoma'da*". So they've said "good day, good week"! If you watch the TV on the first day, or even during the first week of the month, a presenter will often sign off with, "*kali spe'ra, kali ebdoma'da, kalo mi'na*"! We listen to the local radio station here in this part of Rhodes, which is Radio Arhangelos. It's not uncommon to hear the DJ's greeting their enraptured audience with all three expressions during the first week of a month. It doesn't necessarily stop there either. If you're unfortunate enough to meet someone during the first few days of the year, especially if the year starts at the beginning of the week, you could very well hear "*Kali me'ra, kali ebdoma'da, kalo mi'na, kali xronia*" (good day, good week, good month, good year). Plus, since it's a new year, they'll add for good measure "*kali evimeri'a, kali ygei'a gia o'lous*" (good prosperity, good health to all) and that's only after first having begun the greeting (before all the "*kalis*") with a "*Hro'nia pola*" (many happy returns)! To be precise, the expression "*Hro'nia pola*" literally means "many years," but it is employed for every birthday, name day, religious festival, Christmas, New Year… you get the idea by now.

Yet another of the company around the table this evening adds more pearls of wisdom.

"If you wanna be truly Greek, you won't use your knife at the table."

"True." Another replies. "In fact, even placing knives when laying the table for a meal betrays your foreign roots, 'cos the Greeks only ever seem to eat with a fork." It's a fact. Yvonne-Maria and I have shared many a meal with Greek friends and I've lost count of the times when I've asked for a knife. The result being that everyone else around the table thinks to themselves "No idea, these foreigners." I don't understand it really. You can sit there and watch as the Greeks will push food around their plates, using a fork in their right hand, occasionally trying to cut meat using the fork's edge. Oh, they'll eventually succeed, but usually only some minutes after someone with a knife and a fork could have sent the tasty morsel down the throat to the tummy with much more efficient despatch.

Of course, my wife now eats this way all the time.

Whenever I make lunch (which, since we moved out here, isn't all that rarely!) I'll always set the lunch table with a knife and fork for each of us. When we're clearing the table afterwards though, there it will be, the untouched knife, ready for insertion back into the cutlery drawer as clean as when it was exhumed some time before. She considers it a personal defeat if she's had to resort to using it.

Why did God invent knives? So Greeks can show the rest of the world how to dine without them. That's the conclusion I've come to after exhaustive research into the subject.

"All talk of knives aside, I reckon the Greeks are a nation of hypochondriacs!" says Peter, who's lived here long enough to be fairly well qualified to make such an observation. So the conversation takes yet another turn.

"I know what you're going to say," I reply. I do, honest! "...Our friends Mahis and Felitsia have just bought a new one."

"New *what* then?" says someone.

"Go on then - smart Alec," says Peter. "What am I on about?"

I beam with satisfaction as I go on to relate how just about every Greek family has their own blood pressure machine. Can you imagine that in the UK? I don't think I ever knew anyone in fifty years of living there who had their own blood pressure tester. Yet here, it's quite a regular occurrence to be sitting around at someone's house having morning coffee only to see the hostess open a drawer and extract this grey metal box, inside of which is the familiar contraption with the tubes, mercury gauge and inflatable thingie for Velcro-ing around your upper arm. Anyone would think it was the most normal thing in the world to do over coffee. Well, to many Rhodeans, apparently it is. They take great delight in taking their turns with the tester, then either pronouncing the patient fit to run a marathon, or in serious need of immediate medical attention. It's almost like a party game. They seem to relate any number of ailments to the "*pi'esi*" …the "pressure."

"Oooh, yes, I'd say it's your *pi'esi*." …a Greek housewife will opine during a conversation in which her neighbour will have told her about some strange ailment or other that either she, her husband or his ya ya is experiencing. Quick as a flash they'll have whipped out the machine and be rushing next-door or wherever to diagnose the victim, sorry, patient.

"Ever been to a Greek wedding?" …Peter chimes in, evidently giving up on the hypochondria theme, as I appear to have rather selfishly stolen his thunder. Something in the back of my brain then takes me back several decades to the marital prospects of my sister-in-law. Feeling a bit woozy and ready to turn in for the night, a feeling it seems most of those around the table are exhibiting, I stretch out both arms in a huge yawn and pronounce to no one in particular:

"I could have been Bryan Ferry's brother-in-law you know."

7 – *A Bridegroom in Briefs*

Timo'theo and his fiancée Sylvia are getting married. It's April and, with two weeks to go before the wedding, they're sending out their invitations. Seems the Greek penchant for leaving everything to the last minute also applies to wedding invitations. Tim and Sylvia aren't Orthodox, they're part of the small group of Jehovah's Witnesses we've come to know in Kalathos. The fact that the wedding won't be a long drawn-out sanctimonious affair is what attracts us to want to attend. That and a healthy dose of curiosity too, of course.

Although Jehovah's Witnesses don't appear to do anything in the same way as other religions, it doesn't mean that there aren't some traditions accompanying weddings that they don't still adhere to. Yvonne-Maria and I were very touched when Tim and Sylvia invited us to the "dressing of the bride and groom." Sounded interesting right off the bat. I wondered whether I'd be able to attend the dressing of the bride as well as the groom. Well, purely out of natural curiosity you understand, in the interests of research and all that.

It's two weeks on and we're eager to experience this tradition for the first time.

Apparently it's only family and close friends who get an

invitation to this particular event, which, as it unfolds, has a lot of significance in respect to family bonds of love and support. We were both genuinely touched that Tim and Sylvia asked us to attend. The wedding is scheduled for 4 o'clock in the afternoon. They ask us to be at the house of Tim's parents for around 10.30am. The house has a small apartment downstairs into which Tim and Sylvia will be moving right after the nuptials as a start to their lives together.

It's going to be a long day. We don't really have any idea what to expect as we pull up outside the house at 10.40am on this Saturday in April. It's a sunny, warm day and the house is surrounded by vehicles. The cars that will carry the wedding party have beautiful floral displays, replete with ribbons and bows literally stuck to their bonnets with some kind of adhesive. They look gorgeous, but I find myself wondering if they'll have any effect on the paintwork. Tim's dad has a new car with metallic paint, it's only months old and it's the one in which Tim will be transported to the Kingdom Hall. The Kingdom Hall is in Rhodes town, so it's a 45 minute drive from the house to the ceremony, followed by a photography session in Rodini Park, then the reception, which won't be kicking off (not that we realise this yet) until around 9.30pm.

We climb the steps to the front door and ring the bell. It's opened almost immediately and we attempt to add to the crush of bodies within the *"saloni."* Once inside we are introduced to so many people I don't stand a chance of remembering who they all are. Apparently some are family from other parts of Greece, some are over from Toronto, where Tim was brought up until he was around 16, and about ten percent of the faces belong to people we know. Drinks are being passed around, as well as a few savoury nibbles and we do our best to give the impression we know what's going on.

After what seems like an eternity, the groom appears along the passage from the bedrooms. He's dressed in a pair of polka-dot boxer shorts, a singlet-type white vest and nothing else.

Now, I don't know about you, but I found my wedding day pretty stressful. And when I got married I didn't encounter any of my guests until I was fully clothed in my new wedding suit, well coiffured by a hairdresser (a present from my best man's mum) and walking along the aisle toward the minister. Now here's Tim standing in the middle of his parents' lounge among guests who are all in their best wedding-guest gear and he's standing in his briefs. I make a quick guess that probably 30% of the guests invited to this wedding are already here in this house, cheerfully now standing in a hastily-formed circle around the almost-naked groom. I wonder where the bride is. I eventually manage a nonchalant enquiry, only to be told that she's downstairs in the apartment, where she's being attended to by women only. Poor Tim, on the other hand, has to parade in his undies among a selection of guests of all ages and both genders. Life can be so unfair sometimes.

Slowly, Mihalis Spanos, one of the guests who also hails from the village, starts off the singing. "*Simera ga...*, *simera, ga'mos ginetai*" "..today, today there will be a wedding". This song is apparently sung traditionally whilst the dressing ceremony proceeds. Gradually the guests pick up the tune and sing along with Mihali. A chair is brought out from under the dining table and turned so that Tim can sit on it and be seen by the majority of guests. He seats himself and raises his chin, just as his uncle Kostas appears from the kitchen with some water in a bowl, some traditional barber-shop shaving foam in a cup and a cut-throat razor. He has a white towel over his left arm. Kostas has predominantly grey hair, which is still thick and swept back from his forehead, which tops off a face that still shows what a handsome man he was some forty years ago. His is large of girth and jovial of expression. In another life he could have been a British pub landlord. He is a kind man, the way his facial lines have set over the decades demonstrating this fact.

Kostas quickly has Tim's beard covered with shaving soap lather and looking more like Santa's than Tim's own, not all that appropriate a comparison when describing some of Jehovah's Witnesses, who don't celebrate Christmas, is it? Still, it elicits the right mental picture. Kostas carefully performs Tim's last shave as a single man, wipes his subject's chin and beard with a hot towel (and a degree of theatrical flourish I might add) and collects his utensils, bows and heads out of the room to find somewhere to dispose of them.

What's next? I wonder. I don't have to wait long. Two of Tim's cousins approach the under-dressed groom, each carrying a sock. In turn they both put the socks on to Tim's feet and then kiss him on both cheeks. I look around at Tim's mum, Lydia, whose eyes are now looking decidedly moist as she sees her son beginning to be dressed for the last time as a single man.

Tim's older sister, Rebecca, already married and with two beautiful daughters, is next and she helps him slip first one leg, then the other, into his suit trousers. These duly pulled up and zipped, she too kisses her brother on both cheeks. A significant number of the women present (which include aunts, cousins, close neighbours and friends both from Canada and the village here on Rhodes) can now be heard sniffling into their hankies and quite a few of the men have eyes that are quite obviously dampening too.

It's the turn of Tim's mum, Lydia. She approaches her son, who now stands easily a foot taller than her, and he turns to enable her to get his arms into the nicely pressed shirt she's holding up in readiness. Once his arms are inserted and the collar nudged up against the back of his neck, he rotates to watch as his mother buttons him up. She's crying like a baby as she finally stretches up, while he genuflects to receive her two kisses. He'll need his cheeks wiped of lipstick before he gets into the car for the trip to the ceremony at the Kingdom Hall! Lydia extends her arms to hug her son.

I have to say that, coupled with the continued singing by most of those present of the traditional island wedding song, the sight of this most touching of ceremonies gets me going a bit and I internally take hold of myself, swallowing hard, to stop myself joining the sobbers. Glancing sideways I see that my wife has a tissue in hand and is trying hard to stem the tears without spoiling her makeup. Dab, dab.

Mihalis is Tim's father, and is also quite a few inches shorter than his son, who stands tall for a Greek at around six foot. Mihalis and I are in fact almost the same age. He has the classically strong Greek features of Roman-style nose, deep-set eyes and pronounced cheek creases from the corners of his nostrils to either side of his full-lipped mouth. He's an honest, hard-working man who's raised his kids in not always favourable circumstances, given the hostility displayed towards Jehovah's Witnesses by the Greek Orthodox stalwarts. Tim's Dad approaches with the groom's tie and begins the difficult task of laying it around his son's neck and then tying the knot, which I've always found near-impossible to do from the front. Tie duly knotted and pulled up to the neck of Tim's shirt, father takes son in a tight bear-hug and they both show the current state of their hearts by the visible raising and falling of their shoulders as they try and check the tears. They aren't very successful.

After a hug that lasts what seems like forever, Mihalis

releases Tim and steps back to look at his son. He places a mock punch on Tim's jaw, lightly brushing his knuckle to Tim's freshly-shaved beard. It's a move that says something like, "Well son, we've done our best by you. It's up to you now. But I reckon you'll be fine. You'll do us proud. Go get married!"

After they can't resist another slightly (but only just) briefer hug, Mihalis steps away and Tim's best man, Pavlos, approaches carrying Tim's suit jacket. The groom is finally dressed and looking like someone who's getting married instead of someone appearing in a Whitehall farce.

Time flies and we realise that we'd all better be getting off to make the drive into town, where the wedding will take place. We have to allow an hour in order to be at the "Kingdom Hall" well in time for the ceremony to begin promptly. Just for once I think these Greeks are going to start something at the time it says on the invitations. In a few moments we're all downstairs milling around the diverse collection of vehicles and Yvonne-Maria and I are asked if we can give someone a lift. No problem we reply and soon the convoy is beginning to depart in dribs and drabs, but not before the mandatory discussions about who should be really travelling with whom and not a few people have climbed into cars, then climbed out again and climbed into others cars, before some have even been gently informed that it may be better if they went back and sat in the car they'd climbed out of a few moments ago!

Of course, the bride and her party keep well out of our way at this point and evidently no one's going to get a sneak preview until the moment she's brought up the aisle by her very proud father. Sylvia's parents are from Albania, but came to Greece over a decade ago and now live in Corinth. They and her two sisters and brother have all made the trip to Rhodes and we won't get the privilege of meeting them until after the ceremony. She has one more sister who is already married and living in London. Sadly, she can't be here today.

A little under an hour later we're narrowly missing fenders and bumpers while we try and shoehorn our little Suzuki Swift into a parking space outside the Kingdom Hall in a suburb of Rhodes town. Mission eventually accomplished, we disembark and walk into the Hall, which is surprisingly large and not at all like the image of a religious meeting place that one would expect. It's comfortable and at the opposite end to the main entrance there's a raised dais, which is decked with beautiful floral displays in honour of the occasion. The seats are modern and padded and the place looks big enough to seat a couple of hundred people in comfort. In the centre of the platform where the presiding minister (called an "elder") will stand is a simple podium of polished wood, in front of which is a microphone stand. Background music is playing and one could almost be about to enjoy a musical recital or a play. There are no religious icons or images to be seen, just one sign on the platform quoting a verse from the Bible. Apparently they have a theme text for each year and this is displayed for 12 months starting each January.

One of the first things that hits me is the sound of voices. Everyone's chatting to everyone else and all have excitement on their faces and there are smiles all round. It's not as if anyone is speaking in hushed tones as they tend to do in churches. In fact I can hardly hear myself think! I must say, though, that I prefer it this way. I have an antipathy to religion in general, so the less like a religious meeting place their hall and its atmosphere is the better I like it. Once the message filters in that the bride is outside a hush does finally descend and the minister approaches the microphone. Good - he's wearing a regular suit and tie. No black robes and dog collars here then. Another tick in the credit column!

I am immediately struck by the speaker's presence and bearing. I learn later that his name is Manos and he runs a couple of children's clothes shops for a living, aided and abetted by his wife and one or two of his grown-up children. That's the very last thing you'd have thought he does, judging purely from his appearance. In Manos' case, it's definitely deceptive. In all honesty, violin cases immediately spring to mind.

He is a big bear of a man somewhere in his late forties, with close-cut thick dark hair, which is just beginning to grey around the perimeter. He has a patch of hair above one temple that seems to have its own timetable for turning grey and it makes him remind me a bit of badger in The Wind in the Willows. His eyes are quite large and very, very dark as they beam out from under a pair of formidable eyebrows. His nose is strong and prominent, for all that without being too big, and he has a square, strong jaw. If I'd just seen him in the street I'd think he ran an "operation" of some sort. Know what I mean? As he begins to speak, at first welcoming all those present and thanking them for being here to celebrate the nuptials of Timo'theo and Sylvia, I am further struck by the gentleness in his voice. He soon gets into the wedding talk and displays quite a talent for gentle humour. This man is all surprises! I find the talk very listenable and notice that quite a sizeable proportion of the audience have Bibles on their laps as Manos takes us on a brief tour through the roles of both husband and wife in a marriage, using various Bible verses to make his point. The whole thing is refreshingly positive, practical and – dare I say – enjoyable! There's not a hint of sanctimony or ritual. It's a talk to remind bride and groom of what each ought to reasonably expect of the other and of themselves as they set out on this untrodden path of living with another human being.

I find myself thinking that all weddings ought to be like this. Manos even finds time to work into his talk an illustration, which sticks in my brain. From somewhere beneath the podium he brings out a china cup and saucer and then a chunky tea-mug. Which, he asks, would you offer to a respected guest for tea? Which, on the other hand would you set out for the builder working on your extension? We all know how we'd answer, and then he drives home his point. Holding up first the china cup and saucer, then the mug he asks:

"Which is the better of the two? Neither is. We can only say that each is perfect for its own set of circumstances. Would you throw the delicate china cup and saucer into the washing up bowl with the chunky tea-mugs and saucepans and stuff? Of course you wouldn't. You treat bone china with care as something delicate, whereas the mug can take a few knocks without sustaining damage. How well the cup and saucer pictures the wife in the marriage – delicate and beautiful, needing to be handled with care and tenderness, whereas the husband is (you've guessed it) the mug."

Point taken and we in the audience all share a brief chuckle. The talk winds up and Manos invites the bridal pair to stand for the vows, which do resemble those we've heard many times before. It's the only part of this quite enjoyable wedding service that bears any resemblance to what one would expect from a religious ceremony. The audience having been enlightened as to the rest of the day's agenda, all stand to sing a closing song. Apparently the Witnesses don't call their songs "hymns" either, simply "songs", which they sing along to with the accompaniment of a simple piano recording.

After the speaker offers a simple and brief prayer of his own words, the bridal party line up at the front of the Hall below the podium to greet their guests. The guests also form a line, which begins to file past the bride, the groom and both sets of parents and then back around to the main entrance and out into the afternoon sunshine. Yvonne-Maria and I assume a modest position way back in the queue and await our turn to kiss the bride and groom and offer our congratulations. When I eventually reach the bridal pair I kiss the impossibly beautiful Sylvia, who looks stunning (Tim's found himself a catch alright!) and share a bear hug with Tim. I whisper a pearl of wisdom in his ear, something I heard years ago and was waiting for the opportunity to pass on one day. I say:

"Now just remember mate: a man's never complete until he's found a good woman. Then he's finished."

I pull back and watch his face as his expression turns from earnest desire to receive a practical piece of fatherly advice to that look that says he knows he's almost been had.

It's now late afternoon and the reception is to be held at a large taverna that's been hired for the occasion somewhere in Kolumbia (pronounced, Kolymbia), which is about a third of the way down the coast back towards our part of the island. At least we won't have such a long drive home when it's all done and dusted, no doubt some time in the small hours of tomorrow morning. We're assigned to transport an older lady called Paraskevi, a name that literally means "Friday," and, as I hold a car door open for her she invites us back to her house for some refreshments. She lives in Afandou, which is en route, so it's not out of the way. I suggest: "Didn't we ought to proceed straight to the taverna for the reception?"

Paraskevi is about five foot nothing and quite portly. She has "permed" hair that's dyed a sort of ginger colour, a round face and a ready smile. She's dressed entirely in black. Well, since she is about seventy it's inevitable that she'll have lost enough relatives including, sadly, her husband (as we later discover), to have to wear only black for the rest of her life. She replies:

"We've plenty of time. If we go straight to the taverna we'll be the only ones there for hours yet. May as well come to my home and I'll make coffee and we'll share some "*parea*" [company] there for a while."

"Hours yet!?" I'm thinking. HOURS yet? Being accustomed to how we do weddings in the UK, this doesn't compute. What does everyone do for hours between the wedding ceremony and the reception? It surely can't take hours to take some photographs, can it? Mind you, the way the Greeks do most things I suppose it's a possibility.

Some fifteen minutes after we leave the outskirts of Rhodes town, Paraskevi directs me through the expected maze of tiny alleys that pass for streets away from the main thoroughfare in the village of Afandou and eventually points to a place where she suggests I can park the car. Her house is just to our left and this postage-stamp-sized parking space is on my right. The women tumble out of the car and head for the front door as I begin manoeuvres. Several near misses and a bashed (though thankfully undamaged) door mirror later I join them in Paraskevi's modestly sized lounge. Can't say I hold out much hope for the other door mirror still being intact by the time I come back to the car, but there's not much I can do about that now.

The floor in Paraskevi's home is crushed and polished marble chips, thus placing the construction date of this building firmly in the post-war era, as during the past few decades ceramic tiles have virtually supplanted the marble chip system, primarily for speed, but also for cost-effectiveness. Her furniture is all heavy, dark wood and it's all covered with photo frames displaying the faces of everyone from her grandparents to both of her daughters, their husbands and their progeny. There are cousins and aunts, nieces and nephews, brothers and sisters and various other village acquaintances all staring mournfully back at me from behind the well-cleaned glass in the frames.

Why is it that most family photographs that you peer at in a Greeks' home look as if they were taken at a funeral? It's only a few of the evidently recent shots that suggest that the subjects may actually be enjoying themselves; notably the ones that feature new grandchildren. Under most of the photographs, as well as the varied and copious selection of ornaments, most of which look like the kinds of thing you're grandmother would have had on her mantlepiece, there are intricately stitched doilies of white lace. In the middle of a modest little coffee table there's a glass dish brimming with individually wrapped boiled sweets. This is something else you often encounter in a Greek's home, the boiled sweets. You even see them on the desk in the office of your local insurance agent or accountant. I reckon a good career to go in for in Greece would be dentistry.

Paraskevi invites us to be seated while she goes and busies herself in the modest little kitchen nearby, preparing some light refreshments for the three of us. As I sit there and both Yvonne and I occupy ourselves by absorbing our surroundings, I can't help thinking that this is far from what I expected to be doing around this time of the day when I got out of bed this morning.

After a few minutes of hearing chinking noises coming through the door from the direction of the kitchen, our hostess appears in the doorway carrying a tray. She has to deftly prop it on one of her legs as she uses one hand to rearrange several glass ornaments of varying descriptions in order to make sufficient room on the coffee table to place the tray down. On it are three small cups of steaming *"Elleniko"* coffee, which is pretty much the same as Turkish, or Armenian, Cypriot etc. Each country where such coffee is found claims it as their own. You've probably tried it. If you have you know exactly how much caffeine is in that tiny cup. If you haven't, then take my tip: don't drink it in the evening if you want to stand a chance of getting any sleep!

I actually do like *Elleniko*, but not usually this late in the day. Still, we both agree, after exchanging a couple of knowing glances, that it'll be quite a few hours yet before we get anywhere near our bed, so hopefully the damage will be slight. Accompanying the coffees on the tray are two small glass dishes on which sits what looks at first glance like a dollop of marmalade, along with a small teaspoon. This is something else you have to get used to if you visit a lot of Greek homes. They all seem to keep a stock of this impossibly sweet cooked fruit in syrup especially for inflicting upon the hapless guest or two. You are expected to eat it with the spoon, with nothing else, not even a piece of bread, and enjoy it! Usually as soon as the first spoonful gets on to my tongue I can feel myself developing diabetes. It is exactly like a rich marmalade only with much larger chunks of fruit in it. I don't have a sweet tooth at the best of times, but my mum and dad raised me to always accept hospitality with graciousness and gratitude so I tuck into this sickly nightmare with feigned enthusiasm.

I sometimes wonder if the Greeks don't actually ever eat this stuff but only put it in front of their guests as a sort of national standing joke, to watch us all suffer while we say "yummy" and pretend to be loving it. The secret is not to eat it too fast or they'll decide you'll be 'wanting some more then!' But if you eat it too slowly they'll be offended and will think you ungrateful. It takes some getting right I can tell you. Mercifully there are also a few small chocolate wafers, a bit like Kit-Kat, awaiting our pleasure as well, so I move on to one of those as soon as I can. It tastes positively savoury by comparison!

Paraskevi is anxious not to see us waste away while we await the appropriate hour to move on to the reception, so she suggests we try a huge slice of some exceedingly sweet cake as well. This time we make excuses and hope it won't offend. At least she's presented us both with the traditional tall glass of water, so we can wash away all that sugar and caffeine residue which is swilling around every corner of our mouths. A plate laden with Petit Beurre biscuits is also fetched, just in case. Once again, Petit Beurre biscuits abound here in Rhodes, as indeed they seem to all over Greece. Walk around any supermarket and you'll see an inordinately large amount of the biscuit aisle taken up with these rather ordinary baked delicacies. There's a "reality" show on TV here at the moment where people entertain four others in their homes in turn until the end of the week, when the one who's been given the most votes by the others wins a cash prize. In the UK it's not uncommon to use digestive biscuits in things like cheesecake bases. Here, it's a-penny-to-a-pound it'll be Petit Beurre.

After what seems like an age I glance at my watch and suggest that we ought really to be getting to the reception by now. It's about 8.00pm, quite dark outside and we're sure to be missing something. To be fair, Paraskevi is very sweet and we've been absorbed hearing about her family and how she lost her husband some years ago. Seems he'd been a good man and they'd had a successful marriage when he was stricken with heart disease, which eventually took him from her prematurely. Then her grandson died, still in his teens, and she still mourns the boy after several years. She's been dealt a rough hand in life. She's told us how her son-in-law is a gambler and a drinker and has placed his once lucrative business in difficulty, so much so that she's had to bail him out by using her house as security for a bank loan. Now she sees him getting into difficulty yet again and fears for her home. We express our concerns and wish there was something we could actually do for her.

Reluctantly she agrees to move on to the reception. I can't understand why she's not as concerned as I am that we'll be showing ingratitude by turning up late for the food and cake-cutting and so on.

After a drive of some fifteen minutes or so we're turning left off the road at Kolumbia, then the road into which we've turned takes a sharp right and then a left and suddenly reveals a mile-long avenue of huge eucalyptus trees. It's quite a shock to see something like this on a Greek island. It would be more at home on one of the countless long straight rural avenues of France. Yet here it is and quite impressive we find it too. Apparently the Italians planted it between the wars.

More recently while working as a "Transfer Rep." on the coaches to and from the airport, I've come to see this road in the way that the coach drivers do. They don't like having to drive along it at all because the trees on either side are spaced, quite accidentally, at just the right distance apart to make it a near impossibility for two modern coaches to pass while going in opposite directions without their enormous insect-antenna-like door mirrors colliding. Mercifully, there are several hotels along the way which afford the drivers the opportunity to take a detour through a car park or entrance "plaza," but not before the obligatory shouting and vigorous waving of hands, which they'll probably also bang on their steering wheel in frustration, and appealing to their "*panagia mou*" while they thrash out which of them is going to reverse and give way, both asserting that their schedule is much more urgent than the other's.

What seems like ages of driving along this road, which is called, rather unimaginatively, "Eucalyptus Road," brings us to a large and fairly unpleasant-looking single storey building on our left hand side. It has the usual dirt-surfaced car park to one side, into which we turn. It's a huge taverna and the plain ugly exterior deceives, since once inside it's not at all bad. It is, however, huge and not the sort of place I'd usually choose for a quiet traditional evening meal. This, however, is a wedding reception and the place looks eminently capable of catering satisfactorily for a big crowd. As we enter I fully expect to see the party in full swing as it's approaching 9.00pm and the wedding took place at four. As we pass through the inner of the two entrance doors I look around to see not more than a dozen people dotted about among enough tables to seat several hundred.

"Are you sure this is the right place?" I ask Paraskevi.

"I told you it was a bit early yet," is her slightly sardonic response. She's probably thinking "These dopey English. They never take telling do they?"

I now notice that I do indeed know a couple of the faces and that all the tables are arranged into long lines, and dressed with white cloths and wedding-style bunting. There are finger buffet dishes along the centres of the tables and bottles of wine placed at strategic points along each line. There is a decent-sized dance floor, behind which is also a decent-sized sound system and a few party lights on a modest gantry, which are already casually flashing to some very subdued background music. I hear the just-audible sound of a bouzouki tinkling from the five-foot-high speakers. Could yet turn into a good night.

We begin examining the little name cards placed all along the tables and eventually discover ours. We're not, apparently sitting near Paraskevi, and so she wanders off until she too finds her place. We are, however, sitting just a few paces from the dance floor. We're well pleased with our vantage point.

Slowly, very slowly it seems to me, people begin coming in through the doors and filtering among the tables. The music gets a bit louder and I glance at my watch to see it is now 9.00pm. No sign of any of the bridal party yet though. When do these things actually get under way in Greece then? The bridegroom's mum eventually puts in an appearance and tells us all, a few at a time, that the cake has disappeared and so the bride and groom have been told that they'd best wait at their apartment until its whereabouts have been ascertained. Can't imagine what they'll find to do there.

I venture the question, "How can the cake 'disappear' then?" to which Lydia replies, "Well, it was ordered well in advance, but it should have been delivered here this afternoon, but it wasn't. So we've been phoning the cake shop but it's closed now and we need to get hold of the owner, who's not at home, so we have to call someone else to try and get his mobile phone number..." by now my brain is already losing interest and the old expression which Gary the builder used to repeat springs to mind:

"Welcome to Greece."

About 9.30pm the cake is finally wheeled into the room on a trolley and positioned on the dance floor right in front of the disco. Within seconds the bride and groom enter the now quite crowded taverna to the rapturous applause of a couple of hundred people, pick their way among the lines of guests seated expectantly along the tables and walk right up to the cake, pick up the already-in-position cake knife and poise while all the budding photographers, including the official one, get into position. After a few minutes during which the official photographer has fought valiantly to establish the fact that he ought to have the best position for taking cake-cutting photographs, the happy couple get right on with the job at hand. It's all a bit sudden for us Brits, who are much more used to the cake being cut some time later, but here we are watching as the cutting of the cake precedes just about everything else. Once Tim and Sylvia have run the knife into the cake a couple of times the music is cranked up and suddenly we have a party on our hands.

Dancing begins almost immediately. Traditional "*Laika*" music blares out at stomach vibrating level and everyone begins pouring drinks, eating and picking at the savouries placed all along the tables. Everyone, that is, except those who are threading their way to the floor to link hands or arms and get on with the serious business of Greek dancing.

At least an hour passes and, just when I begin to think that the only food on offer here will be these savoury nibbles, the "*orektiko*" (starter) begins arriving on the arms of numerous black and white clad waiters and waitresses. We're now seated between various friends of the bridegroom and the best man's brother and his wife and their two sons are immediately beside us. Sore-throat-inducing conversation ensues (in view of the volume of the music) and we gradually progress through a superb three-course meal. The official photographer's assistant, who it has to be said is a rather fetching-looking young woman, passes among the tables snapping photos of all the guests and things finally quieten down at around 11.00pm for a couple of speeches to be given at the mike stand in front of the disco. Tim's Dad says a bit, then Sylvia's dad. Tim of course has to thank everyone and the best man, Pavlo, also gets in the required few good-natured jibes at his bosom buddy Tim. Laughter having subsided, Tim's sister Rebecca now picks up the mike to sing a Celine Dion ballad and Yvonne and I realise that this girl could have been a finalist on the X-factor, she really is that good.

Now it's time for Tim to do his shmaltzy bit and show his new bride just how much he loves her. Tim is an avid (with a capital "A") music fan and one of his favourite bands is U2. So he's arranged for the DJ to put on their song *"With or Without You"* which Tim now, microphone in hand, sings full-on to his beautiful bride, who's seated alone in the middle of the dance floor facing him. He leaves no holds barred as he does his full Bono impression, occasionally putting his face within millimetres of Sylvia's, then going around behind her chair as he strokes her hair, all the while belting out "I can't li--------ve, with or without you!" into the mike. I'm not sure I think the lyrics are totally correct for the occasion, but since the majority of those present don't understand a word of them anyway they're all suitably impressed by Tim's public demonstration of his love and so he receives another round of rapturous applause for what feels like several minutes. His singing, unlike his sister's, wouldn't trouble episodes of the X-Factor for very long though.

All the required constituent parts of the occasion now dispensed with, the music cranks up again, this time interlaced with some Albanian songs too, from some CD's brought along for the occasion by Sylvia's younger brother. The dancing resumes and the similarity between Albanian dances and those of the Greeks permit all those present to join in. Soon the tracks are flitting between both country's music and the dance floor is becoming slippery with so much sweat, spilt drinks and evidently, condensation. Who cares, as the dancing continues unabated for another couple of hours, the floor sometimes totally packed to the point where you couldn't complete the sequence of steps (always assuming you knew them!) without having a major collision or "log-jam" of bodies, other times with just the right number on the floor to enable full expression on the part of those who really can dance.

There are knots of people renewing old acquaintances, others simply holding a glass in one hand while gazing contentedly around the room. There are children running in and out of the foyer near the toilets and generally getting fractious to the point where (way past their bed time we'd say in the UK) there are always several of them in tears; while their oblivious parents, somewhere else in this huge room, dance on, or talk on, or nibble at a chicken bone.

At some time after 2.00am the numbers begin to thin. In the UK the bride and groom would have been long gone by now, well on their way to their honeymoon suite, but Tim and Sylvia are still here, graciously doing the rounds of guests, kissing both cheeks, thanking people. Sylvia has remained in her wedding dress for the duration, the hem of which is well soiled from being dragged around a now very damp dance floor, not to mention being trodden on innumerable times as the evening has worn on. Hope it wasn't hired.

By around 2.30am there are just a dozen or so left, and we're beginning to think about going home. My wife hasn't left the dance floor since Tim did his "Bono" bit, so we haven't actually conversed for hours. I finally get a chance to slip into the dancing line beside her and suggest that we think about making tracks.

After the dancing lesson we'd had from Tim's cousin Mihalis in our home a while back, we are always quick to refute any ill-informed people who assert that Jehovah's Witnesses don't enjoy life, or that they spend all day with their heads in a Bible. Having just had a dance work-out that would rival any programme set by a sadistic personal trainer, once again we're impressed by what a great time these people have when they get together. We've even seen Manos, the "Elder" who conducted the wedding, getting down with the best of them (and surprisingly light of foot) in the line while we all sweated and grunted our way through another traditional dance on the floor, we've seen a couple of hundred people having a thoroughly great party with no sign of anyone having had too much to drink. Precious few had been smoking and we learned that these were the non-witness relatives who, whilst perhaps disagreeing with their family members for not being Orthodox, were kind enough to come anyway and it looks like they didn't regret it.

Best of all, much to our surprise, we've seen a bridegroom, on his wedding day, in his briefs!

Tzatziki for You to Say

8 – *Plants, Pomegranates and Tantrums*

Some weeks ago, Josie, an English female friend who's about 70-something and lives alone for most of the year, asked us to help her decorate the rooms of the new home she'll be moving into come September. She's been living in Lindos, which is arguable one of the most picturesque Greek island villages in the country, but is soon moving to the large village of Arhangelos (why not "Google Earth" it?).

The new home she'll be renting is a fairly old and compact "ya ya's" cottage and was in dire need of a couple of licks of white emulsion on the interior walls. Josie asked us to oblige, so we duly purchased the paint for her and, shoehorning our aluminium step ladder into our little Suzuki Swift, along with paint rollers and tray, we headed the twenty minutes or so up the road to accomplish the mission.

We hadn't been at the job more than half an hour when we heard a loud female voice declaring its presence with a "hello, anyone about?" (...obviously in Greek). We acknowledged with an "IN HERE!" and within seconds a 60-something woman, warm-faced and ample of figure appeared in the doorway to declare that she was the nearest neighbour and enquire regarding who was moving in and when? Her questions continued with all the usual things a Greek will ask like: "How much are you paying? Where are you from? How many children do you have and is any one of them a doctor? How long are you planning to stay? Is it you or someone else moving in?" We established that we were in fact just helping out and that Josie would be the new occupant, whereupon Dimitra (by now we knew her name) proceeded to tell us her life history. Her husband was Adonis and he was useless. He was her second husband and she'd spent 22 years working in hotels and scrimping and saving to arrive at where she was now, with a nice house, which was split into an upstairs apartment and a downstairs one. Upstairs lived Dimitra and her husband whilst downstairs was the home of her daughter (by her first husband, who'd died) and her husband and two (so far) children. Adonis was now the lucky beneficiary of his industrious wife's decades of hard graft.

Her house was right opposite the one we were decorating, with several windows which overlooked Josie's modest garden, in which were several mature fruit trees (oranges, pomegranates, lemons, *moussmoulia* [can't remember what they are in English] and tangerines). She said, "You must be thirsty. I'll fix you a drink!"

Before we could say anything other than "water would be fine" she was gone and, five minutes later, reappeared carrying a tray loaded with long condensation-covered glasses of chilled water, plus a bottle so we could top them up. These were all arranged on a large tray, which also bore a huge plate of chopped water melon, three forks, some serviettes and three small plates to facilitate our water melon feast. After placing the offering on a strategically positioned cardboard box she retreated with expressions like: "You only have to ask."

"I'm right next door," and the like.

Needless to say Josie was overjoyed at the fact that she had the prospect of such nice neighbours and we proceeded to agree and declare how such moments as this just served to demonstrate all that was good about living on a Greek island.

A week or so later a Greek couple, Kostas and Dina, friends of ours from Rhodes town who run their own fitted Kitchen and Bathroom business, had occasion to use their van to deliver a fridge freezer with our assistance to Josie's new home. Josie wasn't with us on this occasion but, as we pulled up outside, Dimitra's now recognisable head immediately appeared over the next door balcony and enquired what was going on. Once she realised it was Yvonne-Maria and I she was satisfied (after checking out what was being delivered) and disappeared from view. As we were "left hand down a bit"-ing and "mind your fingers on the door frame"-ing Yvonne related to Dina about Dimitra's kind gesture from the week before.

"Kindness?" replied Dina, "She was just plain nosey that's all!! She wanted to have a look round and see both what her new neighbour was like, as well as what she was doing with the cottage."

Well, here we are again at "Rafael," which is what Josie has named her new cottage, and this time we're carrying a veritable jungle of plants from the car to the garden, some in pots and some which have been removed from their heavy pots for ease of transportation, in order to settle them into their new home and give them a good watering in. The car is full of spilt compost and leaves, the usual casualties of such a move, but nothing serious though. The Jasmines and Yukkas, the Bougainvillea and Oleander all look like they'll be OK once they become aware that they'll not be moving again for a while.

Back in Lindos, it had been a major logistic operation getting the plants from Josie's courtyard to the car. Josie's old home is a rented "Captain's House" right in the thick of the village and some ten minutes walk (for someone not carrying a heavy Yukka in its pot) from the nearest point at which one can position a vehicle in order to rendezvous with said plants. In fact, the house is part-way up the steep and pebbled part of the well-trodden tourist path up to the Lindos Acropolis and we are still well and truly in the tourist season. Yvonne-Maria had been deposited in the square, beneath the huge plane tree where the shuttle buses turn round and where traffic cops continually blow their whistles at everything with wheels, seemingly without taking a breath. As Yvonne was making her way up to Josie's to let her know we were ready to do a "plant run" from old home to new, I smiled at an impatient traffic cop and drove up from the square a few metres, then took the right fork along the small road that leads down to the main beach, where I was hoping to find a space into which I could shoe-horn the car until we had a large enough load of plants sitting on the ground in the square to warrant my coming back for the car and driving it back to the whistle-filled square for a loading session.

Car duly squeezed into a "pay and display" space, and having endured the pain of actually having to pay to park here on Rhodes (the first and only time I've ever had to do so!) I half-walked and half-jogged back to the square and into the tourist throng in order to join Yvonne-Maria and Josie at the house where we'd begin preparing to walk a car-load of plants down to the square.

You can't walk fast in Lindos when there are coach loads of tourists all being led on foot by guides through the tiny streets and alleys. If you are lucky enough to find a relatively free bit of lane, you are more than likely to run into a clutch of donkeys and their handlers, either trotting acropolis-wards or making their return trip to their "garage," each with a well jiggled tourist, who's trying to look cool, on its back. In some lanes you'll see the resident "pooper-scooper" sitting on a small stool, waiting for the donkeys to pass and ready with his shovel to retrieve any deposits which the donkeys may leave on the floor in their passing. Once the animals have ambled by, he'll scan the shiny flags to see if there is any work for him and, on discovering some steamy pellets, will leap up from his stool to whip them off the ground, deposit them in a plastic bag and quickly wash the spot with a bucket of water before the pedestrian tourists can come by and pick up a greenish brown mess (including the obligatory bits of donkey-processed straw) on his or her flip-flops and tread it into the next souvenir shop they enter.

Having fussed about for a while, we were ready for our first trek from house to square. We steeled ourselves and opened the courtyard door in readiness. Once outside the door we crossed the few feet of external terrace, through a small wrought iron gate under a stone arch, and were instantly among the lobster-red, semi-clad bodies of a thousand Acropolis pilgrims. Within feet of the gate and heading downhill there are postcards and cotton shirts, lace cloths and restaurant menus, books and bracelets and all kinds of other paraphernalia hanging off the walls of the souvenir shops all waiting to be snagged by the abundant foliage of our burdens as we walked, or more accurately, stopped and started, among the tourist throng. Then there are all the bare shoulders and backs, chests and heads, which are at risk of being "speared" by a rather pointed and rigid Yukka leaf.

Extreme caution was required at this juncture. Reason obvious.

On our second sortie, we had only gone a few metres down the lane from Josie's place when a Lindian woman and her friend, standing on the stone step of their little lace shop in the classic stance of the shop-owner's vigil, one arm in the crook of the other, which is extended straight down with an obligatory cigarette burning between the first two fingers, decided they needed to know who we were, what we were doing and whether it was worth learning about it so they could tell something of interest to their friends and other Lindos residents over their next Greek coffee. The proprietor gave a friendly "*kali mera*" to Yvonne, with sufficient volume to ensure that my wife stopped and returned the greeting.

Fatal.

"You moving someone? Who is it? Where are they going and why are they leaving Lindos? Or perhaps they move to somewhere else in Lindos? Where do you live? Are you from here? Have you any children? How do you know the person who is moving? Is your house your own?" (if you answer with a "no" at this point you'll for sure then get a 'my brother has a house for sale, you ought to buy it...') and so on. My wife, having made the mistake of stopping, found herself fielding all these questions from behind a screen of Jasmine foliage, which was effusing from a black plastic bin-liner that was already beginning to tear from the weight of the soil which it was carrying, in which the roots of the jasmine were hanging on for grim death. I was walking behind her and so had to stop too because the sheer volume of pedestrian traffic prevented me making a speedy pass at such a narrow place, decorated on each side as it was with shops selling material and cheesecloth garments, which hung all over the walls and even from the awnings above our heads.

Having eventually satisfied the woman's curiosity, which involved a moment of sheer delight on her part when she discovered that a) she'd heard of us and b) she knew Josie but hadn't known she was moving, we continued on toward the square with our loads, arms now tearing from their sockets with the weight they were bearing.

Once Josie, Yvonne and I had all managed to be at the square at the same time and we'd amassed a sufficient gathering of diverse and variable sized plants, black bags and pots together to (as I estimated) fill the car and still allow room for three bodies inside too, I left them standing beside the wall of a nearby taverna, which was just beginning to acquire its lunch-seeking clientele, and made off to retrieve the car. Minutes later I braved the whistling parking-cop to draw up outside the taverna on one side of the square where I jumped out and proceeded to open the rear tailgate of the car in readiness for its load.

Shoe-horning plants, tools, empty and full pots and bodies into the car via the rear tailgate and all four doors, I was just preparing to attempt to close the last of the said doors when a fat, sixty-something man, evidently the owner of the taverna whose wall beside which we'd gathered, began shouting at me in Greek. The car was right outside the entrance to his precious restaurant and an idiot could see that we were only going to be there a matter of minutes. It was also apparent to anyone who was observant that Yvonne-Maria and I were helping our more senior-aged friend with a major logistic task, which she'd have found very difficult to accomplish alone. In short, we were the good Samaritans here. Even the whistling cop had turned a blind eye as he realised what we were up to, knowing full well that within minutes we'd be away and out of his area of jurisdiction.

I wasn't paying any attention to the shouting taverna man until Yvonne nudged me and pointed her gaze at him. He was going blue in the face and using both hands (as all Greeks do), palms outward and extended in front of him pointing down at the tarmac right in front of my feet, which were positioned right behind the rear of my car, where I'd just succeeded against all odds in closing the tailgate without chopping off a large and delicate part of a carefully inserted plant.

Now I am a peaceful sort of bloke and hate to retaliate in kind, but at this precise moment I was very hot, very bothered, very thirsty and very much in a hurry to get out of that square before I overstayed my welcome in a spot where, during the day, the traffic cops do not like to see any cars except a taxi. You can't all together blame them, as the shuttle bus has to get around the tree there for its run back up the hill to Krana square and, if it has to deal with any unnecessary obstacles like my little Suzuki Swift, the driver gets understandably rattled. He is also trying to minimise the number of gormless tourists he runs over, since they all wander around the square, camera glued to at least one eye, in total oblivion to the fact that buses and taxis regularly turn there. So you have to feel for him, don't you.

So, just as I am about to return to my driver's door and high-tail it out of there, I am faced with a tirade of swearing and *"Panagia Mou"*s from this taverna owner - and over what?

Looking down at my feet I see a small deposit of plant compost, no bigger than a saucer and no deeper than half an inch in the centre. I can't believe that's what's upsetting this bloke, but it appears that it is. So now I tune my brain into his screaming to find he is indeed saying:

"Who's going to clear all that up? What do you think you're doing leaving that mess outside the door of my taverna?" To say he was making a mountain out of a molehill would be an exaggeration. He was making an Everest out of an egg-cupful. Incidentally, I left out all the swearwords in that brief précis of his tirade too.

It was evident that, although he wanted to make me look the villain, he actually didn't expect me, a tall Caucasian male, to understand his actual words. So he was visibly shaken when I replied in Greek, "What's YOUR problem mister? For goodness sake, it's a couple of yards away from your doorway anyway and the weather's hot and sunny (no surprises there then). It'll be dust in a few moments. Fetch me a dustpan and I'll sweep it up myself if it'll quieten you down! Can't you see we're trying to help someone here? You *VLAKAS!*" (which is a fairly strong insult, roughly translated as MORON!).

Well, I felt quite ashamed that I'd let him get to me, but he chose the wrong moment I suppose. But I'm quite glad in retrospect that I responded as I did because, on realising I could not only understand his words, but could respond in his language, plus the fact that I was bigger than him, he hastily retreated into his kitchen and didn't come out again. Evidently, he'd let out his tirade to impress his clientele rather than to actually get me to clear up the dirt, which, by the time I'd finished my response, Yvonne had succeeded in dissipating to nothing with a few sweeps of her hand anyway.

So we exited Lindos Square and the car negotiated all the walking semi-clads on the way up the hill to Krana Square, where we took a right and headed off to Arhangelos, some fifteen minutes drive up the road towards Rhodes Town.

So here I am forking some soil in order to insert a Jasmine in what will eventually become Josie's modest little garden. Yvonne-Maria and Josie are busy in similar pursuits with Lemon Geraniums and more Jasmine when Dimitra appears from next door, so we all down tools and proceed with the obligatory kiss on both cheeks, exchange pleasantries and listen as she tells us why her leg is all bandaged up. We have to have all the fine detail so we can fully appreciate why she has only narrowly escaped joining her parents in the village cemetery.

This particular day it's late in September and there are two pomegranate trees in Josie's garden. Both of these trees are laden with heavy fruit, which is so abundant that it weighs down several quite large branches. My wife asks Dimitra how one knows when to pick pomegranates, as they seem to be as big as they're going to get and, on one of these trees, turning very red as well. The other tree has fruit of the same size, but they all seem to be still green. We're not actually very keen on eating them, as the seeds always tend to make it too much hard work. But we understand that pomegranates are very good for you, a fact which Dimitra confirms with her life-acquired wisdom.

"When you pick them? You want to know?" Asks Dimitra, "When the rains come. When the first rains come they are ready. These are ripe now." We had indeed had our first thunderstorm a little early this year, during the first week of September.

"But," replies my wife, "these on this tree are still green. Ought they to be left a little longer?"

"Different type." Dimitra replies, her voice resonating authority on the subject. "Look, I show you." She takes a few steps over to the tree with the green fruit and picks a tennisball sized example. She tears it open with her fingers and proffers a piece to me, plus one each to Yvonne and Josie. "Eat!" she says, "This one is very sweet."

She's right, it is. I take a bite out of the pinky-red flesh inside the fruit and ask, while I chew, "What do you do with the seeds? Seems it'll take a month of Sundays to spit them out."

"You chew them." Replies our Pomegranate expert, grinning from ear to ear, this despite her recent brush with death from her now-bandaged leg. "What do you think?"

I have to say, I'd never tasted a Pomegranate like it. Still can't say I'm a convinced fan, but it did taste very nice.

We drive home with a plastic bag full of pomegranates.

"I'll make smoothies." Says my creative wife.

Tzatziki for You to Say

9 – I Kid You Not

A lot of British people living out here are either viewed as totally eccentric by the locals, or even as a flaming nuisance in one particular field, that of animals and their welfare.

We have one lady-friend (no names, no pack drill) who couldn't bear to see the often-emaciated-looking feral cats hanging around the waste bins provided by the local authority and so, a year or so ago, began to put a plate of cat food out on her terrace. Now, apart from the three dogs and a couple of domestic cats she already keeps in the house (to the horror of the locals), she's now acquired upwards of 40 cats living outside her front patio doors and regularly places enough saucers of food out there to make a crockery shop proud. She's even taken some of these animals to the vet in Rhodes town (some 55 kilometers away) for treatment when they've been ill. This exercise is, of course, fraught also with the danger that the vet will say (and often does):

"I'll have to keep her here overnight. Come back and collect her tomorrow about this time."

She has close neighbours who are Greeks and they have recently begun to express their disapproval and so she worries about whether her neighbour-relations will break down further as she can't find it in her heart to stop feeding the little furry breeders (yes, they're mating again at the moment and so will be producing goodness only knows how many litters in her garden).

When you go to visit her you can cast your eyes around her very nicely manicured garden and see a cat under every tree and bush to be found. They're sitting on her patio table and chairs and nestling into the soil atop her terracotta plant pots. They're lazing atop her pergola and stretched out on the dividing wall between her garden and those on either side. In short, it's cat city! The problem is, look next door on either side and you'll notice the cats colonising their gardens too, and that's why the problems are escalating. The locals see the feral cats as a nuisance, as vermin, and even cull them on occasion. Now, right next door they have someone who, in their opinion, is nurturing them, creating a health hazard and they have begun to make their feelings known to our friend, sometimes in high voices.

She's a good friend and we've tried to encourage her to get a bit "harder" and pack in this feeding malarkey, which would save her a considerable monetary sum into the bargain, and she agrees she ought to do something, but keeps putting it off. She'll confess to us each time we visit that she's at the end of her tether with it all and still can't make the decision to cut off their food supply in the knowledge that they'll soon drift away and revert to getting their meals from the local bins down the road. The fact is, she's too soft and is the first to admit it, but it's doing her head in none the less. But then again, she's British and we look after our animals.

But it isn't only cats and stray dogs that seem to infest many an ex-pat's home, much to the bemusement of the

Greeks. Recently we fell about when one couple who we know locally told us about another set of British neighbours, who we are also on excellent "cup of coffee or glass of wine" (depending on the circumstances you understand) terms with, who looked out of their window one day recently to see that a very young baby goat had become separated from its mother and her family by accidentally straying onto their side of the chain-link fence that surrounds (well, to be accurate, almost surrounds ...obviously!) their garden. There was no sign of the mother or the rest of the herd, but there was this cute little kid bleating and trotting back and forth inside their garden, evidently in some distress over being separated from mum against his or her will.

You often see such scenarios in the countryside around here. There are innumerable chain-link fences surrounding ancient olive groves or citrus orchards, most of which have seen better days and so are full of stretches where they've been breached. Along comes the local herd of goats and some will graze to one side of a fence, whilst the rest will find themselves on the other. It seems that whilst they're grazing (which is most of the time) they're not really paying enough attention to where they're going. Pretty soon you'll see some of them getting all worked up about being on the wrong side of a particular fence from the rest of their group. It doesn't ever seem to occur to them that, if they'd just retrace their steps by just a few yards, they can pop through the breach and rejoin their mates. I don't rate goat IQ all that highly.

Anyway, to return to our couple, who now find they've a kid in their garden. Hubby told his missus that she shouldn't worry as the herd would be sure to come around again soon and baby would be reunited with mum. Missus said she couldn't stand to see the poor thing in such a lather and so went out to try and catch it and bring it into the house as it was sure to either starve or catch its death with a cold night expected, as it was January. Against hubby's wishes she and he were soon running back and forth themselves in an attempt to trap the little soul and bring it in for some sustenance. Despite his protestations that nature ought to be left to take its course, hubby went along with his wife's whim, as we so often do don't we chaps?

Sure enough, after much puffing and panting they eventually cornered it and took it inside their very nice modern newly-built villa, where missus insisted it ought to spend the night. Hubby tried to suggest that the herd may even pass by in the small hours and so the kid should be out there and ready to rejoin its family; but no, missus was steadfast - "it stays inside with some warm milk and a heated room with which to pass the night." The subject of a potential problem with goat droppings didn't even enter the conversation.

They eventually retired to bed and attempted a night's rest. Soon the little kid's bleating downstairs was tugging at the Missus' heartstrings and she just couldn't lie there tossing and turning while it relentlessly expressed its distress. While her hubby turned over and pulled the duvet further over his ears, his compassionate wife slipped out of bed and into her gown to go and see what was to be done. When hubby awoke the following morning he noticed a slight whiff in the room and was more than a little surprised to see the young goat curled up at the foot of their bed!! It seemed that his good wife had found that the only way to stop the bleating in the end was to bring the lucky creature up to bed with them and give it a blanket to sleep on. Bit of a far cry from a Greek mountainside eh?

This, then, was the final straw. Hubby now exited his bed,

threw on his gown and, after a couple of failed attempts, managed to pick up the bovine visitor, carry it downstairs and out into the garden at the crack of dawn where - sure enough - the herd could be heard (almost a pun there, don't you think?) chomping their way up the nearby slope. By the time hubby had got back up the stairs to take a peep out of the bedroom window, the little formerly-lost soul was tucking into mother's teat and a few moments later trotting off into the Greek beyond once again in the bosom of its family.

I kid you not. Only the names have been withheld to avoid possible embarrassment, not to mention legal action!

Tzatziki for You to Say

10 – Just Being Careful

Petros and Lena are about our age. They've also been married about the same number of years as us. We've known them almost since first moving out here and so are now good friends. Petros knows how to be careful with his money.

They were both born and bred in Greece, he here on Rhodes and she somewhere on the mainland. They met in Canada, where they'd both emigrated some thirty years ago, he to avoid the draft and she as part of her parents' family at the time, in search of a better life. They'd raised a few kids there before coming back to Greece to settle on Rhodes in the 1990's. They brought a lot of "stuff" back over here with them, kids and all. Such "stuff" included their electrical appliances as well as a load of furniture, all of which was crated up, packed into a "container" and shipped here to southern Rhodes at some considerable cost. Petros felt it was still cheaper than replacing everything once he'd got back here to start building their new home on family-owned land.

Standing around in Lena's kitchen I remark on how large her cooker is. It's a lot wider than your average European cooker and although sporting only the usual four hobs, they are further apart than normal. It has two ovens side-by-side instead of one-above the other, as is the case with most European "doubles". Behind the hobs it has a "splash-back" panel, at the top of which is a horizontal glass strip into which are set the switches to control the hobs, ovens and timer. These days you seldom find such an arrangement, since it means reaching over boiling saucepans or spitting skillets to adjust the controls; all in all, a health and safety nightmare.

"That's some beast. I bet it would cost a fortune to replace." I remark. This elicits a sideways glance between Lena and her husband, who's sipping coffee from his mug, as indeed we all are, as we stand around the kitchen talking. A hint of a sardonic smile passes his lips.

"Sore subject." Says Lena.

"Oops, sorry." I retort.

"It's been a sore subject for about fifteen years, actually." Continues Lena, evidently now developing a keenness to make it "sorer" right now. We're all ears.

"Shame about the cracked glass on the control panel, can't you replace it?" Asks my delicate wife, fishing.

"It came with us from Canada. You can't buy them over here. To get the part shipped would cost a small fortune and, anyway, there's more wrong with it than that. Two of the hobs don't work any more and the larger of the two ovens is on the blink. It gets more and more difficult to cook for friends or family I'm afraid." Lena says, casting a further askance look at her beloved husband, who's now got a sort of crooked grin behind his coffee mug. "Oh, and the timer's gone wrong too."

"Better get your loving hubby to buy you a new cooker then." Says Maria. "I'm sure he can afford it!"

Petros almost spurts coffee all over the kitchen and Lena flicks the tea towel she's holding at the appliance in question and says: "What do you think I've been trying to get him to do for fifteen years? He's too tight and that's all there is to it."

"I'll get it repaired!" appeals Petros, but not very convincingly.

"You've been going to 'get it repaired' for fifteen years. Maybe by the time I'm pushing up the daisies it'll be back to it's former glory. Not likely to be before."

They have a good marriage. It's evident from this exchange that, although his "carefulness" with money drives her up the proverbial, she loves him dearly. It's reciprocated, although Petros isn't the world's best at showing his appreciation for his wife's virtues and qualities, especially where parting with money is concerned. If ever we've been out with them during the day and suggested we drop into a bar for a coffee, it almost gives him apoplexy. He'll invariably say, "Come back to the house, we have plenty of coffee."

He actually gets on like a riot with Yvonne-Maria and often teases her, in return for which she'll insult him good-naturedly, although not without knowing how much nerve she can risk touching. He usually ends up guffawing, in a manner which no one else seems to be able to elicit from him. All in all, he's pretty placid and good-natured. It's an effective weapon against having to open his wallet.

"You mean to tell me that you don't love your wife enough to make sure she has a decent cooker – the heart of every woman's kitchen – on which to make you all your meals! She's a saint managing with a situation like that! After a few years of enjoying her cooking I can't believe she manages it with that cooker! How hard can it be to phone up an electrician then?" My wife is prodding nerves now, no mistake. I'm wondering if we ought to be going. The front door suddenly looks very attractive.

But Petros is starting to laugh, which is his usual defence. He never takes offence at Maria's jibes, thankfully. My wife is now warming to her mission, "When was the last time you took your wonderful wife out then, eh? I bet you can't remember!" If I were Petros I'd be well on the way to "mind your own business" territory by now. He is, however, "killing himself" laughing. Maria's not finished yet: "If you were MY husband I'd have kicked you out ages ago!" Now he's hysterical. He's very clever really. I mean, what can you do? How can you argue with a man who's laughing uncontrollably, as if he's just watched a brilliant stand-up comedian. He always wins in such situations.

Lena's smiling, but you can tell she would like something of what Maria says to register. She does want a new cooker, oh how she does. Petros gains some control over himself and says,

"It's not as simple as you think. That cooker is an unusual width. If I took it out and put a new one in, there would be a huge gap between the kitchen units, which have been installed to match the width of this cooker. So it wouldn't only be a new cooker, we'd have to re-model the kitchen!" This of course would seriously injure his wallet. It may even require intensive care.

They're not badly off, to tell the truth. Lena would say that they could well afford to replace the cooker. In fact it's something you have to afford, as it's an essential. Petros would say that the reason they're fairly OK financially is the fact that he's always "being careful." You never know when that unexpected expense may hit you. You can't be too careful. He doesn't have a credit card and doesn't have a mobile phone. He's deeply suspicious of such tools of the Devil.

A few more verbal prods from my wife about how-he-ought-to-be-ashamed-of-himself later, we take our leave and exit the front door, which is across the hall from their kitchen, and descend the stone steps to the terrace below. Since they live on the first floor of their house and let the three apartments that they've now built below, they do all right.

A week or so goes by and we turn up one day to witness a very unexpected scene. As we exit the car and look up we see a couple of burly men struggling to get down the steps from the front door with the aforementioned cooker between them. It's evidently causing them some grief due to its size and also its weight. Lena is standing on the terrace above, looking like a mother does when she watches her child being carted off to hospital. Petros is beside her and looking worried. If I were a betting man I'd wager a tidy sum that he's calculating how much damage to the wad in his wallet he'll be facing imminently.

We stand aside while the struggling workmen finally make it to the bottom of the steps, readjust their grasp to relieve fingers in danger of amputation and then make their way to a waiting pickup truck, its rear tailgate down in readiness to receive the stricken appliance. Oven duly loaded and tied down, they shout something relating to how long they'll probably take to fix the thing, slide into the doors on either side of the cab, gun the engine and zoom off in a cloud of dust and blue smoke.

Lena and Petros beckon us upstairs. Once inside we all stand around the kitchen again, this time staring at the gap left by the absent cooker. As is usually the case, the space where it had been is full of cobwebs, various bits of vegetable that had managed to fall down beneath the cooker over the years while it had been *"in situ"* which had now dried to wrinkled solidity, plus a dustpan's worth of dust. Lena decides it'll be her that needs to clean up while the appliance is in intensive care. She goes to the cupboard in the hall and fetches her small hand brush, together with one of those dustpans which the Greeks seem so fond of, the type that don't have a top and sport a long vertical handle that's about hip-height. No matter how hard I try I can't get along with this type of dustpan. They seem to have a mind of their own. Usually they come with an equally long-handled brush, but to do the kind of brushing up that demands the use of a dustpan and brush usually necessitates the operator of said tools getting on their knees. With this type you have to do it standing up; but to brush into corners and other nooks, then aim the offending matter into the pan with a long handled brush I find a near impossibility. A Greek will never give up though. Suggest to them that a regular-type dustpan and brush would be much easier and you might as will be speaking a foreign language. You'd have no more success getting them to try using a knife at the dinner table, or perhaps the directional indicators in a car rather than switching on the "hazards."

While Lena struggles to look comfortable with the impractical clean-up tools, Petros suggests coffee and we accept.

Another thing that amuses us about the modern Greek home is that they virtually all have, usually visible on the kitchen worktop, what we northern Europeans would call a "camping gas burner." You know the type I mean, it's got one smallish gas cylinder, on to the top of which is screwed the burner, which has four fold-out metal rods, bent over at the top to support your billy can, while you sit round the camp fire and sing about riding along on the crest of a wave or some such subject. Why, in this day and age, would a modern kitchen need such a thing?

The answer is twofold. Firstly there's no mains gas in Greek island homes. They all have electric hobs. To cook with gas, many buy those double gas-hobs you see at outdoor events and use a gas bottle to supply the gas. Often you'll see one of these portable hobs plonked on top of a modern electric hob in someone's kitchen. They do this because the electricity supply in all parts of Greece is still prone to frequent and often quite long power cuts. If you have an electric hob but no electricity, bang goes your boiled vegetables or fried anything. At least with the gas back-up they needn't go hungry. But why the small camping gas burner?

It's still the time-honoured way of making Greek coffee. Even today they have TV adverts for these burners. You can see all kinds of fancy-coloured ones from various manufacturers. One TV ad running these days, in 2010, shows a very smart gold-coloured contraption with a case that entirely obscures the gas cylinder inside. It looks so swish. The ad shows an ultra-modern kitchen and your usual slim and attractive mother, who would be more at home on a catwalk than making the bed for her three growing kids. Her friend from next-door drops in and she immediately reaches for her trusty gas burner to make Greek coffee so she and her neighbour can catch up on all the goss. They're busy sipping their dark, syrupy caffeine charge when our heroine's teenage daughter (Teenage daughter? You have to be kidding with a mum looking like that!) comes in through the kitchen door and reaches for the burner. There's one thing a schoolgirl needs when before anything else she gets home from school it seems, that's a nice rich Greek coffee. So the camping gas burner is an essential in any household where they frequently make Greek coffee. It seems that the electric hob is simply too slow for the job. Where in Britain these days would you see a supermarket shelf brimming with a selection of those little blue camping gas cylinders, which tend to be used more often in a blowlamp in the UK than for anything else? Yet no self-respecting supermarket here would be without them.

Anyway, it's just as well Petros and Lena have one, since they are now hob-less for an unspecified period. What about the kettle? You ask. Well, the electric kettle is still only just beginning to gain acceptance in Greece. Many, Lena included, still heat water for a coffee or tea in a saucepan, whilst retaining a healthy suspicion of such American inventions as an electric kettle. Kettles use electricity, that means they cost money to run! Try explaining that to heat water on a hob tends to do something similar. You won't get far. It seems that Greek psyche still sees the hob as a leftover from the wood-heated stoves of yesteryear, when they would heat water on a "range." So psychologically it feels better to use a saucepan. Greek logic, eh?

Today, though, we're grateful for the Greek idiosyncrasies of our hosts as it means we can have a hot coffee rather than no coffee at all.

"Dare I ask if they've taken it away so you can take delivery of a new one?" Asks my ever-tactful wife.

"Lena makes as if to look out of the window, "I don't see any pigs flying past." She replies, no hint whatsoever of humour in her voice.

"It's gone for repair. They said about a week." Says Petros.

"That's a Greek week I presume?" I enquire. Lena finally gives up attempting to sweep up and tends to the coffee, since her husband's bold attempt at hospitality only made it as far as the verbal offer. He having not done anything tangible about it, she lights the camping gas and sets a saucepan on top of it. My mind immediately goes back to the English countryside of forty-plus years ago, when my parents used to take my sister and I on camping trips in the summer. Maria enquires as to how Lena is going to manage to cook without her oven. Lena replies stoically that she's managed virtually without one for years anyway. A camping gas cylinder and a microwave (one of the few concessions to modernity in their kitchen) should suffice temporarily.

A fortnight later we visit the couple again and Petros proudly beckons us into the kitchen to view the revitalised cooker. There it stands, back in its custom-built cubby-hole between the kitchen cupboards. I can't help noticing that the formerly glass panel above the hobs, which sports all the circular knobs to operate the hobs and ovens, not to mention the smaller knobs that operate the timer, is now simply black and looks like a sheet of plywood. In fact, it is a sheet of plywood, painted matt black and with a selection of circular holes cut in it to allow the existing knobs to poke through. It looks smart enough, but now the temperature markings and other various information printed on the cracked glass panel that was there before are gone, all evidently now beneath this new addition.

I risk my life in Petros' presence to ask how Lena is going to know what setting she has the oven on, or how hot she's set a hob, since all the markings are now gone. Lena replies:

"Oh, I know the thing so well, that an educated guess ought to do. They couldn't get a replacement panel, so they fitted this black one to make it look better. With time I'll just get used to knowing what's going on! I ought to be able to tell from the positions of the knobs.

"Anyway, the hobs are all working now, as are both ovens." She continues, although not very enthusiastically.

"How much did they charge?" Yvonne-Maria asks.

"Don't ask." Says Lena.

"Nearly three hundred Euros." Says Petros. My better half and I exchange a glance that says "not a good idea to venture to suggest that they'd have been better off buying a new one at this moment."

Petros is quite pleased with himself, as the fact is he got it repaired and his wife ought to be grateful. He's being careful.

A few weeks later we're invited around to their house for a meal with a few other couples. As we step through the front door, the smell of Lena's cooking transports me. She is a good cook, a very good one. In fact, since she can't see the controls on her revitalised cooker, the subsequent meal, which we all enjoy, is proof positive.

But as we enter the house at the start of the evening we can't help but notice that all along the hallway there are various mechanical parts of all shapes and sizes on the floor, all sitting on sheets of newspaper. There are some which I don't recognise at all, but the part nearest to the kitchen is a huge grey metal drum, with holes all over it. It looks awfully like something out of a washing machine.

"What are all these pieces then?" I ask Petros as he takes my jacket.

"The washing machine has gone wrong, so I'm fixing it." He replies with a confident smile. Now I don't know if you've ever been to an American or Canadian household, but I did have such a privilege a few years ago. They still often have large utility rooms (often in the basement) where they keep their washer and drier and the washer is often much, much larger than your average European front-loading washing machine. In fact they still seem to go in for top-loaders. The washing machine on that particular continent could well be described as similar in size to what we Europeans would call and "industrial" sized one.

Well, Petros and Lena's washing machine is one such beast and they keep it in the bathroom. Yes, they brought it back with them all those years ago when they returned to Rhodes from Canada. Apparently it's been on the blink for a while and Petros, despite his desperate wife's appeals to buy new, is going to fix it if it's the last thing he does. "It's still got years in it yet, you'll see." He declares.

It's several weeks before their hallway is absent of all the components of their washing machine. Petros brims with confidence and satisfaction when we eventually visit and find the parts gone.

"I managed to get the parts shipped from Canada in the end." He says, "My cousin over there organised it."

We decide not to comment when we're told how much it cost. But we know what he's going to say as a concluding flourish to his latest success story:

"There's no substitute for being careful with your money."

11 – The Fledgling Thespian

Bertolt Brecht doesn't immediately spring to mind when I think about a school play. Well, he doesn't spring to my mind, I don't know about yours. He's a bit "heavy" for school kids in their early teens, don't you think? Apparently, there are those who feel that the "greatest play of the twentieth century" was "*Mother Courage and Her Children*," Brecht's epic set during the Thirty Years War of the early seventeenth century. When you consider how many people you know who've actually heard of this play, I'd venture a guess that you may think, as do I, that there are plenty of other plays that spring to mind which could lay claim to that particular title. The "*Rocky Horror Show*" for example? OK, maybe not.

Nevertheless, when Mario, son of Manoli, the "Six Million Drachma Man" told us he was starring in the forthcoming school play at his school in Arhangelos, we expressed warm congratulations that he'd landed a plum part (Cook) and promised that we'd attend the performance.

According to some, Arhangelos is a bit down-market. It's the equivalent on this island of that slightly troublesome housing estate you hope your kids won't go and play in. I've always rather liked the place though, largely because it has no pretensions. Yes, if there's going to be any crime of the breaking and entering variety it'll doubtless occur in Arhangelos, although it's rare even here. No, the roads through the village are not the best surfaced asphalt roads in the world, but you still pay a fair price, nay a cheap price, for your frappe and you don't see very many tourists ambling along the pavements even in the high season.

Arhangelos has a generous enough selection of tavernas, all of which are cheap and their food is most certainly acceptable. It also has an epidemic of coffee bars, making it a delight to go shopping for your fruit and veg there, which always of course calls for a coffee stop. The bars range from traditional cafenions where the old guys sit and play backgammon with a Papas, or read the daily paper whilst tutting over their *Elleniko*" at the latest scandal, to trendy places with brightly coloured plastic chairs where the young ones sit and sup and bury their heads in their mobile phones.

There is a Police Station and a Medical Centre which falls somewhere between a doctor's surgery and a small hospital. There are three olive presses, a large cemetery and, apart from a selection of infant and junior schools, there's also a fairly large school for children between the ages of eleven and sixteen. Manoli's two younger children, Mario and Christina, both attend this school, the main entrance of which is along the main shopping street, between a coffee shop and the "river" bed over which the main road runs on a flat bridge. The word "river" is in parentheses because it only sports a trickle of water during the winter months. It's entirely concreted and more resembles a road than a river and you could drive your car along it during the hot rainless summer months.

Manoli, as you'll know if you've read "*Moussaka to My Ears*", is the "Six Million Drachma man," because he was badly injured by an explosion whilst doing his military service in his youth, which left him with one and a half legs, one hearing ear and one seeing eye. He also has no fingers remaining on his right hand. For all that he strides through life with a very positive attitude and does his level best to raise three children on a shoestring, since he and his wife are separated, she having battled with her personal demons (which come out of a bottle), for most of her adult life. We genuinely feel sorry for Manoli and his children. They don't have an easy life. For all that, Mario is always ready with a one-liner and is irrepressible in his humour. If the truth be told, he has a bit of a crush on "*Thia*" Maria [my wife]; which is born of the fact, or so I theorise, that his own mother is largely absent from his life and, on the rare moments when their paths do cross, she usually verbally abuses him.

Mario is an immature fourteen and loves the theatre. He has genuine acting talent and is cock-a-hoop to be playing Cook in the Brecht play. It's a demanding part and requires that he be on stage for most of the play's duration. When he invited us to attend (something about which we were genuinely touched to be asked) we assured him that wild horses wouldn't stop us coming. He looked at us askance nevertheless, since as a Greek he's used to being promised things by those who, on a whim, may choose to break that promise without so much as an apology. It's just the way the Greeks are. If they fail to show up for some appointment or other, they'll act as though nothing's amiss the next time you see them and will be totally baffled if you remind them of their failure. You either learn to live with such traits or you never settle into life on a Greek island.

In the weeks leading up to the play's performance, Mario repeatedly reminds us at every opportunity that he has rehearsals several times each week. During the last ten days or so he informs us of the dress rehearsal he'll be attending and frets over his lines. It's a hot summer's Wednesday evening when we set out to go and watch Mario in his moment of Thespian triumph. We arrange to meet Manoli outside the school gate at around 6.45pm and, for once, there is a need to be punctual. We arrive five minutes late to find Manoli waiting and glancing at his watch. The shoe is on the other foot for once, no pun intended, since Manoli only has the one to begin with. Mind you, you wouldn't necessarily notice as he walks surprisingly well with his prosthetic. He waves our little Suzuki in through the gate, slips into the back seat and directs us across the fifty metres or so of concrete school yard to an appropriate parking slot, one of only a couple remaining. We get out of the car and I silently tell myself that there will surely be someone parked behind me when I come out later, and so not to be too wound up about it when it happens.

The school building has that slightly neglected look about it. The school staff and teachers evidently make the best of a low-budget bad job and, what they lack in resources, they surely make up for in dedication. We walk through the main entrance into the lobby, which is a hard-floored corridor with areas where the concrete rendering is crumbling under yet another coat of cream paint. People stand around in knots smoking, many of these evidently students at this very establishment. Anyone under seventeen is gazing robotically at the front of their mobile phone while their thumb works overtime tap-tapping away at the keys. We turn a corner, proceed along the corridor for another twenty metres and turn right into the school hall.

Notwithstanding the fact that this is a school in a large village on a Greek island, it has that air about it that tells one instinctively that it's nevertheless a school hall. The whole school complex is easily as big as the ones I attended in the UK and so I hazard a guess that there must be several hundred pupils who attend. In size, the hall closely resembles those in which I used to stand during assembly in the days when I was a spotty youth, while listening to the headmaster (I seem to recall that for the greater part of my Grammar school days our headmaster was a Mr. Les Scott, a slightly distant, placid gentleman) as he expounded the reasons why we should all want to make the school proud through our endeavours. I distinctly remember being embarrassed about not having a Hymn book when I was a "first-former," and being equally embarrassed about having one when I was in the sixth.

The whole of one wall, to our left as we take our seats, is comprised of windows which have huge thin black cloths draped all down their length in a vain attempt to make the auditorium dark. With the strength of a Greek early evening sun outside, they never really had much of a chance. The chairs are all slightly too small and comprise curved grey tubes of metal, attached to which are plywood seats and backs, once again almost identical to the ones I used to sit on in my school in Bath, England. Our school hall sported a wooden floor, although this one is made of crushed marble, making the acoustics somewhat more echoey. The stage looks like any school stage you have ever seen or imagined and the curtains are drawn tight, awaiting the moment when the performance will begin. People are still filtering in at 7.30pm, when the play is due to start. I can spot the teachers easily. Why is it teachers always look like teachers? That's not meant as a criticism, merely an observation. There's a forty-something man, slightly stocky with a hairline that's just beginning to lose the battle, and he's creeping over to a door to the right of the stage at regular intervals to consult with an unseen cohort from behind the said door. He glances at his watch, then moves to the microphone stand that's been set up on the floor in front of the stage to ensure all is in order, before once again resuming his seat while a female teacher whispers something in his ear from her seat behind him. He wears yellow cord trousers, a check shirt and the jacket hanging over his chair has leather elbow patches. It's all very reassuring somehow.

Every now and again a face with a manic grin appears between the tightly-drawn stage curtains as some member of the cast or crew can't resist the temptation to see what sort of a crowd they've drawn. By about twenty to eight the lights are dimmed, making precisely no difference whatsoever to the level of light in the hall, and the yellow cord trousers approach the microphone on the floor at the front. The expected feedback noises having been dealt with by a male student deftly twiddling a few knobs on the mixing panel to the right of the stage, yellow cords begins to say a few words.

He expresses deep gratitude to all parents, relative and friends of the school for coming along to this cultural event, which will consist, of course, of a performance of the aforementioned Brecht play, then, following a short interval, there will be a live Bouzouki band of school pupils, to be accompanied by some traditional dancing.

Yvonne-Maria whispers dismay over the fact that we have other plans for later in the evening; since Mario, in his excitement over his part in the play no doubt, had omitted to tell us about the musical section of the evening to follow.

Yellow cords drones on among the throng of bodies of

those still arriving, who are shaking hands with everyone they recognise while finding their seats. While he talks, a distinguished-looking fifty something man with his elegant wife also walk right past his face and sit themselves down in the two seats next to his, at the front of the audience. Yellow cords isn't phased. Visibly relieved at their tardy arrival, he now introduces the local Mayor, who has graciously agreed to say a few words.

Distinguished-looking fifty-something now approaches the *mic* and begins his speech about how wonderful it is for the pupils to have staged such a fine event. He mentions all the preparation that must have gone into it. He praises the teaching staff and the women who've worked night and day to make the costumes. He says how impressed he is by the dedication shown by all connected with the project and how thrilled he and his wife are to be able to support the event in person.

As with the speech by yellow cords, the Mayor is also frequently obscured from view by yet more latecomers walking in front of him while acknowledging all their acquaintances and finding some seats.

Finally, the Mayor senses that the audience has had enough of his ramblings and winds it up, handing us back over to the play's director, none other than yellow cords himself. I actually like yellow cords. He reminds me of all the qualities my favourite teachers used to have when I was at school. You can tell he loves his job and his kids. Not to mention probably the rather attractive female teacher who's seated behind him and hasn't missed an opportunity to lean toward him and whisper conspiratorially whenever possible.

At somewhere around ten past eight the music begins and the curtains part for the spectacle to unfold before an audience of a couple of hundred. Right from the outset as I gaze around

I am hit by the fact that there are enough video-cams whirring to stock your average branch of Dixons. Some are on tripods, making those behind strain their necks to get a view of the stage, while others are strapped around hands and permanently affixed to the right eye of their operators. Correct me if I'm wrong here, but I understood that, owing to the current moral climate in this lovely modern world of ours, EU regulations forbid the use of video recording equipment at such school functions as this. After all, I mean, every other video recordist is a paedophile isn't he (or she)? I'm delighted to say that no one is concerned by the presence of such morally dangerous equipment here tonight.

Yvonne and I are only about five rows from the front. This is just as well because, no sooner has the play got under way, than some of the radio *mic*'s attached to the costumes of the actors immediately begin to malfunction, something which is evidently not fixable and so the play runs its course with some of the participants shouting their parts and others trying to lean toward their less fortunate fellow thespians whose microphones are rendered useless.

Throughout the entire performance people continue to walk in and out and the back couple of rows seem to consist of a social get-together of some sort, the talking from that area certainly giving such an impression anyway. Add to this the fact that the double doors that open on to the corridor are half-way along the hall's length and propped open to aid air circulation and you can see why it proves extremely difficult to concentrate on the spectacle taking place on the stage.

This is a pity because the set is impressive, as is the acting. Mario does a superb job with his part, which he discharges very professionally, while frequently having to pretend to be preparing a stew, or chopping a dead (plastic) chicken. The play is set during the "Thirty Years War" in Europe in the 1600's and is a strong statement by the playwright against Fascism and war in general. It successfully counters great tragedy with humour and we both, seeing it for the first time for ourselves, find it quite amazing that the teachers and a bunch of 11-14 year old pupils have taken this project on and discharged it so well, notwithstanding the constant distractions going on around us.

Eventually the final curtain falls. Well, to be more precise two smaller pupils drag the two sides together from either side of the stage, each making sure that the audience get a view of their grinning faces as their extremely brief moment of glory arrives. They get a second chance as yellow cords gesticulates wildly to tell them to open the curtains again for the cast to take another well-deserved bow. We stand up, shake a few hands of people around us who evidently know Manoli and to whom he feels he should introduce us, then we file out among the melee into the corridor, where we find a small table, upon which are a few plastic cups of fruit juice for the refreshment of the audience. It's hardly the Bar at the Theatre Royal, but gratefully accepting one of these each from an eager teacher, we wait for Mario to emerge from the classroom next-door, which has been turned into the boys' dressing room.

He eventually comes out, now in his regular clothes, but still with stage makeup all over his face, and he breaks into a huge grin to see Thia Maria and Theo John waiting to congratulate him on what was indeed an excellent performance. He evidently hadn't really believed that we'd come and didn't see us out there in the audience during the performance. His dad beams with pride too and we both feel so glad that we'd made the effort. On balance, Brecht had indeed been a better choice than "*Rocky Horror.*"

Mario's mum wasn't anywhere to be seen.

12 - Industriousness

If you wander through the lanes of Lindos during a mid-March day you can be mistaken for thinking that, barring the whitewashed higgledy-piggledy cottages and tiny lanes, you were somewhere else, perhaps in a different country even. Why is this? It's because March is the last full month remaining before the summer season gets under way. Why does this make a difference?

The season begins in earnest immediately following the Greek Easter, which you won't need me to remind you is usually a week (sometimes even two) later than the Easter celebrated by the rest of the world. Trust the Greeks to be different. If you know something about Greece you'll also know that Easter is bigger than Christmas, which means that huge numbers of Greeks are on the move. Many return to their families and the villages where they were brought up, in order to be with a huge family gathering as they roast their lamb (although more often than not nowadays it'll be a pig) on the spit over the barbecue. The barbecue in a Greek home on an island like Rhodes isn't going to be that metal thing on wheels that you can get from your local B&Q. No, no, *no!* The barbecue you'll find on the Greek *avli* will either be a huge stone-built thing with a chimney, or half a metal oil drum that takes enough wood or charcoal to fuel your average power station. You don't barbecue for a handful if you're a Greek. You barbecue for numbers approaching coach loads.

Other Greeks will use Easter as a good opportunity to take that long weekend break. Those lucky enough to be fairly well-heeled, like for example those who have businesses in Rhodes town, will pack up the four-by-four, often with the boat on its trailer behind, and high-tail it down to Kiotari, or further south still, where they'll pass the weekend in their beach-side retreat, of which there are many in this part of Rhodes. Athenians too, will hop on to the *Karavi* (ferry) or plane and head to the islands to enjoy a break before the season begins and they get down to the serious business of worshipping at the altar of commercialism. It's not only the put-upon employees who work seven days a week for six months or so every summer. The boss, his missus and mother-in-law will work no fewer hours than their waiters and bar tenders, more often than not.

This, of course, means that the last few weeks before Easter are the time when things need doing. Walk through Lindos on a January day at around noon and you could be forgiven for thinking you were on an abandoned movie set, or that the bomb had finally been dropped. But when it's only weeks to go before Easter and the start of the tourist season, there are walls to be painted, bars to be re-fitted, stock needs to be dusted off and replaced on shelves in shops that have lain empty for months. There are signs to be renovated and menu boards to be re-affixed to the walls that they were taken down from the previous November. There are glasses to be cleaned of several months worth of dust behind bars where the cane tables and chairs need extracting from lock-ups in which they've languished under polythene sheets for ages. There are studios and apartments to be aired, there is linen to be laundered and made ready for fitting to innumerable beds, which will be slept in by a different body every week or two for the succeeding six months. In Lindos, particularly, there are donkeys to be gathered from diverse locations, saddled up with their wooden saddles and brought into their "garage" in the village in preparation for their long months of trudging up and down to the Acropolis which towers over the village, with overweight, under-clad, lobster-skinned and videocam-wielding tourists perched on their backs.

Wherever there are trees along roadsides, like, for example, the main road by-passing the village of Lardos, they must be drastically pruned. Many of these trees are eucalyptus and very fast growing. So a pick-up load of locals will turn up, chainsaws at the ready, and vigorously slash away at the majestic limbs until all that remains is a thick trunk maybe eight or ten feet in height, and no branches whatsoever. The pickup trucks drive away, laden with foliage which will be discarded in the countryside somewhere, often on land owned by the perpetrators, and the thicker boughs will be sectioned and stacked to dry for the summer months before feeding the log-burner or open fire during the winter months.

Walking through Lindos today I take my life in my hands. It's March 15th and every street where it's remotely possible for a three-wheeled, lawnmower-engined cart to pass, that's exactly what happens. I plaster myself against the wall on more than one occasion whilst the earnest driver trundles past, waves a "*kalimera*" and rounds the next right-angled bend in a cloud of blue smoke. One such vehicle, with handlebars for steering and no cab whatsoever in front of its modest flatbed, driven by an old man who probably competes with the cart in age, sports across its rear tailgate the huge letters (all capitals):

FERRARI

On many streets I pick my way around wheelbarrows, spades and piles of sand and cement, which someone's busily mixing up to repair the terrace of his bar. Men with pencils behind their ears stand in knots and discuss how to go about reducing the pile of shop fittings they've got heaped outside some tourist shop or other and I'm put in mind of the old (very old, actually) Bernard Cribbins song, *"Right Said Fred."* You remember the lyric:

"Right" said Fred, "ave to get the wall down. That there wall is gunner 'ave to go…"

Near where we live there are several low-rise hotels, all of them fairly up-market. During November, groups of men turn up with huge rolls of green material and an ample supply of re-bars, those steel bars that are used to reinforce concrete, hence the epithet "re-bar." These raw materials soon become a goat defence, which completely surrounds the grounds of the hotels in an attempt to ensure that, come the next season, there will still be some flowering plants and shrubs in place to make the tourists admire the hotel's gardens with appreciation. Of course, this means that, come March, these temporary fences all need to be dismantled again to allow access to the hotel grounds for innumerable coaches bringing new arrivals and shipping those whose holiday is over back to the airport, plus other coaches which will turn up at the crack of dawn to take daytrippers off on their often-exhausting one-day jaunts, plus innumerable hire cars, which will turn up and be parked all around the grounds in whichever nook or cranny the driver can find.

It boggles the imagine just how much of a mess the local

business owners can make during this frantic season of preparation and yet have it all cleared up a few milliseconds before the first coach load of package travellers is set down outside their sprucely cleaned and aired accommodation in preparation for their seven or fourteen days of escape.

While I'm thinking about coaches, I'm reminded of the 2007 season, during which I did two weekly excursions for a travel company from Pefkos. A number of the well-known tour operators booked their excursions through this local Greek-owned firm, and I was enlisted to take a group of holidaymakers to Symi every Monday, and on the "Rhodes-By-Night" jolly on Friday evenings. Yvonne-Maria also did a few of the Symi "runs", since during the high season there were often two coach loads of guests making the trip and it was a near impossibility to make a few stops beginning in Kiotari, give the guests all the information they needed about the procedure we'd follow once we arrived at Mandraki Harbour, then jump coaches at Faliraki and enlighten another fifty people with the same information in time for the driver to pull up near the Symi ferry. So I negotiated a deal with the "boss" to let both my better half and I do the trip whenever there were two coaches required.

This necessitated Yvonne-Maria coming with me on a "training run" before she took the bull by the horns and grasped the microphone at the front of a coach-load of sun and fun seekers for herself; something which she's never been that comfortable with.

So there we were seated at the front of the coach and chatting with George, one of the two drivers who regularly did the excursions for this particular company. The other driver we worked with was called Stefanos and he came from

Arhangelos. He's a dead ringer for Silvester Stallone and would feign embarrassment whenever I'd mention this for the benefit of his female passengers. Needless to say both George and Stefanos weren't averse to the pleasures of looking at those of the female gender, especially the more attractive specimens. No girl was safe from the horn-honking of these two if she walked along the roadside when they passed. That's always assuming she met the criteria that merited a honk of course. I did say "honk" there by the way. Any imagined alternate spelling of that word was yours and not mine. Well, maybe George & Stefano's too. Ever the optimists those two.

George hails originally from Symi. Since the trip by coach from the first pick-up in Kiotari to Mandraki Harbour in Rhodes town took around two hours, there was ample time to chat and hear all about George's background. George has two grown up children. His son is a footballer, as was George. Leaving Symi, as a younger man George had emigrated to the USA and, since he had evident soccer talent, had ended up playing in a soccer team as a semi-professional whilst on that side of the Atlantic. He likes to make the point that, had it not been for a leg injury that prematurely ended his football career, he could have reached the top in his favourite sport. But the knee injury he sustained cut that dream short and so he eventually returned to Greece with his young wife and small children, eventually settling in Gennadi, here on Rhodes.

George seemed to be happily married, but then, when all said and done, he IS a Greek. It was while Yvonne-Maria and I were conversing with him as he drove into Rhodes town in the pre 9.00am traffic one hot morning, that he spotted a particularly fine example of womankind, strolling along the pavement in very (and I mean, VERY) short shorts and a miniscule top that barely (appropriate word used again there) covered the essential bits. He was soon honking and waving and expressing his approval to the extent that it prompted my dear wife to reprove him with the words:

"GEORGE! KAKO PEDI! [bad child], and you a married man too!" To which our driver replied, much the way the child with his hand in the cookie jar may intone his words,

"NO! No! Only in winter I'm married, not in the summer!" He then proceeded to explain his position. "I mean," he continued, "if you spend your life eating vegetables, however good for you they may be, you want a little meat sometimes, eh?"

All through the winter, here in Kiotari, there are several modestly-sized hotels which have mature rose bushes in their roadside flowerbeds. Very often these will sport superb many-coloured blooms throughout the winter months and I often get the urge to whip out a pair of secateurs and prune them as I pass, on seeing all the developing rose-hips that, if left unclipped, would sap the energy of the plants and prevent them blossoming in the following season. Come March though, the owners, or someone employed by them, just go totally over the top and you'll pass one day and see that the bushes have been cut right down to a couple of inches above soil level. No careful thinning out, no specific cutting back to the "knuckle" here, no. Just hack it all away once a year.

It seems to do the rose bushes no lasting harm. Usually just a few short weeks later you can pass and see the new growth, all those gorgeous shiny, almost wine-red leaves and an abundance of new buds all about to burst out in a riot of colour as the new blooms shout their presence for another year. The fact that the bushes are left uncared for all through the winter months serves a purpose too. Albeit, not one which the owners would necessarily realise.

One winter's day we were driving back home from Gennadi when we stopped to pick up a "ya-ya" who was struggling with a few shopping bags and trying to flag down a lift on the coast road.

"Where are you going?" We asked as we pulled up beside her.

"Asklipio." She replied, already pumping the door handle and tumbling inside, along with her bulging bags. We had the time so we decided, yea we'll take her up to the village, which was a little out of our way, but we could always drop into the Agapitos Taverna and see if we have any mail. We pulled away and she added:

"Would you mind just a small detour? I have to feed a dog that's tied up near Kiotari Beach, at my family's beach house. It'll only take a minute or two." We looked at each other, and my wife replied, "OK. You show us where to go."

In what could best be described as Kiotari-proper (since the name is applied to quite a large coastal area in this part of the island), there are a few tavernas by the beach, behind which are probably twenty or thirty prefabricated beach houses, each no larger than what in the UK we'd call a mobile home. Some of these are very well cared for, all painted up in blue and white with modest little terraces out front, on which are barbecues and patio furniture, usually under a canopy of some sort or other. There's even the odd pot plant. Others are in a very bad state of disrepair and evidently haven't been used for some years. It was to one of these "cabins", whose state of repair was about midway between the two conditions just described, that our passenger directed us.

"Stop here! Yes this is fine. Don't get out of the car. I'll only be a moment." She said, rummaging in one of her shopping bags for a huge packet of dry dogfood, which she extracted and took with her, leaving the rest of her load on the rear seat of the car. Why didn't she want us to get out of the car? We wondered. Approaching the nearest cabin to where we'd stopped the car, she whistled and a huge Rottweiler appeared, as if out of nowhere, and doing a passable impression of the hound of the Baskervilles. I thought it was going to attack our passenger and had visions of blood all over the car seat as we rushed at breakneck speed to the Arhangelos Medical Centre, but no, it barked a lot and then tucked into the huge dish full of doggy-treats that the woman prepared for it. Only then did we see that it had a huge chain attached to its collar. The chain evidently prevented the dog from roaming too far, but looked like it wouldn't have been short enough to stop the animal taking off one of my legs had I decided to stretch them at this particular moment.

I was reminded, as I so often am at pivotal moments, of an old joke I'd once heard. What do you get if you cross a Rottweiler with a St. Bernard? You get a dog that bites your leg off and then goes for help.

Back in the car, the woman now said, "OK. We can go now. Thank you so much. Oh, before we go up to Asklipio, could you go back along the beach road and turn right at the Kabanari Bay lane please? Thank you, thank you."

Our generosity now beginning to wear just a little thin, we did as instructed. Turning right and away from the beach, up the short lane which runs past the Kabanari Bay Hotel and up to the main coast road, I made as if to increase speed a little when our passenger said: "Stop here! Please, STOP!"

I pulled up as instructed and we found ourselves right outside the entrance to the now quite empty hotel. Here beside the lane there were low white walls, maybe only a foot in height, surrounding rose beds, which sported an abundance of roses of all colours and sizes, none of which was being appreciated, since this was winter and precious few people passed this place for months; certainly none of them tourists. Deftly the woman exited the car, a pair of secateurs in her hand, with which she was soon clipping a nice bunch of roses. She must have once been a Girl Guide, since she evidently went everywhere well prepared. Once she had clipped a sizeable bouquet, she climbed back into the back of the car and smiled this comment:

"I have to visit my mother's grave in the cemetery before you get to the village. These will do nicely. I'm ready to go up to Asklipio now, if that's OK."

We finally dropped her off, all her missions having been accomplished and most of them with the use of our petrol, in the village. As she climbed out of our car for the last time she uttered profuse thanks over and over again and waddled off across the village square.

"That'll teach us to stop for a ya-ya who's thumbing a lift, won't it." I ventured.

"Aaah, she was quite sweet really." Replied my wife with largess. "I'll tell you what. I'm putting the secateurs in the car from now on!" She added, satisfaction at the prospect of putting fresh flowers in the lounge at nil cost to the wallet brightening her disposition considerably.

So it was that some weeks later, after we'd driven past the unappreciated blooms on several more occasions without having remembered the secateurs, we eventually did pull up outside the empty hotel, intent on bringing some scent and colour to our dining table, only to find all the rose bushes had been hacked down to ground level. It was now the month of March wasn't it.

Musing these experiences from previous winters, and wandering the streets of Lindos amongst all the March-time industriousness, I decide it's time for a coffee. Ikon Bar here I come. I only hope you don't smell too strongly of emulsion.

13 – Choice of Footwear

One of the most pleasurable aspects of a Greek island is finding a taverna with a distinctive character that makes it just that little bit special. If you've been to Greece a number of times you'll know what I mean. You make the effort to take a taxi or drive your hire car out in the sticks, or along a very rough track beside the sea to that taverna that someone's told you about and when you find it, it lives up to or even exceeds expectations. If you're crazy like my wife and I, you may even walk it. For "crazy" above, perhaps read "cheapskates," …whatever.

It was while staying at Poros, Kefallonia in 1986 that we found "Grandad's" Taverna. Poros is way down on the South-Eastern coast of the island, some three quarters of an hour by road from Argostoli, the island's capital. The last couple of miles of road drop down through a gorge, or canyon for you American folks, which used to put me in mind of Cheddar, a beauty spot not far from where I was brought up. At the bottom of the gorge the narrow coastal strip in which sits the seaside village of Poros awaits you. A few miles further down the coast, on what was in the 1980's a potholed dirt track, one which, I might add, succeeded in puncturing my brother-in-law Paul's hired Vespa's rear tyre, is Skala, even smaller and even sleepier than Poros, and that means seriously sleepy.

At the southern end of Poros is a small "*limani*" (port) where some of the more modestly sized island ferries occasionally tie up. There were a few tavernas there in the 80's, and not much else. If you stood at the quayside and turned to your right, you could see the pine-covered hill, which jutted out a little further into the Ionian sea than the quayside area, thus affording it some protection and making it an ideal location for a small port. If you were to move to the South of the harbour area you could pick up the dirt track that hugged the coastline all the way to Skala, a few miles to the South. The journey was fraught with boulders and potholes, but if you took it slowly you could make it on a 125cc Vespa, but you wouldn't have wanted to tell the guy you hired it from that you'd been down that track, for fear of him suffering an attack of apoplexy.

Yvonne-Maria and I spent a couple of very leisurely holidays at Poros during the late 1980's, the second of which was especially fun because my wife's brother Paul and his then wife Yvonne (yes, another one) were also on the island for most of the time we were there, although staying in Argostoli. We raved about the good old Vespa 125 automatic and told them they ought to hire one. They were much cheaper than a car and would whizz along at 65 mph, which was plenty fast enough for the roads on a Greek island. Paul had his doubts.

"I have never driven a motor bike or a scooter." He told me.

"That's not an excuse!" I replied, "It's so easy you could do it with your eyes closed, which, incidentally, many Greeks appear to be doing much of the time. Why not let me teach you on mine. Then, when you've got the hang of it, you can go and hire one." If I remember correctly, they had travelled down to Poros by taxi and were going to spend a night or two in our apartment with us.

So, the long and the short of it was that we were soon to be found on a quiet stretch of road (is there any other kind in remote corners of Greek islands I wonder?) where I sat Paul on the back and drove him a few hundred yards, narrating instructions all the way, which pretty much amounted to, "twist this grip on the right here to go faster, and use your right foot and left hand lever to brake. There are no gears, it's all automatic. Easy peazy. Now you try."

Paul and I exchanged seats after I'd done a 360 and pulled over. Paul in front, me riding pillion, I urged him to gently open up the throttle by twisting the right hand grip. Within seconds we were snaking all over the road, making a pretty good attempt at suicide should any vehicle decide to approach us from the opposite direction at the time. Fortunately, as I've already made clear, this was a "quiet stretch of road" and thus we survived long enough for Paul to begin getting the hang of the thing and cranking up his speed until I was sweating from more than just the Greek sunshine. Once I'd finally persuaded him that it was time to stop, change places again and re-join the girls on the beach, he was a convert.

Thus the four of us made intrepid excursions all over the island on our two trusty Vespas, including the coastal trek from Poros to Skala, where Paul sustained his rear wheel puncture. The amazing thing about these old Vespas is that they carry a spare wheel under the rear housing, to the inside of the passenger's leg. So it was that we could have been seen changing a wheel, while Yvonne and Yvonne took the opportunity to take a dip from the ever-present beach along that particular "road."

If you'd walked South of the harbour on to that road, or
"track" as it would more accurately have been described at the
time, you could, with a little perseverance, reach "Grandad's"
Taverna, which peeped out from among the trees part-way up
the hillside above the harbour. There were two ways of
reaching the taverna. One involved walking out to the end of
the headland, then taking a small dirt track back along the
ridge, before descending a few yards into the trees and coming
upon the taverna's terrace that way. This was the more "sissy"
route to take, since there was even a sign as the coastal track
rounded the end of the headland pointing up the goat track,
which consisted of a bit of red paint on a piece of driftwood,
which was nailed to a stake. The other, more macho way, was
to strike up through the pines from just beyond the harbour in
the hope that your sense of bearing would reward you by
bringing you out on to the same terrace from below, and in
somewhat less time, always assuming that you did make it to
the taverna and didn't get lost among the woodland that
covered the hill, as the sun went down.

After having been told on several occasions by others
who'd made it there about what an interesting evening could
be enjoyed at Grandad's, we decided one night, after waving
goodbye to Paul and Yvonne, that Grandad's would be where
we would eat. Apparently, since the terrace there is very
compact, the taverna can only cater for a dozen or so hungry
diners each night and they prefer to do it in one sitting. So,
those in the know are encouraged to spread the word that you
turn up around eight for aperitifs, then spend the evening
there in an intimate group, while you sample that particular
evening's dishes and get to know some other diners in a
convivial atmosphere, all the while gazing down over the small

bay below at the lights of the Poros "limani."

As was our usual routine while staying in our modest little apartment (in fact our routine over innumerable Greek holidays), we'd return from the beach at around 5.00pm, then sit out on the terrace with a drink and a book for another couple of hours before starting to get ready to got out for the evening. On occasions when the evening involved a promenade along the front before deciding which establishment to patronise, there was never any pressure to be ready to leave by any particular time. In fact, we always found that the later the better, since if you arrived at a taverna any time between 7.00pm and 9.00pm it's usually packed to the gills with tourists, who, having rushed through their three courses, then repair to a bar to try and kill the remaining evening hours before turning in for the night. Watch the Greeks, that's the key. Firstly, watch where they go to eat. Secondly, take note of what hour they start turning up at the establishment of their choice. In our experience Greeks often don't arrive at a taverna before 10 and often 10.30pm, long after most of the tourists have eaten, left their tip and nestled into their cushioned cane chair at a nearby bar for the remainder of the evening, large draught lager carefully positioned on the table in front of them.

This particular night required that we be ready to leave the apartment before eight if we were to stand a chance of arriving at Grandad's in time to be accommodated. We'd heard that once the family who ran the place had decided that they had enough guests, they were quite firm in turning any latecomers away with the invitation to try again some other night. They didn't feel they could do their guests justice if they allowed too many in at any one time.

Since our apartment was some ten minutes walk along the

coast from the harbour, which itself was a further ten minutes from the taverna, we knew we'd need to be strolling briskly along by the stroke of eight.

Now, I know I'm going to strike a familiar chord with a lot of people here. But there I was at 7.45pm, all sprayed up against the mozzies, nice pair of sharply pressed chinos and a half-decent polo shirt already gracing my slightly tender body (sunburn, …I never learned in those days), slip-on sandals (those plastic "Buffalo" brand ones that look a bit like leather from a distance that I'd seen all the Greek men wearing) already gracing my naked feet, hair all wet from my shower and slicked back to help my head keep cool for a few more minutes, tapping my watch and trying not to sound too irritated as I delicately asked my better half how much longer she was going to be, since although she had at least finished her shower, she was now sitting naked in front of the mirror, hair still very wet and, as yet, not a scrap of make-up on.

"I'm on holiday. I'm NOT going to be rushed while I'm on holiday!" Was the reply, which for my money, may have been a little more terse than necessary. I decided to take a risk.

"I know, but we did agree that tonight we'd go to Grandad's and, if we're not there by half past eight, we'll be turned away." I braced myself.

"So? We can always eat somewhere else and go to Grandad's another night." Now at this point I could have said, "True, no worries then." But I didn't. We never do, do we chaps? Instead I ventured the postulation:

"Yea, but that would mean we'd be having this very same argum… ah, conversation then instead of now. It's not 'hurrying' to be ready on time if you plan it right, is it."

"Look, I won't be much longer, alright? If you keep talking to me I'll end up taking even longer now won't I." Women's logic eh guys? I ought to have left it there, but couldn't resist…

"I only wanted to make the point that we'd agreed to go there tonight, and that it would mean leaving by eight. Plus, if you know what time you need to leave, it's only a matter of working back from there to the time when you ought to start getting ready. I mean, I did tell you when it was seven o'clock didn't I, but you hung around out on the terrace for another quarter of an hour, didn't you?

"I mean, it's not rushing, or hurrying to plan your schedule is it." Now, we fellas know that we can never win these kinds of discussion, so why we don't just let it drop I don't know.

"Look, read your book. I'll be ready in time, ALL RIGHT?"

At somewhere around 8.15pm we finally trotted down the stairs and out on to the road to begin the walk to the taverna. All the way to the harbour I was getting earache for walking too fast, to which I was replying that I was merely walking at the pace required to make up for the time we'd lost while I was awaiting my wife's pleasure before leaving the apartment. This didn't improve the atmosphere much. Can't imagine why.

In view of the time pressure, I suggested that we'd be best advised to take the route up through the trees, rather than walk out to the end of the headland and back along the track behind the taverna. After all, there was a path of sorts, wasn't there? My wife having reluctantly agreed, we struck up through the pines and diverse Mediterranean undergrowth as the sun dropped below the hidden horizon and the daylight soon became the murk of dusk.

"For goodness sake, slow up a bit!" Said Yvonne.

"'I'm not rushing, I'm just going at my normal walking pace." I replied.

"All these years I've known you and I never knew before that you were an Olympic walker, OUCH!" At this I had to stop.

"What's up now?" I asked with great concern.

"This ruddy undergrowth is like spears. It's scratching my arms and if you don't slow down I'll end up breaking a heel."

Now chaps, as you know, we men always wear the appropriate footwear for the occasion, don't we? It's logic isn't it? Since on this particular night we knew we'd be going into the "sticks' it was only sensible to wear flat shoes wasn't it? Of course. The problem is, my wife dresses up for an evening out. She ALWAYS dresses up for an evening out. Sit in any Greek taverna during a hot evening and you'll see most tourists in t-shirts, shorts, sandals, that sort of thing, won't you? This applies equally to the women as it does to the men, doesn't it? Not so with my wife I'm afraid. She will wear that little black dress, or a trouser/skirt/blouse combination that – although very fetching – isn't all together practical for a rural Greek taverna after dark, especially a rural Greek taverna up a small track through the pines and other undergrowth after dark.

So here we were now having an argument over not simply the fact that we were running a little late and stood the chance of being turned away, which would have led to us having to make the return journey whilst still unfed and unwatered (a fact which would have exacerbated things immeasurably), but also over the fact that I considered her choice of footwear quite absurd for the conditions we knew we'd meet en route to our chosen eatery for the evening.

I ventured, rather unwisely in retrospect, the following, "Don't you think it would have been better to have worn flat shoes?"

"Oh yes. With THIS dress that would have looked great

wouldn't it. Anyway, if I can't dress up for an evening out when
I'm on holiday, when CAN I?"

Just when things were becoming quite fraught and voices
getting fairly edgy to say the least, we suddenly exited the
undergrowth to find ourselves right on the terrace of
Grandad's taverna, staring at a long table around which sat a
dozen or so other would-be diners, who were all sipping their
ouzos and looking in our direction, eager to clap eyes on
whoever was having this heated row from behind the pines.

We immediately flipped into congenial mode and began
greeting those whom we hoped would be our company for the
evening, both of us hoping that our little contretemps in the
undergrowth hadn't been overheard too much, whilst
mentally resigning ourselves to the fact that it must have been.

Grandad himself and his plump wife both emerged from
the kitchen, which resembled a flat-topped garden greenhouse
just large enough to house the charcoal grill and a couple of
work tops and situated a couple of yards away from the taverna
building itself. A metal flue broke through the smoke-
blackened glass (or perhaps perspex) roof and reached at a
dangerous angle toward the darkening sky, discharging its
delicious char-grill aroma towards the gradually emerging
stars. The taverna walls showed signs of neglected plaster,
with some areas of the rendering having given up trying to
cling to what was beneath and fallen away to reveal the fluted
terracotta higgledy-piggledy blocks, evidently thrown
together by someone in the belief that, since they'd hopefully
never see the light of day, it didn't matter if they weren't
particularly well laid. Some of these patches had at some time
been whitewashed, thus revealing that the process of the
external plaster cracking up and tumbling ground-ward wasn't
altogether a recent phenomenon.

The table, around which were seated our fellow guests, was laid out in a straight line, with five or six guests along each side and one at each end. There were two chairs remaining to be claimed. We claimed them gratefully.

Grandad now proffered Ouzo for us both as his wife began to explain in half-English-half-Greek what was on the menu for the evening. While he added water in our Ouzo glasses to our respective signalled levels, his wife explained the mouth-watering provender, which we could imminently expect to see before us. There was to be a homemade *Briahm* (a sort of Greek version of Ratatouille), *stifado* and baked feta. There would be *Marides Tiganites* (fried whitebait) and *tsipoura* (Sea Bream) done over charcoal. To accompany the foregoing there would also be *patates tiganites* (chips!) and *horta* (green beans) done in lemon juice and olive oil, seasoned (as many of the rest of this evening's offerings would be) with *ri'gani* (oregano). In those days my wife and I still ate meat, so there was nothing we wouldn't be sampling during the course of the evening.

The conversation livened up as fresh bread in baskets began to appear, along with Grandad's home-made retsina in the ubiquitous plastic water bottles, which was soon being generously poured into short tumblers. No wine glasses grace the table of a traditional taverna. You always know if the retsina is genuinely home-made. It's a safe bet that it will appear in 1.5 litre mineral water bottles. Re-cycling may be yet to reach these islands, but at least the plastic water bottle is frequently seconded into an alternative use once emptied of its original fluid.

By the time a couple of hours had passed we felt safe in the belief that our fellow diners had forgotten all about our little discussion in the pines and all were getting along famously. By now Grandad was seated at one corner, glass of neat ouzo in one hand, self-rolled cigarette in the other (almost burned down to his fingers and with a perilously long and crooked ash-stick dangling precariously from the other end), as he regaled us in barely understandable English with tales of his past glories at sea. The table was groaning under a clutter of soiled dishes covered with the remains of the stupendous repas which we'd all just enjoyed and the evening had entered that "all's right with the world" phase that only a good meal with a few glasses of wine can induce.

Once Grandad's wife had served up the fresh honeydew and water melon chunks in two huge dishes, which she placed at strategic points along the table, Grandad decided it was time for the fun to begin. Just when we had all reached that "I can't even move, let alone stand up" moment, he rose, went inside the taverna, then leaned out of the front window and invited us to decamp from the table, which was off to the side of the taverna's main terrace, on to the terrace proper, which was about thirty feet square and overlooked the whole of Poros Bay and *limani*. The stars twinkled as he placed the most battered old cassette stereo I'd ever seen (what we'd nowadays call a "Ghetto-blaster"), minus the front of the cassette compartment's door, on the outside window-sill.

"NOW YOU LEHRN TO DANCE!!" he exclaimed as he wedged a piece of folded, torn-off beer mat into the play-button to start the cassette running. Out blared a scratchy and heavily treble-biased *Sirtaki*, evidently one that had been played on vinyl until it was almost transparent, before being badly recorded on to the cassette tape. Never mind, it sufficed to get Grandad's mood into gear as he disappeared from the window, only to emerge seconds later from the front door of the taverna, now wearing a bandana and a huge pair of those "elephant" sunglasses which were popular a couple of decades ago.

Evidently of the opinion that he looked well-racey and debonair in his *"mangas"* togs, he approached each of his female guests in turn and tugged them onto their feet and into some sort of unsteady line. To look at him you'd never have credited him with the amount of energy he displayed over the succeeding hour or two, which he passed gleefully leading all his guests in a series of disastrous versions of a selection of Greek dances, all to the accompaniment of the scratchy tape recordings on the battered old ghetto-blaster, of which he was evidently very proud. All this went on to the backdrop of the twinkling lights of the Poros *limani* below and the impossibly deeply contrasted black and starlit sky above.

It was altogether another of those tingle-factor evenings, spoilt only by the fact that our argument over the type of footwear which my beloved had chosen for this evening's sortie resumed where it had left off once we'd begun the stumbly walk home along a few hundred metres of dirt track, which had to be negotiated in the darkness (neither of us having had the foresight to bring along a torch), until we reached the harbour below.

Only this time the discussion was carried out in whispers, since we had a dozen or so fellow walkers as company.

14 – The "Whining"

The Mediterranean mosquito is only a small little chap by comparison with some of his more beefy tropical cousins, but he can be a major pest nonetheless. Actually, I ought to refer to them in the female, since it's the ladies that bite us humans, not the chaps.

Most of us can remember our first encounter with these little devils. I certainly do. It was during my first ever visit to my wife's cousin's villa at Kalamos, on the North coast of the mainland, up the road to the North of Athens and along the coast from Oropos, where you can catch a "landing-craft" type ferry over to the large island of Evia, that I was introduced to the kind of misery these tiny insect pariahs can cause.

If you've read "*Feta Compli!*" you'll remember the account of the night when Cousin Christina's husband Takis went "over the top" with his fellow conspirators, secateurs in hand, to gather their illicit grape harvest for his next batch of Retsina. Well, it was during this first visit to the villa at Kalamos when I was to learn about an enemy that I would spend years doing battle with. The villa is set into the hillside, with a terrace running around all four sides, at the front affording breathtaking views of the island of Evia shimmering across the waters of the Aegean. To the rear the terrace is at road level and is accessed by a small gate from the road (well, track would be more accurate a description) directly on a level with the terrace and the "front" door into the villa. On the side facing the coast, owing to the fact that the land drops quite steeply, the terrace becomes the first floor with a cellar room beneath. The door to this cellar room is at one end of the villa and can be approached from the lower track which passes below the building by entering the lower gate and climbing up some steps, or conversely by descending those same steps from above.

Once inside, the room is long and narrow with a door half-way along the rear wall, which leads into the cellar proper, the walls of which are hewn out of the earth and rock of the hillside and the floor of which was packed earth. This rear room makes a perfect storage area for the huge barrels in which Takis stores his retsina. The front room was made over into a bedroom, which looked quite comfortable, with solid tiled floor and plenty of room either side of the bed, which had its headboard against the outside wall, placed centrally between two shuttered windows. The ceiling was comprised of exposed beams and wooden laths and the walls were stucco, plastered in that "cantina" style which consisted of great swirls of relief created by doing half-circles with the trowel when applying the stuff wet. This kind of wall can only be whitewashed, since no way could you apply wallpaper (not that a Greek has ever heard of wallpaper anyway) to such an uneven surface. It never even crossed my mind for an instant, when we first heaved our bags on to the bed on our arrival, how much of a problem such a wall-surface would prove to be at around 3.00am the next morning.

After a pleasant evening spent at one of the local tavernas in the village, just a short way along the beach, we bade our hosts goodnight, descended the steps from the terrace to our room and set about retiring for the night. Teeth duly brushed, all vestiges of clothing having been removed, we slipped into bed beneath the single cotton sheet, which usually suffices during a Greek summer's night. It wasn't long before even the sheet was proving too hot for me and I, as is often the case, began slipping it further down my body, thus exposing my hugely impressive (well, when seen through one of those distorted fairground mirrors anyway) torso.

Of course, little did I know at this time, since I was still a "Greco-virgin" and very inexperienced in all things Greek, that by exposing more naked flesh I was simply offering a more extensive menu to any mosquito which was fortunate enough to have entered the room before we retired to bed.

After tossing and turning for a while and finding it too hot for a pale English lad to sleep, I became conscious in the darkness of a tiny but incessant whine near one of my ears. It sounded a bit like hearing a Formula One car from a distance, or maybe an ill-tuned radio from the next room. I didn't have any idea what this was, until the first bite.

"OUCH!" I said, whilst at the same time sitting bolt upright and reaching for the bedside light switch. After sending my watch, rings and wallet, plus other diverse items from amongst my "stuff", flying in all directions, I eventually found the switch and shed immediate illumination around the room. I sat there gazing in all directions, fully expecting to see a huge flying horror somewhere nearby, but there was nothing. My beloved rolled over and in a detectably irritated tone said, "What are you DOING? I WAS FAST ASLEEP! Put that light OUT!"

"Something BIT me!" I replied. Rather naïvely expecting a modicum of sympathy, whilst inspecting the area on my right arm where the skin was already going red and a weal rising.

"Well it wasn't ME." Came the reply, whilst my better half simultaneously rolled over to face the far wall, pulling the sheet a little higher over her ear.

"Why can't I SEE it?" I asked, sort of to no one in particular.

"Probably a mozzie," she replied, "I did want to get a tablet machine but we didn't go near a shop today."

"What good's a machine when you can't even see the thing you want to use it against?"

"It's not a machine *per se*, it's a little plastic thing with a small metal plate that gets hot when you plug it into a wall socket. You slide a little blue tablet into it and it gives off a vapour that kills mozzies. All the Greeks use them. Don't you know ANYTHING?"

"Well I didn't know did I? You haven't mentioned it before. Anyway, where's the nasty little bloodsucker that's pinched some of my blood gone now?" I sat there staring at every inch of wall, in sections, in series. The relief pattern of the plaster didn't make it any easier. I saw nothing apart from white swirls casting deep shadows from the light of the bedside lamp.

"I'm not switching that light off until I've found it. It'll only have another go if I do. It's GOT to be SOMEWHERE." This sufficed to elicit further movement from the other side of the bed. Yvonne sat up and took a brief look in both directions. After an expert sizing-up of the situation, she offered:

"Not much chance of finding it with these walls. Ceiling's

good camouflage too. May as well live with it. Put the light out and try and get some sleep."

With some degree of reluctance I conceded that she had a point and switched off the light. Much against my body's desire for air, I pulled the sheet up to my ear and rolled over on to my side, telling myself, "SLEEP! JUST …SLEEP!"

Fifteen minutes later the whining began again. This time it seemed to be right beside my uppermost ear. I whipped a hand up and smacked myself across the side of the head in a vain attempt to kill the enemy. Once again stuff flew in all directions as I reached for the light switch. My better half was now also being bothered and so was just as much in earnest about nailing the beast as I was. Her bedside light also went on as we took stock of the situation. There we were, stark naked and kneeling on the bed, heads swivelling in all directions in the hope of spotting the cause of our sleep interruption.

You've probably been there, got the t-shirt. So you'll know just how frazzled one feels at half past two in the morning, when the temperature's around 30 degrees Celsius, you're covered in sweat, as is your pillow, and you're bolt upright reaching for a piece of tissue or anything else that may serve as a mozzie-swatter and studying the walls in the hope that she'll show herself just long enough to die.

Mosquitoes are very quick with their reactions too, ever noticed that? Just when I was feeling mightily pleased with myself for spotting the fiend as it sat on the wall just a little higher than I could reach without standing up on the bed, it evaded my first swipe with dextrous ease and once again became invisible. I was frustrated, but I was even more rattled by my wife's helpful comment:

"You MISSED IT! Honestly! You ought to have got it. It's easy enough. NOW where's it gone? You've missed probably our only chance now."

Surprisingly, I wasn't feeling all that happy. "Well YOU said you know all about these machine thingies! If you know all this stuff about mozzies then I'd have thought you would have been a bit more diligent about buying the tablet thing!"

There followed a few moments of symbolic wound licking. Who was in the lead with this particular argument? It didn't really matter. We were both so dog-tired it made more sense to concentrate our efforts on uniting in the common cause.

Once again we got down to the serious business of staring at sections of wall in the hope that the diminutive pest would settle somewhere. Of course while you have the light on you never hear the whine do you. More often than not you can't even see the thing hovering around. They seem to have an uncanny knack of disappearing until that moment when you've given up the hunt, once again turned out the lights and resumed your attempts to get a bit of shut-eye. Then they put in an appearance again, usually right by your ear. Probably already taken another blood sample beforehand too. What's worse, while you're staring about trying to spot the offender, you feel a tickle in the small of your back which you're convinced is the opponent coming in for a crafty blood-suck on your blind side. This results in you trying vainly to swipe an arm around your back in a frantic attempt to swat it while it's off guard. This manoeuvre, of course, never succeeds.

On this particular occasion, as I remember, we just gave up after the third or fourth attempt at swatting the little aerobatic monster and tried sleeping the rest of the night with the sheet entirely covering us, rather like a pair of corpses in the mortuary. It must have been around 4.00am at the last "lights-out." Oh joy.

Next morning over breakfast we examined the weals,

which both of us were sporting in various locations on arms and necks and resolved that the first task that day would be to visit the local "super-market," which rather more resembled someone's front room filled with various grocery supplies than what we would normally recognise as a "supermarket," and purchase a pristine new "mozzie machine," of which, needless to say, we nowadays own several.

I remember thinking, as we plugged it in the following evening before going out to eat, that I'd marginally have preferred to have Jack Nicholson smash my bedroom door in with his axe than live through another night of the "Whining" like that one.

Kalamos beach, circa 1977.
Left to right: Dave (my wife's step-father), Yvonne-Maria,
Cousin Effie, Lela (my mother-in-law) & Christina

15 – A Neighbour's Siesta

It's March 25th and we've just come away from the locked gates of the garden centre on the main road in Arhangelos feeling most frustrated. One of the irritating aspects of living here in Greece is the fact that you hardly get past one *yiorti* (celebration, festival, feast day) when another comes along before you can draw breath! Apart from the fact that there are twelve bank holidays here every year, there are also all kinds of local religious and civic festivals that spring their surprises on you, just when you were hoping to do a bit of shopping.

When you live as far from Rhodes town as we do, it represents quite a lot of planning to do a shopping trip, especially if you want to visit the stationers near the main Tax Office, which is some way out of town on the East coast, then perhaps visit a furniture store or get your car wheels balanced, maybe buy some clothes (if you can get the mortgage that is) and then try and fit in a frappe in Mandraki before heading back to the food stores on the edge of town and hitting the road home.

If you don't leave home at the crack of dawn you can often find yourself part-way round the list of shops you wanted to visit when they're all starting to close down for the afternoon. Soon after 1.00pm this happens and they don't re-open until 5.00pm. It's totally impractical to kill all those hours just waiting for the shops to open again, so we tear about in a blue funk trying to make sure it's all done by 1.00pm. Mercifully the food stores (Lidl and AB, which is the Greek equivalent of Sainsbury's) do stay open all day.

The trouble is, you can get so fixated on planning your trip that you don't factor in the imminence of the next *yiorti*. One time we drove the fifty minutes or so from home to Lidl, on the southern edge of town, wondering all the while why the roads were so quiet, only to find when we got there that they were closed, as was the AB store across the road. The traffic conditions ought to have signalled alarm bells, but you don't always think of the obvious, especially when you have the distinct impression that "they had a *yiorti* just last week, didn't they? There can't be another one this week, surely." Yes, buddy, there is.

So as I said, today is March 25th and we'd forgotten. It's a Wednesday, for goodness sake. Why can't they have all their bank holidays on a Monday like in Britain? We were going to get some seedlings for the vegetable plot, some cord for the strimmer, post a letter at Arhangelos post office, then do some fruit and veg shopping at the excellent grocery store in the centre of the village. Instead, after the disappointment of the garden centre we drive through the main street and spot the tell-tale dais, all set up with chairs for the local dignitaries, we see people in national costume walking towards the centre of the village and various uniformed youths standing around waiting for their turn to march.

At least we can accomplish one part of our mission. We are to paint the walls of two newly built raised flower beds for

Josie, plus do a few other odd jobs at her place. While Yvonne-Maria gets busy with the paintbrush I begin clearing out and re-organising Josie's out-house. The hot sun is beating down and I'm grateful I remembered the sun-block when we hear the music starting up in the main street, a couple of blocks away. Gradually people begin emerging from their front doors and walking towards the sound of the music. The women are all dressed up in their best frocks and the men sport dark sunglasses, black leather jackets and shirts and ties. They look like they'd be at home standing around Marlon Brando or Al Pacino in those famous movies of some years back. I'm surprised no one's carrying a violin case. Funny, no horses about either.

So, what is this Independence Day all about then? Apparently it's meant to be the time when the Angel Gabriel appeared to Mary and told her that she was going to be a mum. It seems that in 1821 a certain Bishop Germanos of Patras raised the revolutionary banner this very day and set in motion an eight year struggle for freedom from the oppressive Turks, under whom the Greeks had laboured for centuries. Quite why Gabriel's chat with Jesus' mother-to-be should have anything to do with a political struggle in a distant land some eighteen hundred years later isn't all that clear. But then, the Greek Church, like so many other national churches, assumes God is on their side and so they invoke his support for their "struggle" at every opportunity.

Some time later in the afternoon the music has finally died down and people are filtering back to their "*avlis*" to sit and eat and sup together for the rest of the day. Of course, it's "Lent" so many of the more devout among them will not be eating any meat, but the smell of charcoal makes it abundantly evident that a fish or two will be consumed instead. We finally pack up the car and head for home, mentally planning another time to try and do a simple bit of shopping.

When you consider how much money is lost in this country due to the more than frequent "*yiortes*", it's not surprising that the country's economy is in a state is it? Still and all, we find the "Flevaris" supermarket open at Kalathos on our way home, pick up some odds and ends, including some still hot, fresh bread, which we soon turn into chunky salad sandwiches, washed down with a nice bit of chilled, dry, white wine as we sit on our terrace and gaze down the valley to the blue, blue sea. The thermometer on the *avli* says it's 24°C in the shade. Yes, warts and all, it's alright living here.

Next day we drop in to see Roy and Cynthia, a British couple who, a few years back, retired to their new home in Pilona, a small village between Lardos and Kalathos. It's also a fairly strong stone's throw from Lindos, although the other side of a mountain. When Roy & Cynthia first arrived to take up occupancy, theirs was the only one of what would eventually be a clutch of new houses in the area, on the edge of the village.

Their garden backs on to a small agricultural plot, which is lovingly tended by Ileas, an old Greek who grows the majority of all that he and his wife of many decades eat. Cynthia tells us, as we sit around on their terrace drinking cool juice on an August evening some four years after both they and us arrived here on Rhodes, that within days of their arrival Ileas was at their door with plastic bags full of fresh produce for them and so it has continued in the years since.

They hadn't been here long when he invited them to share in his olive harvest, which is something a Greek will always do because it's backbreaking work and they need all the help they can get. They kind of bank on the fact that us dumb British will jump at the opportunity, thinking - as we invariably do - that we'll be "assimilating" into the local community by doing so.

So Roy and Cynthia got stuck in and Ileas, despite the fact that he (like many of his compatriots) first involved them in order to make his task easier, duly arrived at their door at the conclusion of the harvest with a good supply of extra virgin oil which they had had not a small part in wresting from tree to mill and thus into the barrels in which it would be transported home.

Cynthia tells us that some time ago Ileas arrived on their terrace one hot afternoon, around 4.00pm and seemed a little put out. It transpired that, since they had company and were all sitting around putting the world to rights over a bottle or two of wine, they were making too much noise and Ileas was trying to take his siesta. Using sign language which involved him placing his hands together not unlike the "praying" attitude, then resting one cheek on the back of one of them while simultaneously slightly tilting his head, he made them understand that he was asking them to quieten things down a bit as he was trying to sleep.

"No problem," they replied, whereupon he retreated, satisfied in the knowledge that now he'd get his forty winks without further interruption.

"We didn't really mind," Cynthia continues, as I give her my undivided attention and imbibe of my freshly chilled juice, "it was just that we didn't realise he was only yards over the fence and that he sleeps every afternoon from about three until five."

She continues to tell us, however, about how they'd been awoken at some dark hour before the dawn on numerous occasions after having first moved in, to the sound of what could well have been described as someone practising on their steel drum! Opening the blinds and peering out into the murk they'd discovered that it was none other than Ileas, evidently cleaning out some metal drums in which he stores his fresh something-or-other!! Evidently he always rises at around 5.00am and goes out to work in his huge garden 365 days a year. Once they'd got used to this, even though Cynthia says it still wakes them up regularly, they are in the habit now of awaking to his banging, sleepily telling themselves "it's only Ileas," putting their pillows over their heads and drifting back off for another few hours!

"So, when he came round to scold us about disturbing his siesta," says Cynthia, "we were tempted to ask him if he realised that some people prefer to let the sun wake them rather than to herald its imminent arrival with a percussion session, but thought 'discretion and valour' and all that!"

After all, we are guests in their country. It's important for the ex-pat British people living here to understand that principle.

Whether Ileas gets up just as early when it's a *yiorti*, we didn't ask.

Tzatziki for You to Say

16 – You'll Need Surgery

So here we are on a hot June day doing some gardening for a friend. We're weeding and pruning, we're also checking the nozzles on the irrigation system for the tell-tale signs of clogging, which is a perpetual hazard with the hardness of the water on this island. We're rearranging the gravel areas, to hide the membrane beneath, which is meant to inhibit weed growth and does nothing of the sort. What it does do is annoyingly begin to show through the gravel and, in some cases the edges become so proud of the stones that were meant to conceal it that a pair of scissors is called for and drastic "membrane-pruning" begins in earnest.

We're planting a few cuttings where some original plants have died, although it's a bit late in the year really, and we're also dreaming of that frappe which we're going to walk into the village of Gennadi for in about half an hour's time.

We both use foam kneeling mats, purchased from the gardening department of the local Tesco during a recent visit to the UK, although sometimes when you move from one area to another in the garden you forget the mat and kneel on the gravel just long enough to embed a couple of sharp stones in the skin over your kneecap before cursing and going in search of that abandoned mat.

We're experts now at weeding gravel walkways, which a lot of gardens over here tend to sport. It's the quickest and most cost effective way to get from "builder's debris-cluttered bomb-site" to "well planned decorative garden" in no time at all. A few rough rocks nicked from the local quarry or simply gathered in the dirt tracks that criss-cross the rural areas on the island laid out to border the beds and gravel everywhere else and you have a garden that Alan Titchmarsh himself would take a look at and emit a "wow."

I say "experts" because all you need to weed gravel areas effectively is a substantial screwdriver and a bucket for the exhumed weeds. You thrust the screwdriver into the gravel at a 45° angle just to the side of the weed you're going to extract, much in the manner that a medic would insert the needle of a syringe when taking a blood sample or injecting his or her terrified patient. Now you're not going to protest that you're not afraid of needles here are you? No? Thought not. So anyway, screwdriver duly inserted a few inches into the gravel, you wiggle the end around to loosen the soil where you estimate the weed's main taproot to be, then gently lift the surface of the gravel by changing the screwdriver's angle as you grab the weed with the other hand and wiggle it free.

There, see? The whole root is out. Then you cast the offending plant into your bucket and use the palm of that hand to exert a gentle pressure on the surface of the gravel where the weed used to be as you extract the screwdriver, once again doing your very best "there, that didn't hurt much, did it?" impression.

At about midday we take that break we'd promised ourselves and wander into the village square for a frappe and watch the world go by for half an hour or so. Jinny, a friend from along the beach road, drops by and joins us for a chat. Then Ileas the bus driver, who we met in Rhodes town through mutual friends a year or two back, arrives in his big orange bus, switches off the engine at the "terminal" (which consists of a wooden bus shelter beside the café's terrace) and bounds into the café, takes a look in our direction and breaks into a huge grin as he comes over to be introduced to Jinny. He doesn't know we live near Gennadi and we tell him we didn't know he drove a Rhodean bus. He's a great character who speaks sixteen to the dozen and tends to spit on you in the process. But he's very genial and doesn't really look very Greek. He's got fifteen minutes to kill and he's going to execute them with a cool drink in the café.

We eventually drift back to the garden, do a bit more, then pack the tools into the car and head home. The evening comes upon us like a warm bath and we potter about in the garden. I notice for the first time that my right knee is a little tender when I attempt to kneel down and pull an onion for the kitchen table. I think nothing more of it until a couple of days pass and now it's looking decidedly red and swollen and I can't kneel on it at all. I mention it to Yvonne-Maria.

"My knee's a bit tender. Can you see where it's swollen?" She agrees that it's "got something in it" although all I can see is a tiny mark at the front of the kneecap, which isn't even for sure the cause of the problem. Nevertheless, there is an infection there and she suggests it's time to go and see the doctor. Today's Wednesday and he decides I need a course of antibiotics and a visit to the Health Centre in Arhangelos. He tells me that the almost golf-ball sized swelling on the front of the kneecap may well be an abscess and that there they may need to lance it to see what's inside. He also explains that, since the problem is on a joint, it is important to get it diagnosed or sorted out quickly because an infection in this spot can even enter the bone, which is serious.

As it happens we're going to town this very evening so we decide to drop by the Arhangelos Health Centre en route. At around 6.00pm I drive into the car park – which boasts the grand total of one vehicle - and along to the far end of the building. Here there is a ramp for ambulances to drive right up to the portico and a sign telling me it's the "First Aid" entrance. This place is somewhere between a local doctor's surgery and a small hospital. We have been here before, when my thrifty wife had once slashed herself deep in the palm with a carving knife whilst using it to try and extract the last few inches of cling film from the cardboard tube it was wrapped around. That little drama had resulted in a highly embarrassed wife and a few stitches in her palm.

Although the staff levels here are "economical," I have high hopes that they'll be able to sort out my swollen knee with one visit, perhaps telling me to finish the course of antibiotics for good measure. I walk into a reception room to find four or five staff lounging about around two desks, feet on blotters, ever-present iced coffees half-consumed and a distinct smell of recently extinguished cigarettes in this "non-smoking" facility. One of them, a thirty-something man in a white coat who seems to be in charge asks me in Greek if they can be of any assistance.

"Yes," I reply, pulling up my trouser leg to reveal the offending swelling, which is now considerably larger from the knee to the ankle than it's near (well, its only) neighbour, "I've been recommended by the doctor in Kiotari to come and see you about this. He says there may be an abscess and if you would…"

"You'll need to go to the hospital in Rhodes town about that. We can't do anything here."

"But if I could just explain. It's not twist…"

"We can't help here. Look, you'll probably need surgery. You'll have to call this number. Look I'll write it down for you, see…" He obviously thinks that the best way to deal with the likes of me is to talk as though I'm about 5 years old. He now tears off a bit of scrap paper and scribbles a phone number on it, then thrusts it towards me, a look of 'What do people think they're doing coming in here disturbing our cosy little chit chat' written all over his body language. "Call this number and make an appointment with the Orthopaedic Surgeon. You'd better not leave it too long."

"But the doctor said you could perhaps lance it…"

"Look, I have TOLD YOU, OK? We can't do anything here. Call that number. They'll deal with it. Thank you, good evening." He now made it very clear by turning his face toward his waiting colleagues and placing his hands back behind his head, where they'd been when I'd walked in, that their conversation was of much more importance than helping out a stupid English person with his swollen knee. Having gauged the situation as beyond recovery, I accept defeat and walk out.

My wife looks decidedly surprised to see me so soon, having turned up the volume on the car radio and settled into some serious listening for what she thought would a good half-hour session with "Max" the local station that only plays "*Laika*", the traditional bouzouki music that's played and danced to in all the self-respecting Greek clubs in Athens and Thessalonika. I climb into the car and immediately reach for the volume control before offering an explanation for the extraordinary brevity of my Health Centre visit.

She gets a blow-by-blow account of my ever-so-short consultation with the caring staff of Arhangelos Health Centre and we agree that there's nothing for it but to call the number at the hospital, which the medic had scrawled on a scrap of paper, first thing tomorrow morning.

I call the hospital at around 9.00 am on Thursday morning. I explain in my best Greek that I need an appointment with an Orthopaedic Surgeon and ask when this may be possible.

"You'll need to call the appropriate department. Do you have a pen? I will give you the number." I decide against getting irate and asking why on earth she can't put me through herself and obediently scrawl down the number she gives me.

Now, the doctor in Kiotari had told me that it was fairly urgent. That it ought to be seen by a specialist within 24 to 36 hours. It's now Thursday morning and I finally get through to the department that makes appointments for the Orthopaedic Surgeon.

"The Orthopaedic Doctor is only here on Thursdays and Mondays," I am told. I've already missed the boat for this week then. She asks me what time on Monday I would prefer. I say as early as possible. She gives me 10.30am. I hang up the phone and resolve to be patient and hope that the antibiotics do their work so I won't need an amputation or something.

Monday morning at 10.25am we're walking into the main entrance of "Andreas Papandreou" Hospital. We approach the Reception desk and enquire as to the whereabouts of the Orthopaedic Doctor's morning surgery and we are given directions. Down this corridor to the fork, take the left then first right. We follow the directions and get hopelessly lost. Eventually, after asking a passing white-coated woman, we arrive at the small corridor (at the entrance of which is a compact reception desk, behind which sits no one) off which are four doors with A4 inkjet print-outs of numbers 19-21 Sellotaped to them. There is already a crowd too large for the small waiting area that recesses to one side of the corridor, with bodies lining both walls of the corridor's thirty metres or so leading up to a small cupboard-sized office at the end. There are even people standing in front of the doors, behind which we correctly surmise that the visiting consultants are conducting their interviews with their patients. We squeeze into a gap between a couple of people who have already been waiting for a period unknown to us, but judging by their faces, it's already too long. I soon find out that I'm leaning against the door to a toilet, which I am obliged to open with my outstretched arm at regular intervals as various patients or their hand-holders decide they have to elbow past me and make use of the facilities within.

We are hopelessly inexperienced at this type of thing, having only been to the hospital twice since moving out here almost five years ago and one of those times was a visit to someone else. After a while one of the numbered doors opens. It's number 19, which is on our side of the corridor, the other two are facing us, and a white-coated girl pops her head out and, glancing down at a clipboard calls a name that ends in "…opoulos." Four or five people simultaneously attempt to enter the room. She's obviously skilled at this and gives no ground.

"You only come when your name is called, please!" She states with as much authority as she can muster. This causes a percentage of her problem to relent, leaving a few people now saying things like, "I've been here hours," or "my aged mother can't be left on her own, so I have to get in first," "See my child, he's only eight. Haven't YOU got children?" She repeats the name on her list and finally someone sitting in the waiting area recess realises it's him and gets up shouting, "ME! IT'S ME!" whilst almost breaking a leg falling over all the feet of the others who are seated in the area in his attempt to get to the door before the girl allows one of the queue-jumpers in his stead.

I notice that most of the hopefuls are holding NCR printouts, white top copy and pink second copy. I surmise that perhaps they've been referred from another department. I look to my left to find that Yvonne has miraculously found a seat and is now engaged in a warm conversation with a kindly faced Albanian woman. I continue my visual sweeps along the corridor, studying my adversaries. I start trying to work out who's going to get in for their consultation before me. How many of these people are patients and how many are just those who've come with them to hold their hands? It's evident from the chats and body language of some that they are together, some in parties of three or four. This causes me to become far too optimistic about how long I'm liable to be waiting in this hot and stuffy corridor.

Having lost concentration for a moment or three I look around just in time to see my wife disappearing around the corner at the end of the corridor in the wake of the Albanian woman. "Where the Dickens is she off to? " I think. Now I'm panicking because what if they call me in while she's away. Where could she have gone and why?

Door 21 opens; another "...opoulos" is requested. The same scenario develops as before.

"Please! Sit down," chance would be a fine thing for the majority "...and WAIT until your name is called. Fact is, it's most people's name that gets called out most times. That's the thing here in Greece. So many people have the same names. If you've ever wondered why there are so few different names in Greece it's because it's considered disrespectful not to name your child after its grandparent of that particular sex, whatever one of the three it is. There's the remnant of an old joke in there somewhere, think about it.

So, for instance, if your dad was called Spiro and you have a first son, you have to call him Spiro too if you want to avoid a major family upset. The upshot of all this is that hardly anyone dare insert a new name into the family tree, unless they want to be sent to whatever is the Greek equivalent of Coventry by all and sundry (Coventrios? Nah, maybe not, probably Florina). This is why, whenever you are required to fill out an official form here in Greece, which is far too often for my liking, you have to provide all kinds of information that wouldn't be necessary in other countries. When we applied for our Tax Numbers on first arriving over here, we had to provide our grandparents' names, plus our parents' first names as well as our own. It really confused the girl behind the desk at the Tax Office when she examined our forms; rubber stamp raised in her right hand in readiness, and found that both of us had written "Kenneth" in the box requiring our fathers' first names. It didn't occur to her that both our fathers might have been called Kenneth. She insisted that one of us had made a mistake and written our father-in-law's name instead of our own father's name. A few heated minutes later, all was clarified and down came the rubber stamp, bomp, bomp. Now take these forms to that desk over there, where yet another rubber stamp awaits to do its bomp-bomping.

So I'm feeling sweaty-palmed as I wonder anxiously where my wife could have gone, when a gurney comes around the corner at the far end of the corridor, bearing a patient and being pushed and pulled by a couple of orderlies, one of which it's impossible to tell if they're male or female (see, that old joke again!) and they're both shouting "FEET! MIND YOUR FEET PLEASE!" Just in time to catch the front foot of a hapless would-be patient whose cross legs are in the way. That ought to read, "crossed" I suppose. Mind you, by the time the front foot of those particular crossed legs had been swiped by the passing gurney they would be cross, wouldn't they. I certainly would.

General mayhem ensues. Where is she? I continue to wonder, when she eventually reappears around the corner of the corridor at the far end waving our very own NCR duplicate paper at me. She approaches, accompanied by the Albanian woman she'd disappeared with.

"Good job I got talking to her," she says, with an air of smugness (I can't help thinking) about the way she says it, "If you didn't have this printout with you then you wouldn't get seen by the doctor. It's proof that you've paid the three Euros registration fee. No proof of fee payment, no chat with the doctor."

"So why didn't they tell us that when we arrived at the main Reception desk then?"

"Oh, well, you know. 'Welcome to Greece' and all that. Anyway, we've got it now so that's all that matters." With that she turns to the nice Albanian lady who'd shown her where to go to pay this fee and get the all-important printout and thanks her profusely. Apparently it was around a few corners, then down several corridors and at the end of one-such corridor there was this desk, a bit like a bank teller's desk, where a fellow with a terrible toupee sat taking the cash whilst staring at a computer monitor and ripping off the printouts and handing them through the small opening in the glass partition that separated him from the infected hordes.

How did I discover this? I get the guided tour from my wife later.

Turning back to me, Yvonne-Maria continues, "She may well have missed her name being called while taking me to find the payment desk, poor thing. Not many would do that, would they?"

"Not many Greeks maybe. Albanians, probably." In our experience every Albanian we meet is polite, friendly and industrious. Fact.

The morning wears on with orderlies trotting into the corridor carrying trays laden with iced coffees, which they carry into the various consulting rooms without bothering to knock. If you're the patient and you're displaying areas of flesh that ought to be for the doctor's eyes only, that's too bad it seems! The sound of an electric saw also drifts out from a pair of double-doors along the corridor, but these don't have a printout with a number on it stuck to them. It's evidently the room where plaster casts are being removed. Either that or someone resembling Hannibal Lecter is in there and one peek through those doors would reveal a bloodbath to rival the Texas Chainsaw Massacre. Probably the former, eh?

Every now and then, but not nearly frequently enough for me, one of the doctor's assistants pokes a head out from their respective room in the wake of a departing patient to call for another "...opoulos" and deal with the ensuing scrum. One woman, sitting next to me (yes, even I eventually find somewhere to sit as the bodies move around following various patients and their entourages finally getting in to see the Ortho Specialist), pipes up when another name is called that she's been waiting two hours already and what a disgrace it is for an old woman like her to be kept waiting so long. I take a sideways glance and decide she's probably no older than me, but she's one of those types that "will" themselves into old age, wearing black years before tradition dictates they ought to and putting on weight and carrying a stick so she looks ten years older than she really is.

About fifteen minutes after she makes the aforementioned comment, another door opens in the usual fashion and she pipes up again, this time claiming to have waited four hours and there was now a strong likelihood that she'd die in this corridor and the hospital would have her blood on their conscience; not to mention the problems that would ensue at her home since her daughter relies on her to care for the children while she works, then there's the dog...

I sit trying to work out how two hours can become four in fifteen minutes. I even fancy that I catch the eye of the white-coated assistant who this woman's trying to emotionally blackmail as she gives me the "I get this all the time" look.

Since my appointment was supposed to be at 10.30am and it was now approaching midday I begin to get the idea that maybe you have to get like the locals, as it were, and try and muscle your way in whenever one of the doors opened. I definitely want to be sure that my name is actually on one of these lists that the doorkeepers always glance down at when they call in their next patient. I resolve that the next time the nearest door opens, which, as it happens, is door number 21, I'm going to be one of the bodies jamming its frame in an attempt to make some sense of what's going on here.

Since we arrived, at around 10.15am, there doesn't seem to be any appreciable difference in the number of bodies waiting in this stuffy corridor as it approaches 12.30pm. I've nothing to lose so I'm going to go for it. Another gurney fights its way along the corridor and enters Hannibal's lair, merrily bruising a few legs in the process, the sound of sawing increasing in decibel level as the double doors momentarily swing open and then close again. I'm on the starting blocks, metaphorically speaking. As soon as door 21 opens I'm gonna be there in the thick of it, just like a Greek. It opens and I almost leap up, only to see an orderly come out and close it behind him again. Well, he attempts to close it, but it swings open a little to reveal some indisposed patient who's blissfully unaware that a dozen or so people who'd almost kill to be where they are at this moment are studying the quality of their undies.

An unseen hand closes the door from within and I settle back on to my blocks. Eventually the patient who's displayed her nether regions to half of those still waiting in the corridor is released and a half a dozen of us poise for the attack, anticipating the next opening of the door for a patient to be called in.

Sure enough the attractive young assistant creaks the door a little and, glancing at her list, begins to mouth a name. Before yet another ...opoulos comes out, however, I beat the others to it and fill her face with mine and, ever the Brit you see, I politely enquire as to whether she could just affirm that my name is in fact on her list as I only booked last Thursday and am beginning to feel that maybe the surgery hours will come to an end with me still sitting here having still not been seen, with - dare I say it - my wife saying: "well, what did you expect? Should have just left the antibiotics to do the job."

She runs her eyes up and down her list. She looks up at me and says, "What was your name again?" That's another problem you have with a name like Manuel, it's spelt quite differently in the Greek alphabet from how it's spelt in the Roman one. You never know which version is going to show up on someone's list. She looks up and down hers yet again and declares, "It doesn't seem to be on my list."

Just when I'm going to explode with a furious "I BOOKED THIS LAST WEEK AND WAS GIVEN A TIME OF 10.30AM, IT'S NOW LUNCHTIME AND I'VE BEEN WAITING HERE…" she changes her story and declares, almost too happily for my liking, that… "Sorry, here it is. It's the last name on Dr. Kiriakidis' list." Quite how it could be the last name, when I was meant to be seen at 10.30am is a mystery to me, like how there's always another knife in the washing up bowl, or why I seem to get bitten by those vicious little flying insects twice as often as my wife, or maybe why British Airways wouldn't sell Concorde to Richard Branson. I could build quite a list here.

Still, once again, although I'm trying hard to behave like a local, my British sense of fair queuing seeps through and I accept what she says, that I am indeed going to get seen at some point, and I retreat from the scrum at the door. It's probably not the wisest decision, but I can't bring myself to jump the queue, even though it's pretty obvious that that's exactly what most of the others are trying to do every time one of these doors opens – from the inside that is.

Finally the Doctor himself emerges from his consulting room and trots off down the corridor to the evident dismay of all those expecting to be seen in room 21. I have heard tales of others who have waited in just such circumstances as those in which we find ourselves, only to find that the doctor's time for "knocking-off" comes round and they're unceremoniously told that he's finished for the day and they'll need to re-schedule their appointment for another day. So I'm now feeling exasperated about the whole scenario.

Fortunately it appears that it was only a bathroom break,

as he soon re-appears and, just as he's about to dart back into the sanctuary of his room, I lock eyes with him and ask if he has any idea as to how much longer it's going to be, since I'll need a shave before long. He apologises and says something like "can't be certain" and nips into room 21, nimbly swinging the door closed behind him. Perhaps he saw the desperation in my eyes, maybe something else registered, but sixty seconds later he pops his head out of the door, yes the doctor himself and not his young assistant, glances over at me and says, "Come on in Mr. Manuel."

For those few milliseconds that it takes him to say "come on in Mr...." I doubt him. I glance to my right and left in double-quick time, confident that it'll be someone else he wants and not me, but then the wonderful word MANUEL also emerges from his lips and I'm galvanised into action. My wife simultaneously leaps up, having been deep in conversation with that same woman all morning, who selflessly congratulates us on our success at being invited into the doctor's room and resigns herself to a continued wait. As we walk in, shouldering a few "...opolouloses" out of the way in the process, she says to me in an undertone, "I hope her name wasn't called while she was showing me where to pay the three Euros fee."

"Not much we can do about it now. Anyway, it's up to her to do a bit of scrumming I suppose."

The doctor is thirty-something and dressed in green scrubs. He's thinning on top, but has a healthy looking complexion – always encouraging in a doctor don't you think? He looks physically fit and is probably a few inches shorter than me. The room is sparsely furnished but resembles this kind of room in just about any hospital I've ever been in. There's the regulation black vinyl couch for the patient, over which, for hygiene purposes, is spread a thin paper sheet. There are a couple of fairly uncomfortable-looking chairs for friends or relatives of the patient to park themselves in and there's a non-descript desk, behind which sits the pretty young, white-coated assistant who's been bobbing in and out of room 21 for several hours by this time. She looks up and smiles and the doctor tells me to pop up on the couch and tell me the history of my problem.

I'm beginning to actually think this place resembles a professionally run modern hospital as I commence with the story of how I'd been gardening when I suspected that something pierced the skin over my right kneecap, resulting in the tenderness that soon became a swelling. The walls boast several charts showing the human skeleton and musculature. There are a couple of glass-fronted cabinets, full of all kinds of medical-looking stuff and some cupboard doors and shelves with reference books on them. The pretty assistant has a PC terminal on her desk and she taps away as I speak. There is natural light pouring in from a frosted glass window and the room is air-conditioned to boot.

I warm to my tale and reach the point where I consult with the local doctor in Kiotari when my professional audience here in the hospital takes a few paces toward a desk in the corner of the room, beside which is one of those sinks with the huge handled tap so they can turn it on and off with their elbows, and, not taking his attentive eyes from mine, turns to pick up something from the desk behind him. As I explain my conversation with the local GP, the Orthopaedic Doctor, cool as the proverbial cucumber, lifts a half-smoked filter cigarette to his mouth like it was the most natural thing to do in a modern, non-smoking health facility and takes a deep drag on it, before replacing it in the ashtray, which here-to-for I hadn't even noticed was situated on a blotter on the desk near the sink in question.

Whilst he exhales smoke through both his mouth and nostrils I'm thinking, "I don't believe what I just saw!" while telling myself that it's best not to react. So with a huge effort of will I continue without showing any reaction whatsoever to what I'd just witnessed. Here we are consulting with a medical professional about my swollen infected knee, in a place dedicated to health and healing and the DOCTOR is having a fag. Not only is he having a fag, he's having a fag while his patient explains what the symptoms of his ailment are.

There's only one way to explain this, and it's: "Welcome to Greece."

He waits for me to complete my tale, right up to the antibiotics and the making of this appointment, then commends me on the quality of my Greek and how he gets fed up with so many British patients coming to see him and expecting him to speak to them in English.

Despite the cigarette situation, I think I quite like Dr. Kiriakidis after all.

See, flattery gets one everywhere.

Tzatziki for You to Say

17 – The "Limey"

There are all kinds of explanations offered (usually by those who make "guess-timates" rather than actually doing the research) as to why so many trees in Greece have their trunks painted white.

"It makes the trees more visible to drivers at night." Say some. Yes, it does. But that's not why the Greeks paint them.

"It's cosmetic, it makes them look bright and summery." Hmm, not so inventive that one, and wrong anyway.

In fact, the traffic explanation is particularly daft when you consider that lots of white-painted trees are nowhere near roads or tracks used by vehicles anyway. Some are on the terraces of houses. Definitely pedestrian territory. Well, unless you count that little battery-powered jeep that the occasional toddler bashes around in as a vehicle.

So, why do they do it? Well, just as a side point here: I used to think that it demonstrated just how sloppy your average Greek is with a paint brush. If you approach any such visually altered tree soon after painting you'll see that the surrounding area is liberally sprinkled with white splashes and spots, not to mention the clothes of the bloke who'd done the painting.

And his glasses, if he wears them.

And his hair, if he has any.

Not the kind of scene that would have you rushing to ask him to do your lounge. Not, that is, unless you want half your tiled or crushed and polished marble chipping floors to look like there'd been an explosion in a cream factory or something.

No, There was little old inexperienced me thinking: I'm pretty good with a paintbrush or roller, but most of these Greeks who paint tree trunks white could do with a lesson or two at the night school for painters and decorators. That was until I tried it.

So, to finally cut to the quick. Funny how we say "*to the quick*" isn't it? In Greece it's a safer bet to say let's cut "*to the slow*," or better still, "*to the slower*." I suppose the "*quick*" here referred to is the quick of one's fingernails. A procedure over which I wouldn't want to spent a long time ruminating because it has the effect of bringing tears to my eyes, pain and the experience thereof not being one of my favourite hobbies. Yes, I know exactly what they paint the trees with and it's not your regular white emulsion from the local DIY store. No, it's lime. It's what the locals call "*asves'tis.*"

You buy it in a plastic see-through sack about half the size of a sack of cement, within which you find a wet white paste, a bit like toothpaste, but with water (well, a very white version of water) swilling around in there too. Having clipped your way into the sack, you squeeze some of this paste into a receptacle, say an old emulsion tub or some such thing, then mix a bit more water with it and stir. No need for any simmering or seasoning here though. Get your four-inch brush out and head for the nearest tree that requires the treatment.

And what exactly is the treatment? Well, lime (as all you experts out there will already know) has some interesting properties. It apparently repels a lot of insects and other creepy crawlies that have the habit of trotting up your average fruit tree and farming its aphid herds while effectively destroying the crop on the tree. Or maybe they don't bother with the aphids and simply chomp away at the foliage themselves or burrow their way into the fruit and destroy it from the inside out. The canny Greek knows that to shell out for manufactured chemicals to protect his fruit trees is not cheap. Not that he's a great environmentalist or anything. Sadly, it's purely economic. A bag of hydrated lime costs pennies (three or four Euros for enough to cover an orchard's worth of trunks) and so is his preferred option, no contest.

So this year, since we care for John & Wendy's orchard, which adjoins our garden and also supplies fruit for our breakfast table frequently through the course of the year, I decided it was time to avail myself of some of this wonder treatment and slap it on a few tree trunks. The fact that having all our tree-trunks limed (including a rubber tree, a loquat tree, several olives, a Jacaranda or two, a Bay and a fig) would make the garden look much more "Greek" may also have been a factor, I admit. I don't admit to a lot of things, but this I do, with all humility.

So I pass by the local builder's yard and buy a wet, polythene sack of the stuff. Though not before having been shafted good and proper by a certain DIY store proprietor in Arhangelos, who, when I asked him if he sold the "stuff you put on trees to stop the ants", since at the time I couldn't remember the Greek word for lime, sold me a plastic pot of interior use emulsion.

I looked at it and, knowing exactly what it was, asked again, "Do the locals actually use this to stop the ants then? I thought that what I needed was something else...[still couldn't remember the word for lime]."

"Oh yes, that's what you need. Nine Euro ninety five please."

Now he obviously thought that I couldn't read what was on the tub. I could, but with the way he assured me that this was what I needed, I had to accept that perhaps these days this stuff actually did contain something that deterred ants and so bowed (well, only metaphorically of course) to his superior wisdom. Subsequently, having painted a few trunks with brilliant white interior use emulsion for walls and watched as the ants barely waited for it to dry before resuming their long highway-lines of workers going up and down (in both directions!), I came to realize that his wisdom had not in any way been superior, but his powers of deception certainly were. Lime isn't green, no, but maybe you could accuse me...

So I go on line and Google my way to the real stuff, which is hydrated lime. Then I discover that DIY and decorating stores here, in fact even some garden centres, don't sell it. You have to go to the local builder's yard to be sure of a supply. Fortunately for us we do have a rather good local builders' merchant, where we've made quite a few purchases over the years, just down the road from us near Gennadi. The fellow behind the desk in the little office knows us and - I'm relieved to add - doesn't rip us off. So, three Euros and a few pence worse off I drive out of the yard in a cloud of dust and head home with my bag of lime. This time I'm going to get it right.

Having positioned my trusty kneeling mat close to the first

trunk that I am going to treat (for a second time!), I give the stuff in my pot a stir and dip in the brush. I very soon realize why the Greeks leave great splashes of the stuff all over the place when they do this because I am very soon doing the same. It's the consistency of the mixture that's the problem. The lime doesn't mix smoothly with the water anyway so you get thicker bits and watery bits, but by and large (in fact, by and even larger) it's impossible to apply it without getting everything in the vicinity covered in white splashes. Not that you realize this right away of course. When I come to treat a trunk that I hadn't previously painted with the emulsion I notice that, as you apply it, it's almost see-through. It looks as though it's not going to "cover" at all. It just leaves a grey film over the surface you've just lovingly and painstakingly brushed. I even try a few stones around our little lemon tree near the car port and they look horrible, just like they did before, only paler.

So, as you leave splodges and splashes all over the place you don't actually realize you're doing it.

That is of course, until it dries.

Then a miracle occurs. It dries totally and brilliantly white! As of course do all the extra areas you've dropped the stuff on to without intending to. I find myself mentally apologizing to all the Greeks I'd criticized in the past for doing such a sloppy job. The trunks look fab and so do the stones I'd experimented with. Of course, there are all kinds of fetching white irregularly-shaped marks in various parts of the orchard and garden too, but these, I like to think, add to the authenticity of the job.

18 – *Pizza to Go - to Stay*

We first had a conversation about the white tree trunks when we were taking a holiday with George and Allison on Samos in 2001.

In fact, it was during that particular holiday when we all decided to visit Ephesus, which is a few miles north of the sprawling port that is Kusadasi, in Turkey. We took the early bus to Samos Town and bought our own tickets on the *"karava'ki"* going to Kusadasi that morning. When you approach the Turkish port you are struck immediately by its sheer size. Samos Town and harbour is positively miniscule by comparison. We stared at a skyline brimming with huge cruise boats, at least half a dozen of which were tied up in the port as we approached. The urban area seemed to go on for an infinity on either side of us as we drew closer to shore and eventually tied up in the blinding heat of a Kusadasi summer's morning.

Having passed through Immigration and had our visas stamped by a couple of burly-looking port officials, we were on the street in Turkey. Without a second's delay, four or five swarthy young men appeared and began to walk backwards with their faces squarely in front of each of ours as we attempted to progress along the bustling pavement.

"You want taxi? My brother take you all day."

"You buy clothes? Come to my uncle's tailor shop for the very best prices!"

"You come and eat lunch. Very good menu, very good price!"

"Where you going? No matter, because my brother's taxi is big and he will be your guide. Very cheap."

We looked at each other and our faces betrayed our frustration at the fact that we could hardly walk without tripping over these fellows, who, it seemed, had relatives to supply our every commercial need. No matter how many times we said no we didn't need their services, or shook our heads decisively, it made no difference. One of these pests managed to wheedle out of one of us that we were planning to take a dolmus to Ephesus, further along the coast to the North.

"No, you don't want take dolmus! Much too much trouble! I get my cousin's taxi for you. Only five million Lire! He will be your guide for the day." In those days the Turkish currency was so many million to the pound that they used to lop off the last five zeros anyway on most menus and tariff boards, just so you could make some sense of it. But verbally they'd often say it longhand!

We were just getting to the point where we were looking for a gun shop so we could cheerfully shoot our hangers-on and happily face the consequences when Allison spotted a Tourist Information Office beside the pavement. Within thirty more agonising seconds we were home and dry inside the air-conditioned office.

Having ascertained that the dolmus stop we needed was

just a couple of blocks away we set off with renewed determination - and a map - to find it. Luckily the pests soon fell away the further we went from the touristy area of the town. Passing a bakery after a couple more minutes we decided that an essential would be something resembling a hot cheese or spinach pie. We went in.

Moments afterward we exited, stuffing our mouths with gorgeous freshly baked savoury pies, getting oily hands and talking to each other in totally unintelligible words like...

"Ummmmph, I thnnnnnnk sthssssway" and "wherrrrrrrrrr dwgo? Numwy crusss uss ro?" You now the kind of thing I'm sure. There were certainly enough flaky pastry crumbs landing on the pavement to satisfy even the most discerning pigeon. We all talk this way, don't we, when we can't decide which should take priority, the pleasure of satisfying a ravenous hunger or the need to communicate important information to others about which direction we ought to take.

Still attempting to get the oily stickiness off our hands with ever decreasing pieces of shredding tissue, we eventually arrived at the correct dolmus stop, where the sign said, among other things, "*Selcuk.*" We waited for our dolmus and the subsequent trip to Ephesus (and back) went without a hitch.

One amusing moment was when I stood on the steps across the square from the famous "Library" while Y-Maria, George and Allison walked across the ancient stones to the library steps. I did the usual tourist thing and videoed their little stroll. I didn't pay any attention to what was going on to my right or left at the time. I was "in the zone," full concentration rapt upon creating a nice mood piece with my ancient video cam. I don't even hear in such circumstances. Some time later, when we watched this piece of avant garde film-making, an American voice could be heard plain as day right beside me saying: "Alvin, stand right there. Alvin! Yes, there, …stand there and …Alvin? Try to look thin."

Some hours later as we returned to Kusadasi, well satisfied and all "ancient ruined-out", we found ourselves with a couple of hours to kill before it was time to board the boat for the return to Samos. We wandered for a while in the older part of the town and soon realised that we were quite lost. After proceeding along various paved pedestrian streets and standing at intersections turning round and round trying to work out our whereabouts, a young teenage boy approached me and asked,

"Can I help you, please?" To which I rather bluntly replied, "Oh don't tell me. Your cousin has a restaurant or a clothes shop and you'd be happy to show us where it is. Or perhaps your dad's got a taxi. Which is it then?"

You know how sometimes you just know you've done the wrong thing. Immediate events following your having said or done something reveal just how wrong you were and you want the ground to open and swallow you up? Well, I now experienced one of those moments. I'll tell you why. The young man's face assumed a look of total dismay and hurt as he replied,

"NO! OH NO! I just thought you were looking lost and perhaps you would like help finding your way."

I bet you know exactly how I was feeling now don't you? Thought so. With more than profuse apologies I ingratiated myself with him as best I could, while making lots of fuss about accepting his kind offer and we all fell into tow as he led us around a few corners until we arrived at an area which we recognised, where there was a small park to one side of the walkway, which at this point was fairly wide with a series of small eateries along the other side from the park entrance. Here we thanked him in a grovelling fashion and he went away satisfied that he'd done his good turn for the day, not to mention scoring a whole bundle of points for his fellow compatriots in the cultural or national characteristics credit column. We went from "Turks are a bit 'in your face'" to, "let's not tar them all with the same brush" in the time it took for him to lead us to safety.

So now, having had our feelings of security immeasurably enhanced, we fell to recognising those familiar pangs of hunger yet again. It was, after all, some hours since we'd devoured our takeaway pies and yet a couple of hours before the boat would be leaving. It was, in short, around three and time for a late lunch.

The nearest of the eateries just a little way down the street on our left proclaimed in English that it was a pizza house. That certainly looked ideal to four British candidates for a "Loudest Stomach Rumblings of the Year" competition. We made our way towards it.

This pizza house was a small kitchen on a corner beside a side alley, with a half a dozen tables and chairs out front, sitting beside those of the eatery next door, and so on along the street. Since it was around 3.00pm it was very quiet. As in Greece, so here in Kusadasi, it was the time when the locals slept. As we drew near to the establishment in question, there was a disappointing lack of cooking smells. No sounds of frantic kitchen activity, no delicious "pizza in the oven" aroma to get the taste buds salivating. In fact, peering into the glassless aperture to the kitchen area, stuffed full as it was with stainless steel equipment of all the kinds you expect to see in such places, we could see that the only sort of activity going on inside at all was that of spanners working on nuts, or screwdrivers tightening or loosening screws. There was a man in overalls, down on his knees, traditional canvas tool bag on the floor beside him; evidently fixing something that needed fixing. The kitchen was closed.

Or so we thought. Standing above this repairman was someone who for sure was the proprietor of this establishment. This man wore whites and a chef's hat and was peering down at his professional guest watching his activity with keen interest, one hand resting on the other arm while his thumb and forefinger stroked his chin. There were no other bodies about the place. No other living ones anyway. This man caught sight of us with the corner of his eye and quickly donned his best "welcome to my humble restaurant" smile and trotted out with some urgency to greet us.

We ventured the opinion: "You're not open for business then?" To which, quick as a flash he responded, "Oh yes! We're open! Please take a seat. Would you like something to drink? I'll fetch the menu yes?"

Turkish beer, notably the *Efes* brand, is rather good. Cold Turkish beer in a frosted glass is even better. Having established that he was able to provide us with that particular pleasure, we took seats and awaited his return with the menus. Seconds later there he was and he handed us one each. As we strained our heads to see what was going on inside his very pristine and decidedly unproductive-looking kitchen, he moved so as to place himself in our line of sight, not an easy feat when you have two people on either side of one of your tables.

"Anything off?" Yvonne-Maria asked? "I mean, is it just sandwiches or…"

"NO! NO! We have whatever you want. You just decide and we have it, certainly, for sure. No problem."

"You have Pizzas?" I ventured.

"Oh yes, you decide and we have your choice. I give you a few minutes, yes?"

We didn't need a few minutes, with a quick glance by each to the other three we piped up with, "A salad and four Margheritas."

To which I added, "And some French fries."

And George said, "And a couple more beers.'

Allison proffered, "Maybe two salads, eh guys?" Looking around for our approval, which she of course received without delay.

Yvonne-Maria, not wishing to be left out, requested a tonic.

Once our genial host had retreated into the decidedly inactive and non-aroma-filled kitchen we started talking in hushed tones about just where he was going to conjure up our pizzas. Could it have been our imagination or was he talking on his mobile phone? He soon came out with our knives and forks, all wrapped in the customary monogrammed paper serviettes. He brought us condiments and the extra drinks we'd requested to keep us happy. Could it be that he was glancing anxiously down the street while keeping one eye on his four hungry customers?

Within minutes a teenage boy wearing the regulation long t-shirt over jeans that had a crotch somewhere between the knees, plus dutifully sideways-situated baseball cap on his shaggy head, came zooming up the street on a skateboard and, rounding the corner where we sat, disappeared deftly into the establishment outside of which we waited in hope. There was no doubt that a plan was afoot to ensure that our enterprising host didn't lose valuable clientele while his kitchen was being fixed.

They talked in hushed tones while squeezed into the furthest nook at the back of the modestly sized kitchen, in an effort to keep the goings-on from us four, no doubt. Within minutes the skateboarded visitor once again emerged from the building, rounded our table with a grin and shot off back down the street, MP3 player cord dangling from one of his ears and soon disappeared round a corner some hundred metres or so away.

We received our salads, together with the customary small plates to eat them from, and so were distracted with the task of pouring oil over them and helping ourselves to personal portions. With something to eat and drinks to imbibe, we continued quite happily to speculate about where the pizzas were coming from, but it was now readily apparent to all of us that it wouldn't be from the kitchen of the establishment outside of which we were seated.

Sure enough, some ten minutes later, skateboard boy was on his way back up the street, a huge white plastic carrier bag suspended from one of his hands containing what was evidently four huge flat cardboard boxes. He made a vain attempt to pass us nonchalantly, as though we wouldn't have a clue what was in them, and zipped into the building as fast as his tiny-wheeled vehicle would let him. The distinct smell of hot pizza followed him.

Before you could say "pizza to go – to stay" our gallant restaurateur walked out from his very quiet kitchen, proudly bearing two huge plates, upon which were laid two hot fresh Pizza Margheritas. Having placed them before the girls with a flourish and a huge self-satisfied grin, he retreated within, soon to return with the other two for George and I.

For all the dodginess of the method used to get the pizzas to the table, for a businessman to keep four punters from going elsewhere, they were very good pizzas. We ate gratefully and in some degree of amazement at our host's resourcefulness and wondered where exactly was the other pizza parlour that had rustled them up. If they were in competition with each other, it was hard to see why the other place would have done such a favour. Probably his brother's joint I shouldn't wonder.

Having finished our meals, our drinks and our time available before having to get back to the harbour for the trip back to Samos, we rose from the table and pooled our millions of Lira to pay the bill.

Before we could actually walk away our host once again emerged and asked if everything was to our satisfaction. At this point we were just discussing the question of leaving a tip.

"So," said George to the proprietor, "Do we leave a tip here or down the road?"

The guy either had a good sense of humour or didn't understand, but he laughed nevertheless. He did alright out of us, and we were happy with the deal.

All we had to do now was run the gauntlet of hustlers as we made our way back to the boat.

19 – The Things You Have to Do For a Free Coffee

To collect our mail we have to go to a taverna in the village of Asklipio, about 4 kilometres up the mountain from our house. There are three ways of getting there. Two of them are dirt tracks winding among the hills and forest, occasionally affording spectacular views along the way, whereas the third is a tar-mac road, which goes up to the village from the Kiotari crossroads. To go by road necessitates driving down our kilometre or so of dirt track to the main coast road, then taking a right and right again some several hundred yards later at the aforementioned crossroads.

In the cooler months of the off-season, between November and April, we often choose to walk it and follow one of the dirt tracks, which lead directly up from behind the house. Usually we'll make a round trip, going up by one track and returning by the other. When we had the fires in the summer of 2008, the flames reached the very edge of the further of the two tracks, just about one kilometre from our house. At that time over half of the sky was an orange-brown colour and people talked in hushed tones while wondering if they'd need to evacuate. Many deer perished in those fires and we haven't seen them in our valley since then. Happily, though, we have seen them further west, so we're just hoping that they'll find their way back to our area some time in the near future.

Since the fires there has been a three year hunting ban put in place, the local councils having erected makeshift road-side signs announcing 'HUNTING PROHIBITED" which consist of a re-bar (those metal rods used in building) with a square metal plate about a foot across welded to the top of it. The entire thing is painted a mucky yellow and the lettering is stencilled on to it in black. It didn't take long for these signs to get their poles bent so that you had to approach them on foot and bend over to see what was written on them, since this rendered them unreadable from a passing vehicle. The thinking behind this, we surmise, being that if someone chose to defy the ban and was apprehended, rifle in hand, they could say, "What sign? I didn't see any sign."

The above fact notwithstanding, we haven't heard the crack of hunting rifles in the hills around the house for a couple of winters, so by and large the ban must be having some effect. In fact, another very noticeable result of the ban is the plethora of Chukars (or maybe Red-Legged or even Rock Partridges, but we reckon they're Chukars) we now have in the valley. When you disturb them, either by coming upon them whilst walking, or driving up the track in the car, they have the habit of running for all they're worth, often for a hundred metres or more, before eventually either finding a convenient spot to veer off into the undergrowth, or taking to the air laboriously after their interminable run before flying very low to a place of relative safety. Despite the fact that they have wings, they evidently don't fancy flying all that much.

You can be forgiven for thinking they're simply partridges. The fact is, unless you get a really good look at them from the front or the side, the least likely angles you're going to approach from, they do look rather brown or grey and uninteresting, plumage-wise. On a few occasions we've disturbed a mother with her brood of maybe six or seven, and they all run away like that procession you used to see at the end of any Benny Hill show, the mother managing to exude an air of: "*Come on children, keep together now! It might be good if we all went in the same direction!*"

We only came to realise that they were either Chukars or Rock Partridges when we found the remains of the head of one unfortunate bird, laying on the track, evidently all that was left after a bird of prey had dropped in for lunch. We picked it up, took it home and searched our "bird books" to find out what it was. Their heads are very pretty indeed. They have a white beard area, around which is a black eye stripe, which sweeps down around the sides of the neck, and a reddish-orange beak. If you Google it you'll see what a handsome bird they really are. Anyway, following the hunting ban we can't move for them in the valley and, since we find them endearing, we're not complaining.

Today, since it's a bright and sunny January day we're going to walk the hour or so up the country track to Asklipio and see if we've any mail. Often we telephone first and talk to Athanasia, who seems to be a permanent fixture in the taverna's kitchen, at which time she usually says quite simply, if there is mail to collect for us or for our neighbours, "*Ela Yianni, ela!*"

On days like this when we thankfully have precious little else to do, we choose to make the walk and, if there's no mail, it doesn't matter anyway. We'll take a coffee on the taverna's terrace, overlooking the huge valley, which sweeps down from a few hundred feet below the village to the coast between Kiotari and Gennadi, and wend our way back along the other lane.

Maria has already bottled our eating olives this winter. There's a simple science to doing it right, as Lena (whose husband Petros is very careful) showed us. First you get your glass jar and half fill it with water. The rest of the volume will be made up by the olives, which you're eventually going to add to it. Into this water you pour enough salt to preserve a beached whale. It certainly seemed that way the first time we did it. Actually, I'm running before I walk here. What I should say is that first you immerse the olives that you'll be preserving in water and either change that water on a daily basis or every other day, depending on whom you talk to. You do this for two or three weeks, depending on whom you talk to. I think you get the picture here don't you.

When your two or three weeks of softening the olives in ever-changing water are complete, you start the salt stage mentioned above. Your olives now sitting in a waiting strainer, you add the salt to the water in the bottle that will be their final destination, as discussed, and stir a while. You'll know when the right amount of salt is in the water by quite simply carefully lowering a fresh egg into it. Once the egg floats with an area the size of a Euro coin (always reminds me of a monk's tonsure) above the surface, you have added the right amount of salt. The first time I did this I added salt by the tablespoonful, stirred and dropped in my egg what must have been twenty times and still my egg sank to the bottom.

"This can't be right." I expressed in worried tones to

Yvonne-Maria, "Perhaps there's something we're missing here."

"That's what Lena said to do." Replied my trusting wife, "Just keep going. I'm sure it'll work eventually." Of course she was right, it did; but not before I'd begun to wonder if I'd have to nip down the road for a further supply of salt. At about that stage when you almost think, "There's no way any more salt will dissolve in that water" you drop in your egg and – wow! It's floating. Now you can pour in your olives.

This is the point where it makes all the difference what little additional touches you add. You can simply fill the jar with olives, seal it and leave it a few weeks and your olives are ready. You just need a little Feta and some fresh bread. But our friend Mavis down the road, who's lived out here a few years longer than we have and also kept her ear to the ground to pick up tips from her Greek friends and neighbours, passed on a little gem which has transformed our enjoyment of "*eating*" olives. When you stuff them into the jar of salted water, add a few cloves of fresh garlic, be sure your olives are all under the water's surface and, just to seal them in, pour a little olive oil on the top before closing the jar.

Olives with that garlic-flavour, which they've assimilated after a few weeks in that sealed jar with those cloves, are phantasmagorical. Take my word for it. Mavis' tip has moved us on from eating them with a salad (after originally not liking them at all), to popping them whole into our mouths and savouring the blighters. We now eat them at every opportunity. Plus it has the added benefit of rendering you unattractive to any passing vampires, leave alone close friends.

So here we are armed with a small jar for Athanasia as we set out to walk up to Asklipio. The sun is out and it's showing

19°C on our terrace. A fleece over a sweatshirt is all we'll need for the walk. We pass numerous *Kou'mara* bushes along the way. Many are still laden with their bright reddish orange fruit and my wife can't resist sampling a few. I have to say that I don't much care for them myself, but each to his own I suppose. They do look attractive it has to be said, hanging cherry-like in bushes which are often higher than my head. I used to think that the *Kou'mara* bushes were what are also often called *Maquis*, even having said as much in my previous tomes. It seems I was mistaken. The *Kou'mara*, or Strawberry Tree, is actually known by the Latin name *Arbutus Unedo*, whereas the *Maquis* is a term more correctly applied to the type of scrub land that covers a lot of the hills in the Mediterranean region and comprises of several kinds of shrub and tree, including the Strawberry tree. See, you learn things when you read my books. Trouble is, after *Maquis*, I keep wanting to add "*de Sade.*" I've no idea why.

After about fifty minutes and feeling quite hot and sweaty from the climb we crest the hill where the lane enters the village. Coming this way we find ourselves on a rise above the major part of Asklipio and so we walk a few hundred metres down the hill to the taverna, which is open every day of the year, bar none. The only time it's closed is during siesta time - if there are no clients present. Otherwise, you can enter the building either through the rear door from the steep lane behind, or through the terrace out front where the locals sit and play dominoes or backgammon all year round and where tourists who've made the trek up here, usually in hire cars and occasionally (complete madness!) on push bikes in the Greek heat, take their cool drinks, their Greek salads for lunch and their fill of the wonderful view.

A little further up the steep hill overlooking the village is

Asklipio *Kastro*, which, although a ruin, has surprisingly intact outer walls and affords a 360° view for those with the energy to make the climb. It was built as a protection for the inhabitants of several villages, including Lahania, Istrios, Gennadi and Vati, probably during the 14th century, during the age of the pirates, when - should they appear along the coast "a rapin' and a pillagin'" as was their wont - the villagers could sound warnings and all make their way there for mutual protection. Within the fortress the remains of a huge water cistern are still intact and if you're not too careful you could succeed in falling into it, since very little has been done to ensure the safety of those who clamber over this battlement.

There is reputed to be a tunnel running from one of the older village houses up to the castle, but no one has dared in recent years to go through it. Some web sites call it a Crusader castle, but it seems very unlikely that it is. The Venetians are sometimes credited with having built it, but the full facts are lost in antiquity. One thing that is for sure is that the stone isn't local and therefore had to be brought from some distance away.

If this castle were in the UK then undoubtedly it would be surrounded by a fence and the only access would be beside a booth where you'd probably have to hand over a fiver each to gain access to it. There would be wooden walkways beyond which it would be forbidden to stray. Yes it may perhaps be a little safer, but the fact that one can clamber over every part of this impressive ruin is what makes it so enjoyable to go there. The views are stunning and it's an exhilarating place to be, especially on a bright day in wintertime. Just watch your step, that's all.

But today we're heading down instead of up. We go down

to the taverna's rear door and walk in. As expected, Athanasia
is in her usual spot in the kitchen, knocking up a prial of Greek
coffees for some of the village men who are absorbed in their
backgammon games. As it's wintertime they are all seated
indoors. The fact that it's almost 20°C outside is irrelevant.
This is winter; it's cold! Athanasia, seeing that we have our
fleeces tied around our waists after the 4km uphill walk in the
sunshine, looks at us with grave concern. You can tell what
she's thinking, "You'll catch your death! How can you be
outdoors in winter dressed like that?"

Rather predictably she asks: "Aren't you cold?" My sweaty
armpits reveal to the close observer what the answer is to that
particular question. It makes no difference. Most Greeks will
be going about wearing fur-collared jackets and thick trousers
at this time of the year. Only the crazy people from Britain
walk around half dressed. The fact that we'd be quite happy
with this kind of day at any time during a British summer
won't wash here. Weather like this in the UK would bring out
the hordes in their cut-off shorts and strappy tops. We know,
we've done it. We have the t-shirt. Well, the strappy top.

Although a half a dozen or so locals are seated inside, there
is still a major mess spread out before our eyes. The ice-cream
chest fridge and the glass-fronted chilled red Coke cabinet are
well away from the walls and great canvas dust sheets are
splayed out across the floor while Agapitos, Athanasia's
husband, is to be seen brandishing a paint roller as he coats the
interior walls with their umpteenth layer of white emulsion.

Agapitos is probably in his sixties, with a round face and
generous white moustache. His wife is probably ten years his
junior, something not at all unusual in Greece, although she
looks much closer to him in age than she actually is. Not for
her the luxury of being able to spend any time on herself, like

...ever. Her life consists of spending virtually every day supplying the men of the village with their coffees and preparing simple Greek fare for the tourists during the season. You won't ever eat Cordon Bleu at this taverna, but you will go away well sated with simple home-cooked Greek cuisine. Agapitos has the sort of kindly face that is always willing to crack a smile and frequently does so.

Just once in the five years that we've lived here and collected our mail from this taverna have we turned up to find their son (who's in his early thirties) holding the fort and telling us that his parents have driven up to town for the day; no doubt to do something that required forms to be signed and rubber stamps to be wielded is our guess.

Just to be doubly sure that Athanasia doesn't ever have time to be bored, the taverna also serves as a sub-post office. This is made evident by a small "Hellenic Post" sign on the wall outside at the front of the terrace, and the booth in the corner of the room where you see a pair of weighing scales and numerous piles of mail in all shapes and sizes and usually in elastic-banded bundles. It looks a mess but Athanasia knows where every envelope, every package, is bound. One of the taverna tables toward the rear of the room, just in front of the "Post Office" corner and to one side of the kitchen area, is dedicated to bills. There are tatty cardboard boxes covering it with different bills stacked, rather like files in a filing cabinet, in each. One box contains the water bills for the village, another the electricity bills, another the telephone bills and there are still others which contain official-looking envelopes that I've no idea about at all. I think that at least some of them are call-up papers for youths whose turn to do their military service is imminent, while others may be of a political nature. One day I'll ask.

Whenever there is mail for us (and we also collect for Mack and Jane just up the hill, while they frequently reciprocate), Athanasia will trot behind the booth, which has desktops rather like you see in a post office, with a lower surface on the inside for the staff member to work on, and a higher surface toward the outside where customers rest their elbows while dealing with their "postal" business, and begin rummaging through what looks like a totally confusing pile of all kinds of stuff. But she knows which pile of envelopes, packets and parcels to go to and quickly extracts an envelope here, or a packet there with our name on it. If we have bills due we flip through the boxes on the bills table ourselves of course, as does everyone in the surrounding area who comes in here to collect their mail.

Having handed us a few envelopes and a package from my mum in the UK, she returns to the kitchen area, figuratively dons her taverna hat again and busies herself as before making coffees. Maria and I order a couple of frappes and begin walking toward the glass doors that lead out on to the terrace when Agapitos starts to grunt behind us. Turning, I see he's making a vain attempt to shove the Coca Cola fridge back toward the wall, having now finished emulsioning that area. I hand my wife the mail, and set to it with him, since he's making little progress with this upright, glass-doored chill cabinet that's packed full of bottles and cans on his own. Between the two of us we elicit that satisfying scraping noise that tells all observers that the cabinet is indeed moving and, before you can say Spiros Papadopoulos, the cabinet is back where it belongs and no doubt will stay for another twelve months. Looking at the ice cream chest freezer I suggest that he may need a hand budging that too, to which he replies with an appreciative, "*Neh, se parakalo.*"

Both cabinets now back in position we repair to the table outside while Athanasia quickly appears with our coffees. She sits down with us and, after we've made her our small gift of a jar of newly preserved olives, for which she thanks us profusely and says we're naughty to have done it, we make small talk about what we do with ourselves during the winter months. All Greeks ask us, even those we've now known for years, things like: "You live here all year round?" The expression they use is *"himo'na kalokai'ri"* which translates as "winter-summer." Or they'll say, "When were you last back in the UK?" ...or the variation on that one which is, "When are you next going back to the UK?" They'll usually ask whether we're growing vegetables too and move their heads approvingly when we list the various legumes we've put in. As I've said before, if you tell a Greek you have a garden and you're not using it to grow stuff you can eat, then he or she will fast assume that you're quite bonkers.

Eventually, our coffee glasses empty, we rise to leave and Athanasia also rises, looks to the village square below and enquires, "Where is your car?" When we reply that we've walked up to the village today she steps back in horror, places her hand over her heart and expresses complete disbelief that we would walk four kilometres when we have a whole day off, rather than get into the car and drive. It only serves to reinforce her view that, nice though we interlopers may be, we're all quite mad.

When I reach into my pocket for my small-change purse to pay for our coffees she waves away my gesture and says, "No! Of course you aren't paying. You have worked for your drinks today! My poor husband would be on his way to the hospital now if you hadn't helped him replace the fridges. That's payment enough."

No amount of remonstrating with her will get her to accept her modest price for the coffees, so we give up, I replace the purse in my trouser pocket and say with my tongue firmly in my cheek: "The things I have to do for a free coffee!"

We walk down the steps from the terrace as she waves, now joined by her husband, who is smiling his appreciation. We both agree once we're out of earshot that they're now probably discussing the belief that we must be so hard up for cash, since we couldn't afford to use our car to come and collect our mail.

Part of the view from Asklipio "Kastro"

Street in Asklipio village, where we go to collect our mail

20 – Kosta's Dilemma

Kostas is around sixty years of age and still bears the evidence about his face of having some decades ago been a dashing, handsome young man. Today his girth is somewhat larger than he'd like it to be, but then, so are his worries. Kostas makes his living, correction, struggles to make his living, on a beach not too far from Lindos. If you were to go and visit the said beach this summer, you'd find Kostas sitting on an old white PVC patio chair, underneath his makeshift canopy, consisting of a few metal posts and crossbars with some cane sticks bound together and affixed to the top of the structure. Cheap and basic it may be, but it serves its purpose of keeping a merciless Greek sun off his flesh in the long days during which he sits here through the tourist season.

Kostas was born in a village close by. One of five children, some of whom now live in Canada, where pastures are greener (not to mention a fair bit whiter during wintertime), others of whom still live in the same village as their aged parents, he is native Rhodean. Some decades ago he started making his living by hiring umbrellas and sun beds on the beach where he is still to be found in the summer season. In the early days he had a good stretch of beach, on which he would place around sixty umbrellas, along with 120 sun beds, most of which would be occupied on a regular basis all through the summer. They were, and still are, always comfortably spaced so as to allow the occupants a degree of privacy, unlike some beaches where you can lie on a sun bed, stretch your arm out and accidentally grope the stranger under the next umbrella. Don't ask me how I know that. The answer would be embarrassing.

Kostas doesn't own his stretch of beach. Every second year before the season begins he has to bid for his patch in an auction run by the local council. This costs him several hundred Euros, but he has no choice.

No bid, no patch of beach. No patch of beach, no income.

Twenty five years ago Kostas and five others all used to put their bids in together, win their plots and equitably share out the stretch of beach won in the auction between the six of them, so that each one would get a fair number of clients. Kostas tells me that although he used to have 120 beds, he now struggles to earn his living from less than thirty. Why?

The answer is a story that has spelt increasing misery for many Greek traders during the last few years, the increase of the *"all-inclusive"* resort. Each year the huge hotel, which occupies the centre of the bay where Kostas has his patch, garners an ever-larger stretch of beach for their all-inclusive guests' sun beds. Kostas tells me he gets depressed as he glances along the beach these days at all the lobster-coloured bodies sporting their "hospital-style" armbands which they wear to identify them as inmates of the all-inclusive resort of their choice, silent bracelets which make the statement that they won't be spending much of their money on privately owned sun beds and umbrellas, they won't be patronizing the local supermarkets or tavernas and they won't be staying in small studios or apartments, many of which in recent years have lost the relative financial security of their annual contract with a tour operator. In fact, many of these holidaymakers will only venture outside the resort's front gates when boarding a coach for an excursion laid on by, you've guessed it, the tour operator.

What's also sad is that, owing to the fact that the area that the sun-bed men are allotted shrinks each time they go to the auction, there are squabbles breaking out between former friends, all of whom worry about how they're going to make ends meet this year.

Kostas has a depth of woe in his eyes that wasn't there just a few years back. It's a look that will, in all probability, grow more pronounced as the tour operators aggressively continue to promote the *"all-inclusive"* option to their customers from the colder climes of northern Europe. He understands why many choose that option, but he also knows that it's killing the local communities that, up until just a few years ago, made their living out of the tourist who stayed in a small hotel, apartment block or village room/studio, the tourist who ate out in a different taverna each night of their holiday and thus enriched their Greek experience in the process.

He could just as easily be the man who runs a small traditional taverna in a village not too far away from this beach. The man who now sits in a chair outside the kitchen, beside one of his rear tables, all of which are covered in their traditional Greek blue and white check tablecloths, and waits for the paltry few customers that he hopes he'll get each night while sipping at his Ouzo and puffing at a cigarette and looking at his fingernails. Tears well up in his eyes now and then as he tries to decide whether to keep his business going for one more year or close it down for good. The latter option would be the wisest one from a financial point of view. But he only knows this business and has done it for decades. His food is good. His family used to make friends of the holidaymakers who patronized his establishment. What else would he do now he's in his late fifties?

Kostas may or may not still be sitting on his familiar stretch of beach during next year's season. The probability is that he won't be there, that the huge hotel just along the beach will have got their wish to squeeze out the small man. What he'll do to support his family heaven only knows. One thing though is sure, the small Greek community of taverna owners, shopkeepers and sun bed rental guys will continue to go to the wall and the holiday experience for those coming to Greece will be the poorer for it.

This cautionary story has innumerable counterparts all over Greece, and probably the world. I make a plea to all those who come here for their holidays: think about my tale. Think about why you started coming here in the first place. If you want every resort the world over to be of the same mould, if you want a few rich entrepreneurs to get even richer while more and more small businessmen go out of business, you just keep reaching for that all-inclusive brochure.

Have a nice holiday. But go home with a clean conscience. Stay local. Stay small. Kostas will probably not now be in business long enough to benefit from your change of heart. But maybe a few younger people will. It's in your hands Mr. & Mrs. Tourist.

See, I understand why an increasing number of families are choosing the all-inclusive option. It does make financial good sense these days. And that's the rub. You have to think of your pocket, it's a fact of life. Everything is a trade-off.

People came to Greece, when tourism itself was young and idealistic, to experience the friendliness of the people. Many businesses were family-run and, by the time you were standing outside the establishment with your suitcases packed for the trip home, you felt as though you'd discovered a second one - a home from home. You'd beamed as the woman who cooks in the taverna's kitchen had come to your child and given her or him a small token, perhaps a free ice cream, perhaps some toy or other that she thought your child might like. You'd begun to shed your embarrassment at being hugged and then kissed on both cheeks by business people you'd patronized who genuinely wanted to see you come back next year and even offered you some extra discount if you did so; or gave you a gift to remember them by. You'd not even begun to understand why some local would give up his precious time to take you out on his fishing boat for a few hours when he hardly knew you, or why his wife would make a point of bringing you a plate of the latest *glyka* (Greek sweets) she'd freshly made. How you'd enjoyed sharing that free glass of *Metaxa* at the end of a particularly enjoyable evening when the bar owner would sit with you into the small hours and put the world to rights.

All the reasons why people would come to Greece are eroding away at the hands of the all-inclusive resort. Sadly, some of the owners of such places here on Rhodes aren't even Greek, so the final profits made by such establishments don't even stay within the island's, or even the country's, economy.

Everything changes. There's no way that we can hang on to the past, I know that. I have to accept it, however reluctantly. But there are some changes that needn't be. There are sometimes alternative ways to implement change, ways that aren't so destructive to communities or cultures.

Experiences like those that I have shared with readers of my books are intimate and life-enriching. Had I been born thirty years later, I wonder whether I'd ever have been so fortunate.

I'm off now. We're going to pop over to Kostas' stretch of beach and sit with him and his wife and their youngest son Andreas, who works with his parents during the high season. We'll pass the early evening together as we stare together at the empty majority of his sun beds, laying expectantly under their umbrellas, offering shade to just a couple of padded cushions instead of grateful holidaymakers. My wife and I will share the humble fare that Kostas' wife Tsambika will rustle up in their tiny little wooden utility hut. Andreas will grill a few fishes on their makeshift barbecue, we'll scoop fresh salad out of a jumbo-sized Tupperware box and wash it all down with a couple of beers from the small beach bar next door. Maybe we'll also drink a plastic cup-full or two of their homemade retsina.

Y-Maria and I will at the very least offer to pay them for the beers, but we know they won't have any of it. No, you don't insult Greek friends by trying to pay for their kindness. They may not have much nowadays, but they do still have a fierce pride in their Greek hospitality.

The small wooden utility hut that serves as their HQ during the season is probably only about five feet square. It has a sloping corrugated roof and inside is lined with worktops, shelves and hooks. By the end of each season they usually have a good clutch of beach towels that their dwindling number of clients forgot to take away with them at the end of their last day, hanging on one wall. On another hook hangs a selection of diving masks and snorkels. Inside this cramped structure Tsambika most days manages to rustle up a meal, as they'll not be leaving the beach until mid evening. She also makes a very good frappe in there too. There is always chopped *karpouzi* (watermelon) on offer. Outside the hut is a large thickly-trunked plane tree, onto which is fixed a rudimentary shower, with mains water coming from somewhere nearby. Behind the tree, just off the short path back to the parking area is a double changing hut. Everything you need to live a simple life is within twenty-five square meters of Kostas' canopy, which serves as his beach office. It's just as well because they spend more hours on this piece of beach during the months of May to October than they do at their home in the village a couple of kilometers away.

I am amazed, when I chew the fat with Kostas, at how ready he is with a laugh. Despite the melancholy in them, his are smiling eyes, with the type of crow's feet that indicate a man with a happy character. He's a man who loves company and loves to make people happy. He also speaks fairly good Italian, which is an asset because during the high summer there are more Italians than British here these days. So as I sit in one of his cracking plastic patio chairs, its legs sinking into the shingle, patting his old mutt who's trying desperately to keep cool by lolling his tongue out of the corner of his mouth in the August temperatures, I wait while Kostas rents one of his modest boats to an Italian family who try to haggle his rental price down a bit. Once they've agreed terms Andreas is off down to the water's edge to prepare the boat and get the guests launched safely after a little pep talk about how to use the craft safely.

"Please be back within two hours." Asks Kostas in Italian as the father waves a hand behind him, his body already facing the other way as he begins to walk toward the waiting Andreas.

Some time later, after my having helped tidy up and wipe clean the sunbeds that have seen "action" today, Y-Maria having also helped clear away the remnants of our modest, yet hugely enjoyable al fresco meal, we stand and bid our farewells. Even the few things that we have done to help were accepted with some reluctance by Kostas and his family. Now, as we take our leave and make as if to walk away, Tsambika calls, "Wait!"

She disappears within the hut and momentarily re-appears with a large carrier bag, which she hands to my wife with the words, "For you."

We thank them yet again and, once out of earshot, investigate the contents of the bag. Inside it there is a sealed Tupperware container containing a generous portion of chopped salad, another filled with tsatsiki, some silver foil wrapped around a couple of huge slices of watermelon, also within its own smaller plastic bag to prevent seepages, plus four or five beach towels.

Fortunately for us we still occasionally receive reminders of why, when we used to take our annual holidays, my wife's heritage notwithstanding, we came to Greece so frequently.

21 – A Lesson in Pest Prevention

Takis lives with his French wife Naomi down the valley from us. He's probably about my age, maybe a little older and speaks passable English. He keeps his straight graying hair just a little longer than collar length and it usually looks like he's just got up, no matter what time of day you encounter him. I think if you were to buy him a comb he'd look at it with a perplexed expression and ask what you're supposed to do with it.

Like us, he finds the "village mentality" a little difficult to deal with and so prefers to live outside of Asklipio, the village of his origin. His attitude is no doubt shaped by the fact that he hasn't married a girl from the village, or even one from the neighbouring village. His wife is a *"Xeni,"* a foreigner, although - as it happens - one who speaks very good Greek. Back when they married it was much more exceptional than nowadays to marry a non-Orthodox, leave alone a non-Greek, and nowadays it's still a bit odd for the more isolated villagers, where marriages are still often a case of two families uniting as they choose which daughter is going to marry which son from the other family.

Not long after we first moved in, Takis and Naomi drove by to make themselves known. Following that occasion we could quite conceivably have never crossed passed with them again had we not dropped in once in a while. This is not to imply that they aren't good neighbours. In fact it implies that they're excellent ones. They never fail to make us welcome if we call, but don't smother us or crowd us in any way. Having passed an hour or so drinking coffee with them we usually come away with a clutch of cuttings and roots to put into the garden, plus assorted fruits and vegetables that they've grown, depending on the time of year. Our visits are more frequent during wintertime as both of them work during the season. In winter, as with many Rhodean residents, it's time to socialize and take coffee in company while solving all the world's problems, not to mention the frequent problem of what we're going to eat for lunch.

This particular March day we've been for a long walk along the beach and managed to scavenge a few nice chunky pieces of wood for the fire. We enter our neighbours' gate in the chain-link fence that encloses the 2,000 square metres or so of their property, walk past a pile of logs large enough to fuel a dozen or so log-burners for the duration of the winter, and tap on their front door. It's probably around 17°C out today, (63°F in the old money), but feels cooler with a keen wind. The huge revolving bird-shaped cowl on their chimney reveals from its plume of smoke that their log-burner is in use.

Naomi opens the door and breaks into a warm smile, while stepping aside saying *"Peras'te,"* which literally means "pass" but is the expression most often used here for "do come in." Before we've even seated ourselves around her dining table, which is laden with jars of preserves, bowls of drying herbs and a colander full of something green, she's got the kettle on.

There is also an assortment of accessories used in sewing and needlework as Naomi is a dab-hand and has made some superb throws, tablecloths and bedspreads. Plus, her walls sport a few hand-made tapestries and her windows are framed with curtains she's made herself. The *"somba"* radiates heat from the glowing logs inside and the entire scene is one that makes you feel like you've just put on your favourite old pair of slippers.

It's probably a good idea to slip in another note here about word endings in Greek. People often ask why the same word, even if it's someone's name, can be spelt with several different endings. I won't bore you with all the ins and outs again here, but I will just explain that if a name is the subject of a sentence then it's a nominative case. This means you'd say, for example, "Takis is here". Note the "s" at the end of the name. However, if you want to talk about someone, then the case is accusative. In this case you'd say, "I can see Taki". Now you don't use the "s" on the end of the name. There are two other cases, but since to most of us a case is usually what you pack your undies in, let's leave it at that for now. So you may have noticed that I use the "s" or change name endings where it's appropriate, even though I'm writing in English. I know, I'm a pedantic so-and-so, but I just can't help it.

Pretty soon we're seated around the kitchen table, hot mugs of coffee cradled in our palms, fingers wrapped around them as we blow across the surface of the liquid within. Takis joins us from another room and we begin catching up on what we've all been up to recently. After covering all the various jobs we've done and how anxious we are about whether we'll get work again next season I raise a subject that's been on my mind for a while.

"Taki, perhaps you can tell me, I notice that in a lot of orchards there are plastic bottles hanging from the trees. I presume it's some kind of pest control, but what do the locals put in them? Is it some special stuff you buy from garden centres? Do you have to go somewhere specific to buy a chemical to use in them? See, I don't really like the idea of using chemicals, but it seems there are so many potential threats to the fruit."

"Nope. Nothing special. Just something sweet."

"Something sweet. Like…"

"Like fruit juice, squash, sugared water, that's all. The idea is that the wasps and other insects that may otherwise bore into the oranges will go for the easier option, the liquid in the bottle."

"So you just hang an old water bottle in the tree and wait for the insects to go into it. How do you stop them getting out again?"

"Easy," replies Takis, "I show you." Finding a 50cl empty plastic water bottle in the rubbish bin, Takis rescues it, wipes off a few tomato pips and other sticky stuff and proceeds to take me back over forty years to the days of Valerie Singleton and Christopher Trace on Blue Peter. I was so innocent when I used to watch that programme. I was far too young to understand all the rumours about their off-screen affair. Sorry, I ought to say their alleged off-screen affair. Or was it with Peter Purves? Oh, I don't know. That's Val Singleton with Peter Purves, not Christopher Trace. Or was it? Sorry, getting a bit side tracked here aren't I.

Takis opens a drawer and ferrets around in it, extracting a pair of scissors, some nylon string and a staple gun; but not before placing various mobile phone chargers, batteries, cigarette lighters and other assorted paraphernalia on the worktop, much to Naomi's annoyance. Though, bless her, she says nothing. Sorry, no sticky-backed plastic or toilet rolls though. Hey ho.

He removes the blue plastic bottle top and consigns it to the bin from where he'd extracted the bottle. Deftly taking one blade of the scissors and stabbing the bottle just below the shoulder, just where it begins to narrow toward the top, he works the blade into the plastic and begins to cut all the way around, eventually separating the top part of the bottle from the rest of it. Flipping the removed part upside down, it immediately resembles a shallow funnel, the bottle's open top becoming the spout at the bottom. He drops this part back into the open part of the bottle, which is now shaped somewhat like a plastic beaker or tumbler. Then, when he has seated it as tightly as he can, he grabs the stapler and fires a few staples through both layers of plastic, to create an effective insect trap. No expense involved.

"To hang it from the tree, you just do this with the string," he says, wrapping the string around one of the indentations which circumscribes the bottle and, quickly tying a couple of knots shoves his thumb into the loop of string he's now created and suspends his newly manufactured wasp trap proudly from his left hand.

"See, they go in here," he says, pointing to the inverted top, now forming an effective funnel down into the body of the bottle, "and they are not clever enough to fly out. So they eventually drown in the liquid and they don't harm the fruit of the tree. Simple and very cost-effective, agreed?"

"Agreed," I conjoin. I do a lot of conjoining, I just don't talk about it all that much.

"Right, if it's that simple I'd better start collecting empty water bottles then." I say, as Takis hands me the trap he's just created and declares that I now have my first one already. Modest it may be, but it's a gift I greatly appreciate. I shall use it as a template.

I'm tempted to reciprocate by giving him my comb, but I think better of it. Anyway, it needs a bit of a clean-out if the truth be told.

Here's one Takis made earlier

22 – Uncle Stamati the Second

My wife has now taken to permanently calling me "Uncle Stamati." If you've read the first volume in this series, *"Feta Compli!"*, you'll already have come across him. You may remember that he was married to aunty Effie, my mother-in-law's sister, and when I first came to Athens to visit them they lived in Kato Patissia. Their "daughter" Christina lived in the apartment upstairs with her husband Takis, who was probably ten years her senior. Effie used to cook spaghetti Bolognese for her husband virtually every day after his retirement, though it was like no spaghetti Bolognese you'll ever have eaten. It's described in all its gory detail in the chapter *"Aunty Effie's Cuisine"* in *"Feta Compli!"*

Takis, as I mentioned in "Feta", was a sort of upmarket Greek version of Derek Trotter, of "Only Fools and Horses" fame. The biggest difference was the amounts of money that he dealt in, which were substantially larger than those that would pass through "Del-Boy's" hands. Takis could never, though, have been accused of being ostentatious. I couldn't understand why, when I first went to visit, a man - whose business was described to me as "importing and exporting" - drove around in a faded old red Mazda which was not only old, but small. It was barely big enough for four people, if, that is, the ones in the back didn't mind having the circulation in their lower legs cut off.

I remember one particular evening in Athens circa 1977-78, when Takis decided he was taking us all out for a meal. By "all" I mean my mother-in-law and her second husband David, Yvonne-Maria and I, plus Takis and Christina themselves. That makes six (yes I know, you've worked it out before me. But I had to take my socks off to get there I'm afraid). Quite how the six of us got into the tiny Mazda is a mystery, but get into it we did. I was thinking at the time, "Why aren't we going in his other car, you know, the Merc or something?" But I never actually discovered if he even had another car. Of course, at the time, as I began to say above, I couldn't work this out. I knew he had plenty of money. The quality of their furniture testified to that. So why the ropey old family means of transport?

Of course nowadays I fully understand. Today, in 2010, when hearsay has it that the government is resorting to Google Earth in an effort to spot swimming pools that don't have a license in their efforts to persuade the populace to part with their taxes, the issue of tax evasion is on everyone's lips. Back in those days, as I now realize, it wouldn't do for a man who was declaring barely enough income to feed a sparrow to be seen taking delivery of a luxury car every couple of years. It would have been a bit of a giveaway really, wouldn't it. Hence the tattered old tiny, faded, red Mazda, in which the six of us set out to go for a meal one Athens September evening.

We hadn't gone a couple of blocks when something was evidently very wrong. The car began behaving weirdly and slewing over the road. Takis managed to bring it to a halt at the kerbside and we all shoe-horned out on to the pavement (that's "sidewalk" if you're American). The problem was a flat tyre. After several minutes passed in which the five passengers waited while Takis swore and fumed about his misfortune, us chaps set to and began to see if we could find the spare.

Of course, in order to fit a spare it helps greatly if you're actually carrying one. Popping open the tiny boot (trunk, guys) we rummaged through old newspapers, cardboard boxes, various ropes and things that were covered with oil and found the spare wheel-well, which rather unhelpfully was devoid of its expected contents. After several more minutes of Takis letting off steam, David, my step-father-in-law suggested we telephone for help. There were no such things as mobile phones (cellphones, …boy is it difficult writing in international English these days!) then, so Takis had to find a *"periptero,"* which is what they call those kiosks you still see everywhere in Greece which sell newspapers, gum and cigarettes. Fortunately, there was one within yards of us and they all used to have a public phone hanging off of one corner, which Takis was quick to wrest from its cradle and dial a friend's number. David called out,

"Takis! There's no jack either. Oh, and better get him to bring a wheelbrace too!!"

Takis understood because he spoke reasonable English. I suppose he had to really, what with being in the "international trading" game and all. He evidently called someone who knew the whereabouts of the Mazda's genuine spare wheel (or at least, one that would fit) and within half an hour or so a Greek screeched to a halt behind us and climbed out of his driver's door, opened his boot and extracted the things we needed, but not before a Policeman had pulled up and ascertained that we had a bona fide reason to be parked in a no-parking area and expressed disbelief that all six of us had been travelling in the same car. Once again, these days he'd have apprehended us for over-filling the vehicle in such a way that not all of us could wear seatbelts.

During the brief time that the Policeman spent with us it was evident that Takis was uncomfortable. He tended to keep himself on the other side of the group from the Officer, so the two of them would have found it difficult to pursue a conversation. Luckily the Policeman soon tired of dealing with a flat tyre situation and drove off into the Athens night.

Eventually, with the wheel changed and our saviour despatched with much back-slapping and cheek-kissing, we continued to our destination, which proved to be a select taverna somewhere on the outskirts of the city, where we ate a stupendously good meal under the stars, with a distant view of the Acropolis and plenty of home-made Retsina to wash it down with. After the meal Takis insisted that we all needed a "Chicago." I'd never heard of a "Chicago" and thought it perhaps was a drink of some kind. But no, it was a huge ice-cream, one of which we all had placed in front of us at Takis' chosen Café-bar. Nowadays you can buy pale imitations of the "Chicago" from ready-made ice cream manufacturers, but these were brought to us in stainless steel dessert dishes, which were filled with vanilla and chocolate ice cream, topped with nuts, those round crispy wafers you sometimes buy in tubes, and plenty of chocolate sauce. Very huge and very enjoyable, even though it processed my condition from "just about able to keep my belt done up" to, "Oh, what the hell! Take the thing off and pop your top trouser button too while you're about it."

Got a bit side tracked there didn't I. I began by letting on that my wife has begun calling me "Uncle Stamati." Now in *Feta Compli!* I had omitted to refer to an aspect of Stamati that

I thought unnecessary to mention at the time. This would have been his flatulence. It seems that my wife's abiding memory of Stamati in his twilight years was of a bent old man shuffling about a be-darkened apartment from bed to table to bathroom, sometimes in a different order, releasing gas at regular intervals as he went.

What is it about getting older that inevitably brings on this physical condition? I mean, I like to think I keep in pretty good shape. During the winter we jog and do loads of physical labour, especially in the garden. We also walk for miles. During summertime we swim a lot and our diet is predominantly fresh fruit and vegetables all year round. Aaah, perhaps that has something to do with it, do you think? Yet I don't remember having quite so much air needing to escape my nether regions in my younger years as I do now. Am I striking a chord with anyone here (possibly even playing the same note)?

I'm not good with mornings. Mornings and I don't get on. I can get up to the alarm, never fear on that score, but I don't really wake up right away. I tend to shuffle about in a bit of a daze for half an hour or so. I can be lying in bed for hours with no problem, and all is silent. But then I get up and before I reach the bedroom door I am doing a passable impersonation, albeit unintentionally, of my wife's doddery old uncle, and it's very audible I'm afraid. I can't work it out, I really can't. Sometimes she says it's like hearing a rough old motorbike going past.

There I'll be, just opening the bedroom door and I'll hear from behind me, "Morning Uncle Stamati! I never would have married you if I thought you'd turn into him!" That's when she's in a good mood and laughs about it.

At other times when she's feeling more negative the

comments are more barbed. I try and counter the accusations with a word to the effect that, in more recent years, she's not so silent in that department herself, but I always lose the argument.

Still, at least she can console herself with the thought that I don't want to be fed Spaghetti Bolognese every single day. Not even if it looks and tastes like Spag Bol ought to.

Mind you, maybe (that's perhaps if you're British. Wait, am I getting myself all linguistically reversed here?) she'd prefer it, since she wouldn't have to keep saying things like, "Oh I don't know. What shall I cook tonight?"

She doesn't particularly enjoy cooking.

23 – Trek to the Hinterland

We once rented a car in Parga, on the West coast of the mainland, across the waters from Corfu and Paxos. We were staying on Paxos at the time, along with a couple of friends, Tom and Christine, plus their ten-year-old son Ben. Over a meal one evening we decided it would be a good idea to visit Meteora, the place where all those huge pillars of rock are topped by old monasteries, most of which were at one time only accessible by a basket lowered on a rope. A James Bond film was once made there; I think it was one of the Timothy Dalton ones, but my memory's hazy on that one. If you've ever sat in a travel agent and looked at the huge posters on the wall bearing the word 'GREECE" in huge letters over a photograph showing great sandstone pillars with buildings atop them, that was Meteora. Poring over a retsina-stained map we decided that it couldn't be all that long a drive from Parga, which was only half an hour by boat from Paxos. After a good meal in a Greek taverna, lots of normally stupid things seem like a good idea, don't they.

Plans were made. Decisions were taken. One subsequent morning saw the five of us on board one of those old curvy boats with the bright blue hull and a modest-sized cabin, inside which we could be seen playing cards, owing to the excessive amounts of spray flying around outside, as we made the short crossing to Parga. Owing to the wind direction there was also a generous amount of diesel fumes to be inhaled by anyone foolish enough to remain on deck for too long, which would result in a swift attack of nausea.

Stepping back into the cabin, I felt sick. The others reminded me with very little sympathy, a little unnecessarily in my view, that I'd been warned to stay in the cabin. The five of us were the only passengers and so I got the distinct impression that the crew (of precisely two) wanted to get the trip over with as soon as possible. There was, I believed, a backgammon board sitting outside a kafenion somewhere in Gaios awaiting the return of the players.

Parga was a revelation. It has gorgeous curvy bays with gently sloping sandy beaches, separated by green rocky headlands, one of which sports a "*kastro*." In the centre of the main bay there's a modest jetty, where the boats tie up and an attractive island out in the bay completes a very good example of a Greek getaway landscape. Once ashore we repaired to a nearby taverna for some midday sustenance, before tracking down a couple of modestly priced rooms to rent. Our bags having been deposited on the firm mattresses of the beds in the rooms we'd found, we then completed the preparations for the drive to Meteora by finding a car hire office, just metres along the road to Agia Kyriaki, the first village we'd be going through on route to our planned destination.

The sign outside declared that this was a well-known and therefore well-trusted car hire company, one with offices in several countries. We enquired from the young bored-looking man behind the desk how much it would be for a day and agreed a fee. He examined a couple of our driving licences, swiftly marked the forms in various places and span the form around for one of us to sign where he'd placed a couple of "x" marks. I perused the form for any hidden surprises and noted that where it said "Kilometer Charge" he'd left it blank. As is the norm these days, few hire companies charge for the number of kilometres or miles covered any more.

The formalities dispensed with, we all trouped outside in his wake to have him demonstrate the controls of the modest little Japanese motor that would carry the five of us into the unknown on the morrow. We were feeling buoyed up by the idea of a nice little adventure as we waltzed off with the car key to find somewhere to satisfy our growing hunger for the evening.

Next morning we arose early, got over those "It's far too early to be thinking straight" blues and all tumbled into the little hatchback to begin our trip. I was to drive the first leg, with Tom navigating. Map duly folded to show the right area spread out on his lap, girls and Ben in the back talking about trying to sleep on a bit once we'd got underway, I turned the key and we were off.

The first hour or so was quite fun. We passed storks nesting on the tops of telegraph poles, slowed down for tortoises to cross the road and generally admired the scenery as we travelled ever further from the coast toward the "hinterland" as it were. No one was too concerned when Tom first remarked that we didn't seem to be covering as much ground as we perhaps ought to have done from our calculations about how long the trip would take us. We'd passed through the villages of Karvounari, Paramithia and Vrosina by the time an hour had gone by and Tom ventured the view that we ought to have reached Ioannina by now. In fact it was two hours before we arrived there and the women were desperate for their first "bathroom" break so we didn't need much excuse to pull up near a café and have a drink and take stock. Having rejoiced and also expressed our disbelief at how cheap the drinks were, this far away from the tourist trail, we once more piled into our little chariot, this time with Tom at the wheel for the next stage of the journey.

Leaving the large and picturesque lake of Ioannina behind us to the right we noticed that we were climbing steadily and that the road, once we'd passed Votonosi, was getting decidedly "curly" as Christine put it. When a road's as "curly" as this one, you begin to realise that you're not going to cover as much ground "as the crow flies" as you may have expected to. We began seeing large vertical red and white poles beside the road and other signs that we were in the kind of country that gets serious amounts of snow during wintertime. There were ski lifts occasionally crossing the road above us and snow ploughs lurking behind glass panels in their garage doors beside the road at regular intervals.

Once past Metsovo and still climbing we gasped as with each hairpin bend another exquisite vista of alpine scenery presented itself, first to the right, then to the left of us; but still we hadn't arrived at Meteora and it was now well past midday. Having set out at around 8.30am, we'd confidently expected to be snapping photographs at the foot of the huge pillars of rock that were the edge of the escarpment which formed what was called Meteora well before lunchtime.

After four hours on the road Christine declared that she now had a thumping headache and Ben said he felt sick. We discussed whether we ought to stop somewhere for lunch, but decided to keep going, as we wanted to be back at Parga that same evening. What had started out as a "fun" excursion was fast turning into a nightmare expedition of endurance. We all knew that we were dehydrated as what little water we'd brought with us had long been quaffed as we hadn't anticipated that the journey would take so long.

Five hours after setting out from Parga, full of excitement and anticipation at the prospect of viewing one of Greece's great wonders, both in terms of landscape and building achievement, we drove out from the claustrophobic mountain passes into a huge valley, the other (Eastern) side of which stood the pillars of Meteora in all their grandeur.

We felt too tired and too ill to notice.

If you've ever been out to the mid-West of the USA, somewhere like the "National Momuments" of Northern Arizona, southern Utah, or Colorado then you've likely seen something of this magnitude and grandeur. There can be little in the whole of the European continent to compare with the uniqueness of this place. The majesty even of the rock formations, many of which have monasteries perched impossibly atop them, leave alone the size of the vista before you, is breathtaking.

Having crossed the valley, we drove up a short distance between the gargantuan pillars and stopped the car. Wearily opening the doors we tumbled out, stretched and rubbed our aching heads. Tom and I gave up trying to get the women to demonstrate any enthusiasm for what lay around them, Ben was still asleep on the car's back seat, so we did what tourists do, we clicked away with our cameras, so that in times to come we'd at least be able to prove that we had indeed been to this place.

Yvonne-Maria spoke what was foremost on her mind. Like some person long abandoned in the classic desert situation that is the subject of so many jokes, she simply said,

"Water! I need WATER!!" Christine immediately chimed in with similar sentiments. There was nothing for it but to repair to the nearest village, which was Kastraki, and find a café. Stumbling back into the car we drove the few yards back down the valley to the first buildings at the outer edge of the village, one of which proved mercifully to be a Bar. Not only that, but it was a bar with a parrot. The five of us (since we'd woken Ben up by now) flopping into the softly padded seats around a table, we were at least glad to see that, whilst we re-hydrated ourselves, we could gaze from here up to the wonder of Meteora, which loomed skyward immediately above us.

The parrot amused Ben for a while, but his nausea wouldn't go away and nor would Christine's headache. There was nothing for it but to clamber back into the car and begin the five-hour trek back to Parga, the expressions "more than one can chew" and "biting off" in all of our minds regarding this excursion.

How we made it back without hurtling off the road and down some precipice to our certain deaths in the mountains is a wonder in itself. We were probably able to re-define the meaning of "tiredness" by the time we drove back into Parga some time after dark that evening after more than ten hours on the road. The day had been successful only in that we had reached and witnessed the wonder that is Meteora, but sadly under less than ideal circumstances. In all other respects, what had begun as an optimistic trip to the hinterland had proven to be far larger a project than we had ever imagined. I think the two women hardly remembered what they'd seen at all, their heads having been so "furry" inside during all the while that we were there. And the day's disasters were not yet complete.

Pulling up outside the car hire office, Tom and I strode

back in with the key and dropped it on to the desk of the young bored-looking man, who looked even more bored than the previous night. At least we'd made it back within the twenty-four hours, thus not needing to pay for another day's rental. Pulling his headphones from his ears he asked us to wait while he checked the fuel level in the car's tank. Yes, we told him, we'd remembered to bring it back full, since that was how we'd received it the previous evening. He still wanted us to tarry while he sat in the driver's seat and noted the kilometre reading on the dial.

"Hmmm," he said, "there will be a surcharge for the number of kilometres you've travelled. Where on earth can you have been in just twenty-four hours anyway to put this many kilometres on the clock?"

We told him. The expression that appeared on his face revealed that he found it hard to believe us. "Wait please, I'll have to calculate this." He continued.

"But there isn't a Kilometer charge!" I replied. "I distinctly remember looking at the form we filled out last night. You left that part BLANK. If you'd written something in there then we wouldn't have made this trip in the first place!"

"I'm sorry, but you must pay." Having tapped a few keys on his desktop calculator he sat down behind the desk, assumed an air of confident authority and declared, "Another 80 please."

"NO WAY, HOSE!! We're NOT paying you for something you didn't tell us about. Sorry. But NO, NO NO!!!" Both Tom and I uttering similar sentiments of outrage simultaneously.

"If you do not pay, then I must pay from my own wages. Please, it is the rules." At this juncture my wife entered the building and the conversation.

"I wondered what was taking you so long. Tell him we don't have the money. Anyway, we don't!"

'Yes, but it is the rules, you must pay 80, because you travelled far too many kilometres."

"LOOK, STAVROS, OR WHATEVER YOUR NAME IS. YOU SHOULD HAVE MADE THIS CLEAR YESTERDAY. YOU DIDN'T. END OF STORY." By now I was fired up. My ire was rising like the flames on bonfire night. The young man may have been trying it on, we don't know. Perhaps he just thought that he'd get a few gormless tourists to part with the cash so he could pocket it. But this impression began to crumble somewhat when he assumed an air of great despair and started to go on about losing his job. They didn't pay him very much anyway and if we didn't stump up the cash then there was nothing for it but that he would have to find it himself. We could go away without paying if we liked, but would we be able to sleep at night with the thought that he'd probably lost his job over this.

We began to weaken. Christine said, "We'd have to go to a cash machine, anyway. We really don't have that kind of cash on us now."

"Well, I leave it with your conscience," said the lad, now really eliciting the 'aaah' factor from the women, both of whom were now standing around his desk with Tom and I. "But, I really don't have the money myself and the boss will want it from me tomorrow morning."

"So," said Yvonne-Maria, now converted to his cause despite the forthcoming pain to our finances, "if we go away and find a cash machine, will you still be open when we come back?"

"Oh yes. But if not, just up the road, on the other side..." he proceeded to describe a house where he'd be if the office was closed by the time we returned with the cash.

The conversation at an end, we trouped out on to the pavement to begin a heated discussion as to whether we could believe him. I tried to stick to my guns, "The fact is," I repeated, "he ought to have stipulated that there was a Kilometer charge when we hired the car."

"Yes," said my wife, "but what if he's telling the truth. I don't want to fork out all that money, but if he is genuine, then he may be in a lot of trouble."

So, even though we really wanted to be finding a taverna by now, we dutifully trotted into the village, found a cash machine and drew out some cash. Having decided that the women and Ben would head for the taverna to begin ordering some food, Tom and I agreed to walk back up the road to see if the young man was still in the office. On arriving there we found it in darkness and locked up for the evening. We then strolled a little further up the road to the house that he'd described and found that also in total darkness.

"Do we slide it under the door?" ...we wondered. In pretty short order we decided that, no, that wouldn't be a good idea, since who knows who may pick it up? After all it was his fault, if he'd still been there he'd have been paid the money. We hastily beat a path to the village and joined the others for our evening meal, where we explained what had happened.

Next morning we were aboard the Parga boat bright and early and quite relieved when the crew of two cast off and we got under way. Unlike the conditions for the crossing from Paxos to Parga, the sea was this time like glass and we all sat up on the boat's superstructure and enjoyed the wonderful light of a Greek morning as we made the trip. My wife was looking a little perturbed. I asked her what the problem.

"I was expecting a Police car to be at the quay to arrest us because we didn't pay that money," she said.

"Don't be daft, sweetie," I replied reassuringly, "they don't even know that we came over from Paxos, so how could they have known where to find us this morning?"

"All the same," she continued, "I shan't be sorry to get back to Paxos."

Right up until the moment we took off from Corfu airport for our flight back to the UK, my wife was looking suspiciously at every male she saw. "They could be plain clothed policemen," she would say. "Perhaps they'll arrest us if we ever come back to Greece. Maybe they'll contact Interpol and have us arrested when we land!"

Women do take on so don't they. Mind you, I can't say I wasn't a tad relieved to get home from that particular holiday. Lots of normally stupid things seem like a good idea, at the time, don't they.

24 – Eating Out and its Hazards

We're going out to eat tomorrow night. We don't do this too often. There are several reasons for this. One is that we jealously guard our "evenings in" during the summer months, since we have fingers in all kinds of pies in order to earn a casual Euro here and there. The schedule is quite varied and so, since going out involves a fairly extensive preparation period on the part of my beautiful wife (guys, you know where I'm coming from here, don't you), by the time we have done all the chores and reached the stage where we stand in the kitchen wondering what we're going to do for a meal it's often already between eight and nine in the evening and the thought of the female of the species and her "preparation period" adds to the notion that it's easier to make pasta, pour a glass of wine and stay in. After all, we do tend to go to bed right after Sakkis.

Who or what is *"Sakkis"*? Sakkis is the best meteorologist on Greek TV. I'd venture the opinion that he's probably the only meteorologist on Greek TV. Sakkis does the weather forecast on ET3, one of the Government channels, each weekday evening from around 9.40pm until almost 10. Other weather forecasts on the other TV channels tend to consist of what we've come to call "Ping" girls or blokes.

Why "ping" people, you're now wondering? Well, if you watch what they laughably call a weather forecast on most channels you'll more often than not see someone standing in front of the chart and evidently wondering what they're supposed to do with their hands. So, after having stood, hands awkwardly dangling at their sides, while they told us how strong the winds are going to be in various parts of the country, they then say "…and the temperatures in Attiki [for example] will range from 18 degrees in the morning up to 25 in the afternoon," at which point one of their arms will "ping", as if sprung, up to the chart and hover ever-so-briefly – hand turned upwards as if they're a waiter who's just found that someone's nicked their tray - under the temperature figures marked thereupon, before immediately dropping back to the side of their body, from whence it "pinged" in the first place. This usually consists of the only movements these "forecasters" make, apart from walking rather awkwardly from one side of the chart to the other; since the shape of this country, when you consider all the islands over on our side of the Aegean as well as the *"Epta-Nisa"* (seven islands) of the Ionian, is rather wider than it is high, the upshot of which is that it's quite difficult to show the entire chart without the forecaster standing continually in front of either the west or the east of the country and thus irritating viewers living in either of those areas.

Britain is designed for ease of television forecasting isn't it. I mean it's nice and narrow and the forecaster doesn't have to be standing in front of any of it while they tell you how much rain you're going to get tomorrow. Greece, however, is different. Here you just know that the entire populace of the

Dodecanese islands will be shouting "MOVE OVER WILL YOU!" as the forecaster concentrates the more extensive aspects of his or her report for the benefit of the only two cities of any respectable size in the entire country, Athens and Thessalonica, both of which are to the west and therefore necessitate the forecaster standing in front of Rhodes and her neighbouring islands. We all watch on the edge of our seats for that all-too-brief moment when he or she moves across to obscure the west of the country and fleetingly gives us a tantalising glance of the symbols, wind strength and temperatures for our area. Blink and you miss it.

Sakkis, on the other hand, is the real deal. He spends ages using his entire body to make great sweeping gestures across various regions while he explains all the minute details of what's going to happen during the various parts of the day. His glee is almost tangible when the first rains of the winter finally arrive and he actually has something to talk about. During summer he almost looks a bit fed up with the fact that it's mainly sunny across the entire country. The best he can do is muster up enthusiasm for wind speeds as they may affect ferry crossings when the Meltemi gets into its stride during July and August. But, come the winter he's demonstrably excited that he has lots of weather to report.

And report he does. He evidently knows his stuff and barely keeps still for an instant. No "ping" guy is Sakkis. He loves his job and we love watching him. His forecast also covers the entire continent of Europe so we get to see what's happening in the UK. Plus, the icing on the cake is that he'll also run through temperatures, cloud and rain charts for the next six days. By the time Sakkis has finished with his trademark *"ena thavma'ssios vrathi se o'lous"* (a wonderful evening to all), spoken so quickly that even a Greek must have trouble understanding him if they're not familiar with the man, you feel that he'll be needing a bit of a lie down. Perhaps that's why he takes quite frequent and often long (too long for my wife) breaks.

That's something that we find amazing and somewhat irksome. In the UK all the major TV stations have several professional forecasters working a duty rota so you always get your trusty forecast come rain or shine (no pun intended. Rather good though don't you think?). Here the ET3 channel has Sakkis and that's it. If he's on holiday we feel cheated as a voiceover gives a brief summary over a chart in front of which no one stands. No six-day prognosis, no analysis of the rest of Europe. Sometimes in the summer he'll have four weeks off and during the entire time we have to make do with this inferior substitute. My wife experiences Sakkis withdrawal symptoms. Each Monday when she's expecting him to return to work she'll have ET3 on at 9.40pm and almost go into apoplectic anger when she finds he's still not back from his hols.

The only forecaster who holds a slightly flickering candle to Sakkis is Tassos on the independent channel Ant1. The name of this channel looks clumsy in English, but since *"one"* in Greek can be pronounced *"ena"*, it makes the name of the station "Antenna" in Greek. Since the Greek for "aerial" is *"antenna"*, they have a rather neat piece of wordplay there, eh? Tassos does a passable job of emulating Sakkis' methods and comes quite close, but isn't quite in Sakkis' league. He's still head and shoulders above the "ping" boys and girls though, no argument. What we like about Tassos is that he's a little older, maybe 60 or so, and always has a warm smile that makes you imagine him with his slippers on sipping his coffee, grandchildren around his feet and loving wife baking in the kitchen. For all we know he could actually be a right git in private, but we don't care, we like him and we reckon it's his real personality that comes through anyway.

So, as previously stated, on our evenings in we tend to watch Sakkis and then retire to bed. My wife lets nothing get in the way of her watching him. She won't answer the phone (she doesn't much anyway to be honest), she won't move from the couch until he's done. Woe betide me if I want to converse during Sakkis' forecasts. If I get a response at all it'll be an irritated rebuke letting me know in no uncertain terms that "now is not the time, I'm watching SAKKIS."

I won't score any points interrupting now for sure.

So, we're going out to eat tomorrow night. We tend to plan it or otherwise it doesn't happen at all. We'll maybe go to Savvas Grill in Lardos because we haven't been there for ages, apart from for takeaways, and we like the family that runs it. I'll throw on a cool pair of linen trousers and a t-shirt, then sit and write while I try and keep my patience during my wife's "preparation period."

Some past occasions when we ate out are memorable for all the wrong reasons. It was in 1998 that we first went to Skiathos with our friends Guy (he's French, so it's pronounced "*Ghee*"), his wife Rebecca and their then ten-year-old daughter Jessica. It was during one expedition to eat out that we discovered a restaurant right at the top of the town, the kitchen of which was inside an old windmill. In those days it was a French restaurant and the menu was - rather alarmingly for my liking, since it indicated a serious dent in the wallet was also on the menu – all in French. Guy and I had gone off in the early evening to do a bit of street-wandering in Skiathos town, while the women and Jessica embarked upon their "preparation period", and were soon climbing through tiny streets, catching occasional glimpses of the harbour below. Eventually we emerged at a steep stone stairway, which climbed up through several terraces, each bordered with rustic wooden balustrades cut from pine wood, to the door of an old windmill. As it was still early in the evening, the staff were busy making preparations to welcome their first diners of the evening and were popping in and out of the windmill's door carrying various items like menus, cutlery, condiments and other stuff you'd expect to see restaurant staff busying themselves with carrying.

Guy and I took in the scene. It was quite a surprise to have suddenly emerged at the top of the town and standing on the upper terraces of this wonderfully-situated restaurant it truly felt like that, the top of the town. The views across the roofs to the sea below were beautiful, both of the new harbour and the old, with the *Bourtsi* Island separating the two. The evening sunlight lent to the feeling that there simply couldn't be a more relaxing or romantic place to partake of an evening meal under a clear, starlit Greek sky. We thought we'd found the restaurant to which we'd lead our women folk a little later. Guy picked a menu up from the nearest table and perused its contents.

"Ah, it's a French restaurant!" he enthused. Well, he did a bit of enthusing until we saw the prices. We were the types who ate economically. This place, stunning environment notwithstanding, wasn't in any way in the "economical" bracket, something to which all five of us would have agreed. The dishes boasted exotic names and were mainly French, as you'd expect. To be honest, whilst my wife and I enjoy French food and Guy (of course) is fiercely proud of his nation's culinary achievements, we didn't come to Greece to eat French food, and having seen these prices, we didn't need any more persuading that it would be inappropriate to eat here, even though the views were among the most impressive you'd find anywhere on a Greek island.

A member of staff approached to ask if we'd like any help, or indeed would like to book a table. We, both being males, weren't going to let on that our eyes were watering over the prices and so decided, without a word needing to pass between us, that we'd play it cool.

"Just looking," we replied, in unison. I asked: "Is the owner, or one of the owners, French perhaps?" If I remember correctly the reply was that yes one of the married couple that ran the place was French and the other Greek (these days I believe, whilst the restaurant still exists, it's not particularly French-themed any more, new owners having taken over in the intervening years).

"My friend is French!" I enthusiastically volunteered, "His brother is in the wine business in Paris!"

The staff member smiled one of those *"I think I have a smart Alec here"* smiles and acknowledged my comment, whilst making it clear that they didn't have too much time to hang about talking to a couple of clever-dicks and proceeded to re-enter the windmill's door. We continued reading through the menu and discovered a fairly elementary spelling mistake on one of the dishes. I can't remember quite what it was now, but I do remember remarking to Guy that he could help these people get these things right, since it looked a bit silly having such basic mistakes in the menu of what to all intents and purposes was an upmarket establishment. Rather rashly I urged Guy to point the error out to the proprietors. We approached the door and popped our heads in, looking for someone to talk to.

The owner (as it turned out) appeared and asked if he could help and Guy, rather wisely replied, "No, it's OK. Perhaps we'll come back later."

"Do you want to make a reservation?" asked the owner. Now, if you're a seasoned taverna eater, you'll know that the idea of making reservations rings alarm bells, since it means that the establishment is going to be rather select and not particularly traditional. Plus it'll sure as anything be more expensive than your regular check-tableclothed trad taverna.

"Oh no, we'll just take our chances," replied Guy.

At this point I did wrong. I know, I know, I should have kept quiet. The problem is I'm a bit pedantic when it comes to spelling and grammar. I can't help it; it's just how I am. I get really irate in the UK when I see the spurious use of the apostrophe that seems to be gaining ground everywhere year on year. If I had a pound for every time I've seen some bloke seated on a pile of potato sacks on a roundabout, with a cardboard sign saying "POTATO'S", I'd not only be rich, I'd probably have suffered a major heart attack owing to the stress I induce in myself when I get started on my apostrophe "soapbox" while my wife adopts that "here he goes again" expression and turns up the radio, or maybe starts taking a great interest in her fingernails.

I remember seeing a van once with the wording "SMART CARPET SERVICE'S" emblazoned on both sides. Now this told me that not only was the driver rather uneducated but so was his signwriter. If I'd been doing the artwork for that vehicle I'd have had to speak up and tell the client that his apostrophe was unnecessary. A simple plural NEVER needs an apostrophe. An apostrophe indicates that there are missing letters, that you're reading an abbreviation. For example, "it's raining so the car had its soft top closed". See? It's simple, the "it's" in "it's raining" needs the apostrophe because it actually should read, "it is raining." On the other hand, the "its" in "its soft top" doesn't need an apostrophe because there aren't any missing letters, it's not an abbreviation. Is it me, or is this principle really that difficult to grasp?

Sorry, I was off again there wasn't I? But at least now you're well up to speed on my feelings about spelling and grammar. So you'll understand why my irritation got the better of me when I dropped Guy right in it at the Windmill in Skiathos. I found myself saying to the restaurateur:

"My friend wants to tell you something."

Oops. I knew right away that I should've kept quiet. I proceeded to put Guy in the position where the Windmill's owner, in all innocence, was interested to know what my French friend wanted to apprise him of, when in fact Guy didn't want to do any apprising at all. In fact apprising was the last thing on his mind at that moment. The man pressed him for his information and so Guy was obliged, in the absence of anything else to say, to mention that there was a fundamental spelling error in the menu.

When a fairly upmarket restaurant gets new menus produced, they tend to cost a little more to print than your average "fill the prices in the spaces provided" menus that most cheap and cheerful tavernas use, have you noticed that? Of course, the Windmill was no exception. Having learned from the owner that he'd very recently changed the menu and had new menus printed at considerable cost, I suppose it wasn't surprising that he wasn't all that enamoured with a couple of cocky holidaymakers turning up one evening, telling him he's spelt something wrong and not even doing him the courtesy of eating at his establishment. Had we been smart enough we could, at this juncture, have walked off feigning disgust and leaving the owner with the distinct impression that we may well have patronised his establishment, had it not been for such a fundamental error in the menu. We weren't that smart.

Needless to say I spent the remainder of that evening eating humble pie and being exceedingly nice to Guy. I should be grateful. Guy's bigger than me and, considering the awkward moment I'd managed to create, with him smack dab in the centre of it, he would have been well justified in decking me. He's a nice bloke is Guy. We're still firm friends, although we don't see much of each other these days, as he lives with Rebecca in South Wales and we're out here on Rhodes. Jessica's now married and lives in West Wales. Maybe it's time to invite Guy and Beccy out here to see us, as long as we avoid any French restaurants while they're here that is.

Tomorrow becomes today (as they tend to, don't they) and during the morning we drop by to see our friend Sandra, where we're treated to some of her delicious homemade lemonade, diluted with some sparkling water. Seated in the shade around Sandra's teak patio table, the conversation turns to eating out, since we don't do it very often and so we decide to swap recommendations with Sandra, since as I stated at the beginning of the chapter, we're eating out tonight.

"It's dangerous making recommendations," states Sandra. We agree with a nod. "Especially if you have a friend who is very hard to please. I remember going out with Nadine and Derek a few weeks back, Nadine's one of those who, although she's a friend, usually finds something to complain about. I've reached the stage where I tend not to suggest where to go for fear that it'll be my fault when we leave and I say 'did you enjoy it?' and she says, 'well, the bread was stale, the steak was tough, or my knife was dirty' …you get the idea."

We do. When ideas are expressed in such terms, we usually "get" them.

Sandra continues, "So I'd suggested that we go somewhere I knew about, which was out in the wilds, for lunch. I thought it was a nice location with a nice view in a pretty little village. When we got there we were immediately struck by the odd appearance of the two waiters. They were evidently aged and in the UK would have probably retired at least ten years ago. One had his hair died so dark it looked like he'd had a bowl of hot liquorice poured over his head. The other only had one eye and a comb-over."

"Twins were they? " I ask. Sandra smiles sardonically and goes on:

"They approached and asked what we'd like, so we asked if there was a menu. One-eye proceeded to bring us one of those "store-bought" menus, which – fair enough - a lot of perfectly good tavernas use and, as he handed it to us, said 'if there isn't a price, it's off.'

"Turned out that we had the choice of salad, chips and bread for lunch. Maybe a bit of *tzatziki*, but that seemed to be it. There was a charcoal barbecue burning, we knew because we could smell it. Locals were now coming in and it looked as if they were bringing their own meat with them. At least the place was authentic! We called liquorice-head and asked if there was possibly any fish, to which he replied, tilting his head toward the valley which led down to the sea (a couple of miles away), 'Yes. …In the sea!' and walked away again. Evidently he thought he was hilarious.

"So our lunch ended up being a couple of *Horiatikis*

[Greek salads], some French fries and bread. You can imagine Nadine's comments during the journey home. Funny thing is she decided to suggest where to go the next time we went out. She was sure this particular taverna that she was thinking of would offer an extensive lunch menu and I certainly wasn't going to make any suggestions. You'll never guess what we had to eat."

We both give knowing nods.

"Exactly," Sandra continues in response to our knowing nods, "Greek salad, chips and bread! I was sooo tempted to get my own back, but thought better of it."

We finish our lemonades and bid Sandra farewell. Once we arrive home the afternoon passes much as any other [well, any other when we have the time that is], with a cup of Earl Grey tea taken to bed at around 3.00pm, where we read for a while before falling asleep.

We rise at around 5.30pm and the inevitable discussion begins.

"So," I tentatively initiate, "where are we going then?" We'd previously decided we'd be going to Savvas Grill in Lardos; a cheap and cheerful taverna, run by a nice family and open every day of the year. The only problem with Savvas Grill is that it's in the village, so it has no view and can be very stuffy when the weather's hot. Plus we can eat there any time of the year, hence the first response from Yvonne-Maria:

"Well… I don't really fancy Savvas tonight." I don't mind this, since I'd already begun to doubt the wisdom of the initial decision. So far, then, so good.

"You know where I'd suggest we go. I know you don't want to get frustrated among the hordes in Lindos, but I would love to eat at one of the tavernas right on the beach in Lindos Bay."

The ones I have in mind are at the end of what's these days called "Pallas" Beach, after the ever-modest mayor of Lindos, Manolis Pallas.

"You remember that time that Katy and Lefteris took us out in Piraeus?" Asks Yvonne-Maria, while continuing to apply mascara in her dressing table mirror.

Indeed I do.

It was probably in September of 1978, when we again spent three weeks in Greece visiting relatives in Athens, punctuated, as was the previous year's visit, by a week spent at Mrs. Mellou's rooms on the island of Poros. I didn't really have a clue as to who Katy and Lefteri were. I recalled the previous year visiting the huge penthouse apartment in a posh part of the city where they evidently lived, which was when I'd first sampled *Kourabiethes* (pronounced coo-rah-bee-eh-thez), those delicious almond shortbread cookies that the Greeks make for special occasions. I don't have a very sweet tooth, but these come literally immersed in a coating of powdered (icing) sugar. The sweetness of the sugar is tempered somewhat by the shortbread cookie, which is usually shaped like a half-moon, but can come in virtually any shape really. Having lived here for some years we've found that the only time you can buy them in the shops is in the run-up to Christmas, so we usually avail ourselves of a few boxes so we can have one with our coffee during mornings when we're at home throughout the winter months. I have a vague recollection of sitting on a huge sofa while Katy (whom I'd never met before and at the time – since I couldn't speak Greek – could hardly be described as having "met" on this occasion, if the truth be told) brought out a plate of *Kourabiethes* and out of politeness I took one. I was instantly hooked. Those were the days when everything used to go on around me when I was in Athens, since I never understood anything of what was being said in conversation. So my knowledge of quite how my mother-in-law knew Katy and Lefteri wasn't anything other than what could be described as "sketchy."

It was a possibility that the two women had been friends when they were young and still single back in the austere Athens of the 1940's, when Lela was swept off her feet by the dashing young British army man who was to become her husband and the father of my wife, while he was posted in the city during the dark days of the famine and the bloody civil war. These were the times when Greeks learned to eat *"horta"*, which you or I would call weeds. If they hadn't begun to sample such wayside fare even more of them would have starved to death than the 300,000 or so that did so in Athens alone during this post-war period.

Something I shall forever regret is not having asked more of my mother-in-law regarding just what life was like for her, living in Athens as a twenty-something girl, looking for some kind of normal life. I never asked her how she actually met my father-in-law and my wife doesn't know the story very well either. I would, though, hazard a guess that it's the stuff novels are made of. My mother-in-law was one of four surviving children that I know about, although Yvonne-Maria tells me that there was definitely another brother of her mother's who died, but she can't remember how old he was at the time.

Since Katy and her husband were of about the same age as my mother-in-law, it was a safe bet that they'd known each other at least since their teens, if not longer. Anyway, returning to the evening in question, having wiped the icing sugar from around my mouth with a tissue supplied by my hosts, I rose along with the rest of the party when it became apparent that we were going out. It was by now around 10.30pm, just approaching a respectable hour for Greeks to go out to eat!

A short trip in their car, which, it has to be said, was somewhat larger and more comfortable than Taki's little Mazda, brought us to a residential door in Piraeus sandwiched between two shop fronts. Having eased this door open we all trooped up a dimly-lit stairway to what was nevertheless a quite impressive front door, whereupon another obviously well-to-do pot-bellied shipping magnate and his fur-wrapped spouse emerged almost the moment we pressed the bell. Introductions over with, having involved (as they usually do) a couple of complete strangers bear-hugging me and mock-kissing both my cheeks, whilst everyone in fact "scrummed" around the others in an effort to ensure that all had kissed and hugged all and no one would feel spurned, we all descended the stairs and this time walked a short distance to the waterfront of a small bay, one side of which was a steeply shelved pebble beach, whilst on the other side of the road which skirted this beach there appeared to be a succession of restaurants and tavernas, fish being the predominant speciality.

Our party now consisted of myself and Yvonne-Maria, Lela (my mother-in-law) and Dave, Takis and Christina, Katy and Lefteri and this other couple who were even more unknown to me than those who'd initiated me into the marvellous world of Kourabiethes. Ten of us descended some very suspect wooden steps from the roadside on to the pebbly beach, which consisted of an area of almost level pebbles perhaps several metres across, after which the gradient steepened considerably and dropped a few more metres into the inky night-time waters, on which a few of the regulation fishing boats bobbed. The time now well after 11.00pm, we came upon a table which had evidently been set for us in advance. It was laid out for four on either side plus one at either end and had a cosy feel, brought about in part by the fact that there were two huge square parasols above the whole thing, plus several oil lamps burning at evenly spaced intervals along the table's length.

When you're a young twenty-something British lad who doesn't speak the lingo, evenings like this are a mixture of complete terror and unbridled excitement in equal measure. The terror arises from the fact that you're quite certain that something's going to be placed in front of you that you don't recognise and you worry whether you'll be able to put on the confident front needed to make those you're keeping company with think you know what you're doing. The excitement comes in no small part from knowing that some else is paying for this spread!

I remember once, when I used to travel all over the UK doing deals (alright then, running errands) for an International Numismatist (look it up!) and was frequently well out of my depth dealing with professional businessmen several years my senior, I had taken my wife with me on one particular trip to somewhere in Essex and, since we were to stay the night, the client we were meeting had decided to take us out for a meal. We arrived at his "pile" in our rented Ford, whereupon he signalled for us to climb into his Jensen FF. We drove back down his much-too-long gravel drive, out through his much-too-grand wrought iron gates and through enough country lanes to make it very certain that, had he and his glamorous wife decided to deposit us on the roadside, we'd have died of starvation trying to return to civilization – and that even in the overcrowded UK!

Eventually we pulled up outside a building that actually closely resembled our host's house. For all I know it may well have been it. Perhaps he'd had his butler drive our rental car around the back so we wouldn't suspect. We climbed out of the Jensen, and walked into this sumptuously carpeted foyer, where some chap in a dickey bow took our coats, and we were shown into a luxurious, though cosy, library, where the light was subdued and augmented by the flickering of a huge open log fire. The smell of cigar smoke and old books hung in the room as we sat down on a couple of plush leather Chesterfields and were served drinks and some tiny stuff that tasted awful served on a tray, but was evidently some delicacy which one was supposed to eat as an appetiser. I was already sweating. The log fire didn't score any points with me.

Of course the menus, which I read with a mounting sense of fear since I didn't understand any of it, were placed into our hands while we "relaxed" in this way. There were no prices besides any of the dishes either. It was the classic "if you need to know the price then you can't afford to eat here" scenario.

Having survived the choosing of what we were going to eat unscathed, or so I thought, we were eventually led into the restaurant proper and seated around a huge circular polished mahogany table. We were so far from each other I wondered how on earth we were going to converse. My sweatiness now ratcheted up several degrees, I perused the bewildering array of cutlery on either side of my as yet still empty plate. Stealing furtive glances at our host I attempted to use the correct knife or fork for whichever course we were attacking by copying him. The starter went off OK, no major disasters there. But when the main course was served I found myself staring down at huge swathes of pristine white bone china, in the middle of which was a modestly sized steak in a pepper sauce. Of course, I asked the waiter what vegetables I could expect to go with it. His response made it evident that he regarded me as marginally more worthy of his attention than something he'd scrape off the bottom of his shoe, or perhaps pay someone else to scrape off, as he informed me that since I'd ordered a la carte and hadn't actually requested any accompaniment to my steak, then it was assumed that I wished to eat the steak alone.

I made a feeble attempt to assure him that I knew what I was doing and had merely forgotten about ordering vegetables, but the damage was done. Most of my memory of that evening was being desperate to finish our meals and get the hell out of there!

That night as we lay in our four-poster bed in the client's guest room I remember us agreeing that they'd done it on purpose to have a good evening's entertainment at our expense. They got their money's worth without any doubt. The only good thing I took from that night was having been for a ride in a Jensen FF, which at the time was a seriously prestigious motor.

At least, in terms of cringe worthiness, this evening in Piraeus didn't even come close to that disastrous Essex evening. The environment was truly wondrous for a young, not-very-well-travelled chap from England. A semi-circular bay lined with twinkling lights, waiters crossing the road dodging the traffic and a deeply black Greek sky above, stars twinkling benignly. Wine was placed in carafes at several strategic points along the table and bread arrived in those little baskets. The first course of what I'd call "white-bait" soon followed, those little fishes that are normally fried in olive oil and breadcrumbs, over which you squeeze some fresh lemon juice and then pop the entire fish into your mouth and crunch away. A few mouthfuls of *Horiatiki*, some *tzatziki* and a few sips of wine and the palate was stimulated for what was to come by the whitebait. Yummy. I even had someone to converse with as I was seated at one end of the long side of the table with my step father-in-law Dave to my left, occupying the table end. Whilst the Greeks got on with explaining over each other what the current government ought to be doing to keep the machinery of running a country from grinding to a halt, or perhaps the females amongst them compared shoes, handbags and diets, Dave and I could happily natter about snorkelling, snooker and afternoon snoozes, oh and the merits of the various blonde beers on offer in Greece at the time.

The plates which had borne the whitebait having been cleared, the next course was soon being lowered on slightly larger plates into strategic spots along the table. Low and behold it consisted of some slightly larger fish. The aroma of fish, which were in all probability still happily swimming in the adjacent ocean not a few hours before, freshly char-grilled, is one of the most enjoyable sensations in life, don't you think? One or two of the women arose from their seats and, using their knives, deftly opened the fish lengthwise, gently easing the flesh away from the bones beneath, squeezed some fresh lemon juice into the newly created apertures on the carcasses and beckoned all to tuck in. Ten pairs of hands were soon carving chunks of delicate white fish-flesh from the prepared victims and we all soon reverted to our happy munching, quaffing and – in the case of the Greeks anyway – shouting over one another, though all with great bonhomie.

Extracting the occasional bone from our mouths with our fingers, wiping hands with paper napkins, scooping more Greek salad on to our individual plates, we allowed the evening to move across us at its own pace. Dave and I, having eaten our fill, agreed that a dessert would go down well. Perhaps some fresh fruit, peaches maybe, or water melon. Some sorbet would slide down really easily. We were ready for the closing stages of the repas.

The now empty plates, save for piles of fishy skeletons and individual bones, on which the slightly larger fish had arrived, were once again removed and we waited in contented anticipation for what was to come next. I was slightly amazed and a little perturbed, since I was already getting into the "belt-loosening" zone, to observe a waiter descending the steps to the beach carrying two even larger plates, upon which, when they arrived at the table, proved to be lain ten *"Tsipoures"*, or Sea Bream, evidently one for each diner. These were excellent examples of the said species, long enough in fact so that, once they'd been placed with steel tongs on to our individual plates, the heads and tails hung at each end over the linen tablecloth, since our plates weren't large enough to hold them in their entirety.

This called for more wine, and "a few bottles of water please!" my wife and I rejoining in unison. More salad arrived, along with more slices of fresh bread and the tsatsiki too was replenished. There was nothing for it but to press on. The skin of my Tsipoura still sizzling from the charcoal, I sliced it long its length, used the tail to pull the main skeleton out from the carcass and threw it on to the pebbles behind me, whereupon innumerable previously invisible feral cats pounced seemingly out of nowhere, thinking "Tonight, boys, our luck is in!" Remember *"Top Cat?"* I bet Benny would be saying *"Gee TC, hope Officer Dibble ain't about to show now."*

There was no question that the fish was absolutely delicious. I have probably never eaten such perfectly prepared and succulent fish flesh in my life. Having managed against all the odds to decimate the carcass before me, I colluded with Dave over whether now we could expect a little something sweet.

The next course came on one single huge plate; on which lay a fish, which I would have thought, rivalled a shark for size. Glasses, lighters, wallets, bottles, ashtrays and tsatsiki plates were all shoved aside to accommodate this new arrival as pride of place in the centre of the table. Dave and I exchanged glances, both of us now seriously hoping that we did indeed have hollow legs, as some have occasionally accused me of possessing. Once again the women prepared the nautical beast and soon began forking chunks of freshly grilled flesh on to our plates. My sips of wine and – occasionally – water became more frequent, as I laboured under the probably erroneous belief that this would help me to continue eating although my body was telling me that my digestive system was probably now backing up to somewhere just below the epiglottis (is that how you spell it?). My belt was now so undone as to persuade any casual observer that there was no way that this belt was ever big enough for my middle and the top button of my trousers had long since waved goodbye to the buttonhole on the other side of the fly. The zip was going south at an alarming rate.

After the ten of us had all slouched around slowly ingesting this huge sea monster, along with copious liquid accompaniment and still more bread, salad and dips, it became apparent that we had finally completed our meal. There now followed the customary interminable phase where Greeks push their chairs away from the table, grasp a brandy balloon in one hand and a cigarette in the other, although in the case of some around this table, it was a cigar. The women talk in hushed tones and frequently appear to be staring off into the distance, their minds perceiving something quite apart from what their eyes alight upon. It's like they're philosophising on what another of their number is telling them and need to lapse into a trance-like state of concentration.

I was making my usual feeble attempts at remaining cognisant of what was going on around me, as it was now probably approaching 2.00am and well past my bed time and my eyes were making desperate attempts to close for the night.

Finally, after one of the well-off Greek couples had settled the bill, the party began to stir and rise from the table. I can't imagine at what hour the staff of this taverna would be getting into their beds on this particular night, or rather, morning.

Fortunately it wasn't too far to the door of the car in which we were to be whisked off to our beds, because I must have looked like an amateur flasher by the way I was clutching at the top of my trousers in my feeble attempts to keep the zip from opening completely beneath my swollen middle.

"Right!" Exclaimed Takis, "Who's for a Chicago then?"

"How's it going?" I tentatively ask my beautiful spouse, now ensconced behind her dressing table, wondering whether it would be worth our while venturing out at all this evening. I must say I'm feeling quite tired as it's approaching 9.00pm already, since we've done a spot of pottering in the garden since rising from siesta.

"You know what?" comes her reply, "I've got a feeling that Sakkis is back tonight. I haven't seen him for weeks because he's been on one of his holidays again. I don't want to miss him if he's back tonight."

I have a feeling I know what's coming, how this evening is

going to play out. She continues, "Why don't I make pasta, and you can open a bottle of wine, eh?"

MARRIED IN ATHENS: Mr. K. Morton White, of Bathford, and Miss Ge Lela Georga, of Athens, after their recent marriage.

At Christina & Taki's wedding in Athens, circa 1960.
Second left is my wife's older sister Christine, while below right
is the cute kid who grew up and married me.

25 – *Diving For Jellies*

In an odd kind of way, I ought to be thankful to Adolf Hitler. Perhaps I ought to qualify that remark. I mean, sure, if you were to ask anyone whether Hitler was a good man or a bad man, you'd probably receive an overwhelming vote in the negative. There may, of course, be a small minority who would reply: "He was good for the German economy." Yes, perhaps there is an element of truth in that, but this was at such a high cost to human dignity that most would still agree that, on balance, Mr. & Mrs. Hitler's son was a bit of a blight on mankind's history, by and large. Poor little Paula, how did she cope with her brother's misdemeanours.

So, why do I say that I should be a tad grateful to Adolf? Basically it's because he invaded Greece in April 1941 and started off the chain of events that led, eventually, to the British arriving in Athens in 1944. Amongst the throngs of the British military was the young man Kenneth Morton White, who was to become husband to Lela Giorgiou, my mother-in-law. So, whilst I must confess to a huge aversion to your other deeds, thanks Mr. Hitler for bringing my wife's parents together, albeit unwittingly.

Here I am now living in Rhodes, and if you'd asked me thirty some years go where I'd have expected to be in three decades or so, you could be pretty sure that I wouldn't even have considered the possibility that I may be living here. All the experiences that I've been privileged to enjoy in this country must be put down to one night in October 1971, when my friend Ian and I went out on the town in Bath (UK), primarily to have a few drinks, and to "pull" would be a bonus as well. Well, we "pulled" and took these two girls home and drank coffee on my future wife's friend's sofa while we eyed each other up and wondered which of the two girls we'd "get off" with, as we used to say. Doubtless they were thinking something similar. What if I'd ended up with the other one? Life's full of such apparently insignificant watersheds isn't it.

I have to say that things could have turned out a lot worse. I've thoroughly enjoyed the steadily growing relationship I've been granted with my wife's country of heritage and am still doing so. I began writing book one of this series, *"Feta Compli!"*, with the thought that one volume would be all I could come up with; yet here I am writing the closing chapter of volume three and still with loads of stuff up there in my brain that I'd like to write about. Though as I said above, if Mr Hitler hadn't done what he did a half a century ago, I wouldn't be writing this stuff now.

Come on now, there's no call for that! It was a bit below the belt for my liking!! Some people do actually enjoy these ramblings I'll thank you to remember.

There was the time when we took a couple of weeks off in Thassos. We watched a pair of spotted flycatchers busily feeding their young in the nest, which they had built in a hanging basket under the portico outside our studio. They had to share it with a spider plant, which didn't seem to mind having a bird's nest constructed right in its centre. We were sitting outside on one magical evening when the fledglings did just what they're named for, they fledged. We watched as one young bundle of feathers took its first tentative flight out of the nest a few yards across the lane to an olive tree where it made an emergency landing and subsequently sat for a quarter of an hour or so, its body language exuding that *"Phew! That was a bit hairy! Might take me a while to get the hang of this flying malarkey. Not to mention landing"* attitude.

It was during that particular vacation that I got myself into a bit of a spot by absentmindedly mouthing the words to "Hotel California" at a beach side taverna, where the live band had just concluded a very nice traditional Greek set, during which, as is her usual form, my wife had bounded out of her seat, grabbing my unwilling hand as she did so and began dancing in and out of the tables, much to the delight of the Greeks present and the bemusement of the seated German tourists, who were only on their fifth or sixth draft lager of the evening and didn't want some banshee of a woman edging past their chairs and possibly spilling some of their drink.

The band decided that to finish off the evening they'd play a few modern numbers and finally broke into the Eagles' Hotel California. There was a drummer, a keyboard player, a bouzouki player who'd now switched to guitar and a girl singer, who caught sight of me mouthing the words, stopped the band mid-verse and called me up to the mike. She didn't speak very good English, but asked me if I was a fan of the Eagles, to which I replied in the affirmative and told her that this was probably one of my favourite rock songs ever.

"I donno the words too good." She said, "but I think you do, yes?"

"I know them all," I confessed, not at that precise moment realising what hot water that was going to get me into.

"Good, then you sing this song!" she replied and counted the band into the intro for a second time. Before I could protest she stuck the mike right in front of my lips and, with a wave of her hand suggested I get on with the job. The problem was, the key was exactly wrong for my not-all-that good-anyway voice. I tightened up my throat and attempted to belt it out in my best Don Henley voice, only to succeed in emptying the taverna of most of its clientele during the next six minutes or so. Plus, although I knew all the words well, my nerves got the better of me and I blanked out half way through verse two and had to improvise a bit. When we wound the number up with the guitarist doing a half-decent version of that wonderful series of guitar solos at the end, there were only the band, the waiters and my wife and I left in the place.

I couldn't help thinking as we walked back to our studio that I'd had precisely the effect that they'd wanted to achieve. As we departed, the band was packing up and the staff knew that they could close up for the night, yippee!!

Once on Leros, in the summer of 1996, we made friends with the bloke that used to change our travellers cheques in the tiny bank in the square at Platanos. There were frequent power cuts when we were there, as indeed there are here on Rhodes, especially when it rains. Since it wasn't raining while we were in Leros, I don't know what their excuse was, but one time we ended up sitting in the bank for half an hour, hopefully awaiting for the power to come on again so we could draw some money. Across the desk was Yiannis, who took a shine to us because Yvonne-Maria is half-Greek and ended up telling us about his family, his life, his mother – who lived on

Lipsi, the next island up toward the North and the fact that he owned a boat.

"Where do you keep it?" Yvonne-Maria asked, trying to sound disinterested.

"It's anchored at Pandeli, but not in the small limani, it's on the other side, near the hillside which goes over to Vromolitho."

"We know it. It's the boat that we usually swim around to give us a target when trying to swim for exercise. We always go to Pandeli when we want a 'beach' day. Looks very nice." I said, my mental picture now complete and showing a sleek speedboat, with leather seats and a very powerful outboard on the back. It also had a below-deck cabin, a fact revealed by the existence of a couple of oval portholes on either side. I had to fight to fend off further images of my beloved and I relaxing on the front of this vessel while Yiannis steered it as it flew across the surface of the azure Aegean.

We didn't let on that we'd often wished that the boat's owner would turn up just as we were swimming around it. You never know what little treats that can result in, eh? Yiannis continued:

"I'd be glad to take you for a ride. But I don't know when I'll be free this week. I do have to go over to see my mother on Lipsi soon though. Maybe if you're on the beach when I am going you'll come with me. But I can't promise anything right now."

Needless to say we went to Pandeli beach as much as we could over the succeeding few days. Each time we arrived the boat was laying at anchor and there was no sign of its owner. On the one day when we arrived much later, after having lingered in Platanos Square for another drink before making the fifteen minute walk down the hill to Pandeli beach, we arrived to find that the boat was nowhere to be seen. What a disaster. We looked at each other and shrugged our shoulders. As it was, we'd already cooked our goose with the fish farmer who lived up at Blepouti (see chapter 27 of *Feta Compli!*, "*A Missed Appointment*"), now it seemed we'd lost another opportunity for a free boat ride. C'est la flippin' vie I suppose.

After we'd been stretched out on the rickety sun beds under an ancient umbrella on the wonderfully sparsely inhabited Pandeli beach for an hour or two, the sound of the deep throb of a huge Mercury could be heard approaching. My head sprung up from under my baseball cap and Yvonne-Maria's from her novel. Coming into the bay was Yiannis in his boat. Perhaps all was not lost. We immediately leapt up and "sauntered" nonchalantly down to the water's edge and slipped in. As we watched the boat approach we began swimming out to the spot where we knew Yiannis had a dinghy tied to the anchored rope, which was marked with a buoy. I'm sure you know what a buoy is, it's an old 2.5 litre brightly-coloured plastic drum, cap firmly screwed into place to keep it airtight so it will float. If you're the nautical type I'm sure that you knew that already though.

As Yiannis killed the engine and fished the buoy rope out of the water with his hooked pole, we approached, swimming for all we were worth, but making great efforts to look as though we always swam like that. We waited for him to hail us. At first it looked as though we were going to be out of luck, but then he spied us and called, "Hello you two! If you had been here earlier you could have come to Lipsi!" Like, yea, thanks Yianni.

That extra drink in the square had cost us dear. We smiled, attempted to show that we hadn't really seen him coming and returned his greeting. I was tempted to ask, "Are you going anywhere else?" but thought it would be a bit too obvious. He spoke again:

"Climb up, I have a few minutes, if you want to see the boat." Yea well, seeing the boat wasn't quite what we'd had in mind. Seeing it zip across the waves with us aboard would have better described it. Still, beggars can't be choosers. We grabbed hold and struggled up on to the platform at the back. It was beautifully laid with wood, superbly finished with several coats of yacht varnish or something like it. This platform was inches above the water, ideal for diving in. the boat looked even better once aboard, all the sides and superstructure gleaming white and the seats upholstered in white leather too. Some panels a deep navy blue, against the white it looked like a couple of hundred thou's worth.

"I have something my mother made, if you'd like to try it." Continued Yiannis. We nodded our assent. He went below and emerged from the cabin carrying a parcel of greaseproof paper, which he unwrapped on his lap to reveal a clutch of honey-soaked cookies, called *Melomakarona*. These are often made at Christmastime, but can me made at any time of the year, as evident by the fact that this was June. They contain olive oil, sugar, orange juice, maybe some brandy, ground semolina, flour, baking soda, cinnamon and perhaps cloves. Yiannis also produced a carton of chilled fruit juice to wash them down with and so we sat and ate and talked and it turned out to be almost (but not quite) as good as having gone for a spin. At least my wife was able to drape herself as though she looked like she belonged on such a craft.

Our snack finished, Yiannis made it clear in as subtle way as he could that time was pressing and he had to get on. His dinghy, which had been tied up where the boat usually lies, was ready for him to row ashore once he'd put the tarp over the speed boat's open area, something which he began doing as we stood and thanked him before retreating to the rear platform in readiness for diving in and swimming back to shore. He did offer to row us in the dinghy, but we were sweltering enough by now and wanted to cool off anyway.

In those days I used to wear my jellies when swimming. As explained in *"Feta Compli!"* I tend to go backwards when using flippers, so jellies protect my feet when setting them down in areas where there are, for example, too many urchins for comfort. My feet were sweaty and so, when I took my dive in such a manner as to ensure to all who may be watching that I was "cool," I managed to slip one of my feet right out of its jelly, resulting in the said jelly popping off the platform, plopping into the water and drifting straight down through some thirty feet (well, it seemed like thirty feet to me) of clear Aegean sea and alighting on the flat sandy bottom some distance below me. Looking down I saw my trusty jelly sitting right-side-up on the sand and decided that I couldn't just leave it there. For a start it would mean walking the couple of miles or so back from the beach to our apartment in Agia Marina with either one foot in a jelly and one foot bare, or with both feet bare; something which I found hard to contemplate. I had no other footwear with me.

Taking a huge breath and securing my mask, I thrust myself downward, and kicked for all I was worth to get down to my wayward jelly. The harder I kicked the harder it became to keep going down instead of back up to the surface like a cork. If I'd ever doubted the human body's tendency to float, I certainly didn't now. By the time I was within inches of the wayward footwear item with my outstretched fingers, I was already running out of lung capacity and thinking, "Shame I'm not going to survive. I'd never worry about drowning again, the human body is evidently that buoyant."

With one last gargantuan thrust of my tired legs I managed to hook the jelly with my little finger and turned my body to thrust my legs for all they were worth in an effort to get back to the surface as quickly as I could.

Have you ever stared up at the surface of the sea from some way below and wondered at how beautiful it is, especially when the sky above is clear and blue and the sunlight is filtering through the ripples? If you're a scuba diver you'll be only too familiar with such a sight. In fact you're probably quite blasé about it. If, however, like me, you're an occasional snorkeller whose dives usually amount to a quick kick in three feet of water to pick up a shell that's aroused your curiosity, then you may perhaps understand that sometimes the briefest of moments can feel like hours, especially after a lot of puff has been expended in order to get this far down to the bottom.

Staring up as I rose, all too slowly for my liking, I remember being fascinated by how schools of little fish have the tendency to hang around beneath the shadow of a floating boat's hull, like a single entity. The underside of Yianni's speedboat bobbing gently yards above, I watched the fish in wonder as I carried on trying to kick my way to the surface. Then, as I was perhaps half-way back up I looked at the rope which ran from the buoy to the anchor on the bottom and noticed how it was all green and furry with the plant life which had taken up residence along its entire length. Everything was so marvellous, except my lung capacity, which was now beginning to cause me some concern. Yes the body wants to rise, but when you're this far down it's not really ready to rise fast *enough*.

Of course, my lovely wife hadn't looked back and was now several yards away and still swimming towards the beach, not turning her head. She didn't even know that, had she turned around she'd have noticed a distinct lack of any part of my body showing on the water's surface. Yiannis was busy fiddling with rope on his dinghy in readiness for rowing ashore, as I could just see the occasional wrist and hand over the side of the small craft from my angle below. Had he noticed that I'd dived, he'd probably have drawn the conclusion anyway that I knew what I was doing. See, the trouble is, if you go and drown yourself in such circumstances, any points which you may have scored in the macho department go straight out the window don't they?

Probably six feet from the surface I remember thinking, "I HAVE to breathe in. I just MUST." Yet the other half of my brain said, "Ahem. May I suggest that if you breathe in about now, it'll be saltwater and not air coming flooding into your lungs. You may not want that." Yet my mouth was metaphorically screaming to open, my nose was symbolically demanding an intake of breathe. My lungs were saying, "Enough is enough, kiddo. We need some oxygenated air right about *now*. This just isn't playing the game y'know."

Quite how I managed to break the surface before giving in to those extremely strong desires I'll never know, but the fact that you're reading this right now reveals, fairly convincingly of course, the fact that I did indeed make it. I shot out of the water up to as far as my midriff, like a cork that had been held down well below the surface and the noise I made when I eventually realised that it was indeed safe to take a breath must have attracted the attention of every living thing for a hundred metres around me. I was well relieved, not merely to be still alive, but by the fact that the only sentient beings close enough were Yiannis and Yvonne-Maria, both of whom whipped their heads around to see where this strange noise was coming from.

I fell back into that Leonardo DaVinci diagram position on my back in the water and lay there, face to the sun, silently giving thanks that I was breathing air and not the Aegean Sea. In my relief I almost let the rescued jelly shoe slip from the grasp of my left hand.

Once ashore, my wife, ever concerned for my wellbeing, told me off in full voice, at full volume and in no uncertain terms (purely out of concern of course) for risking my life for a jelly that was worth maybe a quid or two.

"You silly idiot! You should have just left it there. You can always buy another. I dunno what to do with you sometimes, I really don't!" I looked around at one or two other sunbed occupiers and smiled that *"she loves me really"* smile in an attempt to give the impression that she was only joshing and that I was in control. No one believed it for an instant.

The rest of the afternoon went without a hitch as we fell back into that sunbed torpor that's just delicious, isn't it. A bit of Sandy Denny or "Van the Man" on the iPod and a sleep under the umbrella is all you need sometimes to make everything right with the world. My wife had another George Elliot on the go so she too was quite content. When time came for us to pack up our "stuff" and walk the couple of miles back to Agia Marina, I packed up my rucksack, we slipped on our shorts and tops and searched for our footwear. Yvonne-Maria slipped on her rope-soles and I slipped first one foot, then the other, into my jellies, one of which fell straight off again, as the rear buckle support strap had broken apart completely, meaning that each time I tried to lift the foot, the blessed thing [the jelly that is, not the foot] would just drop right off.

Just behind Pandeli beach that June afternoon in 1996,

had you been there to rummage through the rubbish bin that was conveniently sited for the use of those arriving at or leaving the beach, you would have seen a pair of size 43 jelly shoes, lying atop various empty pop bottles, crisp packets, old fag ends and beer cans.

Later and a couple of miles away, at Tassos II apartments, you may have spotted a bloke on the upstairs balcony complaining about having just walked two miles along Greek tracks and roads in his bare feet.

Pandeli, Leros, in 1996. Yianni's boat is circled.

26 – Where's the Fire?

Several times a year here on Rhodes, we get covered in African dust from the Sahara. It's just one of those natural phenomena that's probably gone on since time immemorial. If the wind veers from its prevailing direction of North to North-West around to the south, the dust is likely to be a hazard.

Parasols, air conditioning units, patio furniture, ceramic tiles, clothes left out to dry on the line at the wrong time, café tables and chairs, awnings, cars, in fact everything that's out of doors can in a matter of a couple of hours begin to adopt a rather ochre-coloured hue. If, as happens during springtime or winter, the dust comes as part of the rainfall, it makes a real mess of everything for a while, with ochre-coloured water stains on everything.

Once the dust has come and the weather man (Sakkis, of course) has told us that it's finally passed on from the country, people can be seen everywhere washing off their yards, their cars and their patio furniture in an attempt to get rid of the stuff.

A rather unfortunate side affect of this plague from North

Africa is, at least so the electricity company tells us, that the dust gets into the contacts on the overhead electricity wires and poles and can cause short circuits and power outages.

Here we are in Spring 2010 and we've just been talking to Mac and Jane from up the hill about the fact that, since DEH (the electricity company) have re-routed the main cables and poles from which our supply comes the half a kilometre or so up the valley to our homes, there have been a lot fewer power cuts than we'd become used to during the first couple of years that we were here. It had even become so rare that you fancied your chances at programming the electric clock on your household appliances and your video recorder (if you have one of course, which we don't!) in the knowledge that they may actually stay accurate for a while and not be found flashing the dreaded 00:00 next time you looked at them.

So I am tapping away at my keyboard and my wife's fixing us some lunch on a rare grey day, when the humidity is high and we've been suffering the dreaded African dust, mingled with misty rain, for several hours. It's only a few weeks since a major change (which entailed a twelve hour power cut) was made to the way that the power cables are routed along this part of Kiotari and some new poles can be seen across the lower part of our valley, carrying the cables from which they now connect our supply. From our front garden we can see these poles, some five hundred metres down the valley below, where the cables run from the main "artery" across to the pole from which they run up to the one at the extremity of our garden. On the pole that holds the first "stays" for the three cables running our way (still with me here?) there are three large 'trips," which consist of rods, perhaps a foot long, which are hinged at the bottom and fit into some hefty clips at the top. These rods need to stay in place for us to receive our 220 volts.

From out of nowhere there is a huge bang. The goats stampede across the hillside to our right and all the birds in the valley take flight. The pigs in the pen down the lane squeal and the dog that's chained up with them 24/7 begins barking wildly. At first I suspect that there's a hunter with his rifle right outside our gate, until I remember that a) the hunting season doesn't start until October and b) hunting is still forbidden in this region following the fires of 2008. The UPS that keeps my Mac and its router from being fried starts beeping, telling me that the electricity has just gone off, so it's definitely not a hunter's gun we've just heard. I have twenty minutes to shut the Mac down safely before the battery power expires.

My wife curses, as she's half way through preparing something and the cooker hood light has gone off, plus the blender is now rendered useless. Bad-temperedly I shut down the Mac and walk outside in the gloom of the grey drizzly day to see if anything will tell me what the source of the noise was. After scanning the valley for a while and at least seeing no corpses, either human or animal, my attention is drawn to the first electricity pole down the valley, the one that holds the three "trips". Do my eyes deceive me? I decide to pop indoors, rummage through the appropriate drawer for my binoculars and come back out to see if what I think I saw is right.

Sure enough, high on the pole one of the three trip rods is hanging limply downwards from its hinge, whereas the other two are still going upwards and lodged in their respective contact cradles. Heaving a weary sigh, I realise that it's Saturday and it's almost noon. We need to call out DEH and we have no idea what number to ring or how long they may take to come, even assuming we can get through. Back inside I grab the phone and them slam it down again. It's a cordless. No power, no phone.

"What are we going to do? I need to finish mixing this and I can't use the blender," expresses my wife, deeply concerned about a possible waste of perfectly good ingredients.

"I'll have to go down to Despina's. She'll know who to call. Plus her husband Nico works for the Dimos, so they'll be able to help. I'd better go now because I don't know what time they close on a Saturday." Despina is the fifty-something Canadian Greek who runs a DIY store just down the road and her husband does indeed work for the local council. He knows how to "get things done", or how to get the right people to come out whenever necessary. He knows people and can pull strings. Despina and Nico are our best hope. Her store is open seven days a week and for long hours but, as it's a Saturday, I'm worried that today she may close earlier than sundown and so I grab the car keys, throw on some outdoor shoes and dash out to the car. Since we often call in at her store, we don't actually have a phone number for it, so we can't even call her using a cell phone.

My wife opens the gate as I drive out and head down the lane to the main road. Five minutes later I walk into Despina's store and ask: "Despina, can you help? The *revma* has gone off in our valley and I think it only affects us and our neighbours, Mac and Jane. I'd call DEH but I don't know what number to call."

"I can give you the number John, no problem." She picks up her mobile phone and thumbs it, then says, "Call 1050, that's the DEH emergency line. Tell them you're without power and they should send someone. If you have any problems, call me from home and I'll see what Nico can do. I'll write the number on the back of one of our business cards."

I thank her profusely, jump back into the car and dash back home, since I'd forgotten to take my cell phone with me. I pick it up and punch in 1050. I get a continuous tone, telling me that the number doesn't work from a cell phone. At least now I have Despina's number, so I immediately call her and tell her the problem.

"I'll call them for you. Don't worry," she says and once more I find myself thanking her and at the same time silently thanking heaven that she's there.

We stand, the two of us, inside the French windows and stare down the drizzle-soaked valley at the offending power line and pole. I grab the binoculars again and stare at the trip rod, which hangs tauntingly, telling me the reason why there's no power anywhere in the house. I find myself willing it back into position. My wife begins that womanly thing where they begin imagining the worst case scenario.

"What if no one can come until Monday? What about the food in the freezer? You'd better get the oil lamps out or we won't be able to see anything once it gets dark. How am I going to do a meal this evening?" She adds a few more too, but you get the picture.

The sky lightens and the drizzle stops. The sun even tries to peek through the thinning cloud and we still stand and look, hoping to see a familiar orange truck or van (orange is the DEH company colour) winding its way up the valley to come to our rescue. Our patience is rewarded when, not twenty minutes after my last conversation with Despina, we spot a bright orange pickup roaring up the lane at great speed, leaving a wake of dust and exhaust fumes. The rain hadn't been enough to dampen the dust completely, evidently. The driver seems to be in quite a hurry. Perhaps he wants to get us sorted and get home to watch the football.

Seconds later the pickup skids to a halt, stones flying from it's tyres, outside our front gate. We are already there to meet it. Two men in dungarees jump out from the doors and run up to us, exuding an air of expectant urgency. The first one asks:

"WHERE'S THE FIRE, THEN?"

Now I am slightly perplexed. Maybe they've come up our valley by mistake and really ought to be somewhere else, somewhere where the need for their presence is even more pressing than ours. I look around at the sky and don't see any sign of smoke. I reply, "Fire? We didn't report a fire. Are you sure you didn't come up our valley by mistake?"

"You are Kyrieh Walls?" Here he uses our landlord's surname, so, as is often the case when explanations would only complicate things, I reply in the positive. He's also looking in all directions, evidently searching for the telltale signs of fire.

"Then it is your call we are answering. We were told there was a fire." He's still looking this way and that, I'd hazard a guess he's doing so hopefully. His eyes are almost out of their sockets with concentration as he surveys the scene around the house.

"*NO*. I said there was what sounded like gunfire, perhaps that's where the misunderstanding occurred, but I didn't report a fire."

"Anyway, we are here so we will do what we can; do you know what is the problem?" I proceed to tell him about the big bang (not the original one of course. That would have taken some hours. Plus I don't feel qualified to go into too much detail on that one, and I'd prefer to handle the subject with a pencil, a notebook and diagrams, it always helps don't you think?) and how at that precise moment our "*revma*" went off and we got our friend down the road to put in a call.

The one that's evidently in charge introduces himself as "Giorgo" and says that today they are very busy because of the "*skoni*", which is a reference to the African, or Saharan dust.

He says that it plays havoc with the connections on the poles and knocks out power all over the place. The pair of them ought to have finished for the day by now, but they still have several call-outs to respond to yet.

I point down the valley to the pole that carries the 'knocked-out' trip-rod and he gives a knowing diagonal head-nod.

"OK," he says, "This is my *kinito* [cell phone] number," while extracting a crumpled piece of card from his pocket and scrawling something in ballpoint pen. "We will go down to that post and you call me if you have power, kala?" He hands me the scrap.

"Sounds like a good idea to me. Thanks Giorgo." Before I finish those few words they're jumping back into the cab and doing a three-point turn outside our front gates and high-tailing it back down the track. I watch with my binoculars as they pull up by the pole, pile out and Giorgos sends his side-kick shinning up it on one of those special pole-climbing contraptions, with a tool belt around his waist. No sense Giorgo getting fried, when the slightly younger assistant can take the risk, now is there?

Yvonne-Maria goes back inside to keep an eye on the cooker hood. Within minutes she calls out from the house door, "IT'S BACK ON!"

I pull my phone out from my trouser pocket and call Giorgo's number. He answers.

"*Great*, Giorgo! The power is on. Thank you so much." With a "You're welcome" he's closed the call and is soon hairing back down the lane in a cloud of dust to their next emergency. Clearly he still thinks he can catch the second half of the match if he's quick enough.

"Don't you think it would be good to call Despina, to

thank her?" Asks my ever thoughtful wife.

"Yea, OK. I suppose it would be a good idea," I reply. I punch in the number from the card she gave me and listen to the ringing tone. She answers: "Giorgiadi DIY and Builder's Merchant," I speak:

"Hi Despina. Just called to say thank you. The guys from DEH turned up very quickly and we now have *revma*. The only thing that puzzled us was the fact that the man seemed to think that there was an electrical fire somewhere. That appeared to be why they turned up so quickly, driving like maniacs into the bargain."

"On a Saturday lunchtime there's always a risk that you won't get them to come out. So I told them you had a fire. Otherwise you may have been without power for a couple of days!"

'YOU told them we had a fire?!"

"Yes, well, it worked didn't it?" She had a point.

Summer of 1972,
outside my mother-in-law Lela's home in Bath. Left to right:
My brother-in-law-to-be, Paul, Cousin Christina from Athens (her
daughter Effie crouches below), Christine, Yvonne-Maria and yours
truly (cool or what?).

27 – *Tzatziki for You to Say*

Five years have gone by very quickly. It's now October 2010 and I'm closing out volume three of *"Ramblings From Rhodes"* with mixed feelings.

We came out here with some ideas, some of which proved correct and some of which have proven spectacularly wrong. But, we're still here, *"Doxa to Theo"*, as so many Greeks say in such circumstances. It's an expression that literally means, "Praise be to God" and you hear it often. In Britain it would simply be an idiom, but here they usually mean it.

I was making a brace door for our newly constructed shed recently. Just along the road from the house is a workshop run by a couple of Albanian brothers who have been quite kind to me on occasion. Several times I've wanted a few modest pieces of wood or perhaps laminated chipboard for some odd job or other. I've wandered into the workshop and either one of the brothers would ask me what I wanted. I'd explain, then they'd sift through all their off-cuts and wave off my attempts to pay them when they'd handed me just the right piece to meet my requirements. One time when it was white laminated chipboard that I was scrounging, they even applied the white edging strip for me after cutting the piece to size. They have an expensive looking machine that does it properly, but no matter, they wouldn't be paid.

One time I did succeed in paying them a few Euros. This was when one of our "hardwood" patio chairs collapsed when my sister was visiting from the UK and we were passing a pleasant evening on the patio, sipping a little more red wine after a splendid meal prepared by my wife, who doesn't like cooking, yet always elicits compliments from guests on her ability. My sister Jane descended floorwards in a hail of splinters and cries of distress. She came off relatively unscathed, but the chair looked terminal.

I took it down to the workshop, with little hope that they could salvage it, but there was nothing to lose, when all said and done. Petros (the older of the two brothers) took a look at it, all the while scratching his chin with his thumb and forefinger, then said,

"Leave it with us for a couple of days. We'll see what we can do."

Two days later I returned to find the workshop closed. I called Petros on his cell phone and he told me that he was in Rhodes town and could I come back the next morning. *Three days* later I finally made a visit that coincided with someone being on hand.

Doxa to Theo, it was Petros.

"Hold on," he said as he turned and trotted back into the workshop. I was fully expecting him to exit the roller-door carrying a still wrecked patio chair, but I was quite wrong. Out he strutted, looking well pleased with himself, carrying a chair that looked as good as new. The only thing that gave away the fact that it had been repaired was the need of a coat of varnish on the newly installed piece of hardwood. He allowed me to pay him ten Euros.

So I asked him, "Do you supply new wood too? I mean, it would save me going all the way to town to the timber yard, so I don't even mind if it's not quite as cheap." When I do go to the timber yard, if I buy anything that's too big for the car I have to wait until they have a lorry coming to our part of the island before I take delivery of the timber. I could be lucky and it arrives only days later. It could, though, mean a wait of a couple of weeks.

"Sure. Just tell us what you need and we'll add it to one of our orders. We often have new timber in stock, so if we've something that suits, you can take it away on the spot."

This sounded good to me, so, when some weeks later I was building the brace door for our newly-built concrete block shed, I drew a nice detailed diagram of what I'd need, complete with all the measurements, and took it down to the workshop in the hope of short-circuiting an expedition into Rhodes town, which usually requires the best part of a day.

Petros was there when I arrived and I showed him the diagram. Could they cut the pieces to the right lengths? I asked. Sure they could. Just come back in three or four days, I was told.

Four days later I drove over the rise from the main road to the secluded location of the workshop to find one of the brothers' several workmen present, but neither of the bosses. I asked about my pieces of wood. The mystified junior replied that he knew nothing about it. I told him I'd left my diagram with Petros and that I was asked to come back today.

"Well," he replied, Petros will be back later this afternoon, maybe you could come back then."

I had no choice but to comply. At around 3.00pm I called

Petros' cell phone, only to get his voicemail service. I asked if it was OK to come to the workshop again later and hung up, hoping to hear from him.

Of course, I didn't hear a thing. Next morning, bright and early, I decided that, if I got to the workshop before 9.00am, I could catch someone senior before they took off to some site or other for the day. Sure enough, as I crested the rise there was Petros' huge shiny black Japanese 4x4 pickup, parked outside. My spirits rose. I almost allowed myself to think that he'd have cut the pieces and that I'd be driving homeward with a selection of lengths of timber poking out the rear of my little Suzuki Swift in very short order. A brace door could well get constructed in a jiffy.

"Ah," said Petros. "Um, ...just a minute." He walked to the back of the workshop where two of his lackeys were conferring. From among a pile of sawdust and shavings he extracted my diagram and explained to them what I needed. Well, from the distance at which I was standing, I assumed that was what he was doing. He always spoke to them in Albanian so it wouldn't have made a lot of difference had I been in earshot anyway.

Their conflab over, he came back to the doorway where I was waiting patiently and said, "Your door pieces will be ready this afternoon. Come back at four o'clock."

What do you do in such circumstances? I'll tell you. You smile and say, "OK" and go home - hoping beyond hope that this will mean that at four o'clock you will have your wood. Four o'clock came and, having got absolutely nowhere calling Petros' cell phone, I decided that maybe someone would be expecting me at the workshop, so I hopped into the car and again drove the ten minutes down the road.

No one there. The whole place was locked up. I do admit

to having now reached irritation stage. How could someone tell me to come at this particular time and then leave the place all locked up like Fort Knox. It struck me that perhaps my timber was indeed all cut and ready and perhaps propped against the wall just inside the roller door. If I could just get in somehow.

Big savage dogs are a bit scary aren't they? Especially the ones that are chained up and, when you approach them, strain with all their might at the chain while snarling at you and baring a very impressive set of gnashers. These guys have just such a dog, which is always chained up outside the workshop when it's open, but just far enough away from the door to enable customers to enter and leave without having become the dog's latest plaything. No matter how many times I have visited the place, the dog always makes it plain that, were he not restrained by that huge chain, I'd be in hospital suffering multiple bites and severe blood loss within minutes. That's if I survived the attack, of course.

But here I was standing outside the workshop, along a secluded lane over a rise from the main road in a rural area and there was no dog on that chain, which lay on the ground, looking a bit suspicious. I drew the conclusion that perhaps Petros or his brother, who I hadn't seen in a while, took the dog home with them when the workshop was closed for business. One of the reasons for coming to this conclusion was the fact that there was no sound to be heard, apart from the birds and a light breeze.

To the left of the main roller door there was a narrow panel, about eighteen inches wide and as tall as the door, blanking off the gap between the door and the workshop wall. In my frustration I kicked at this panel and was surprised to see it give under the impact. In fact, there was even a gap at the bottom where the panel didn't reach all the way to the ground. Inspecting it a little closer I saw that the panel was composed of a thick piece of polystyrene foam. A couple of good punches would see it give in and I'd be able to check out my theory about the possibility that my timber was perhaps ready and waiting for me just inside the roller door. Maybe they had in all good faith intended to be here for me, but some woodwork-related emergency had come up, meaning they had to leave the workshop unattended.

It was now already a week since I'd first approached Petros about my brace door and I was pretty frustrated. Wouldn't you be? I got down on my hands, as if to do a press-up and took a look through the gap under the panel, whence I was afforded a good view of the length of the workshop. There didn't appear to be anything resembling the kinds of sawn lengths that I'd ordered for my new door to be seen leaning against a wall anywhere.

What *was* visible, though, was that dog, standing just a few feet back from the roller door, rear legs ready to spring, head low and mouth salivating as it stared menacingly at the back of the roller door, no doubt expecting a tasty meal of intruder-leg for supper. I decided I'd not bother to attempt a break-in after all. My timber wasn't ready anyway.

Driving home and fuming over developments, I made a policy decision to bite the bullet and make the trek to town the next morning, get the timber cut to size at the yard and drive home with it. I'd get it all into the car somehow if it was the last thing I did. I wasn't well pleased with Petros at this moment in time.

The next day I did as planned and succeeded in cramming all the various lengths of tongue and groove and sawn 4x1 for the braces into my gallant little Swift and drove the 55 kilometres home with the rear tailgate just a little open. That evening, I had occasion to drop into my friend Tony's place, having collected some mail for him from the taverna up at Asklipio, when he asked if I knew about Yianni.

"Yianni who?" I asked.

"You know," continued Tony, "Yianni my next door neighbour, the Albanian fellow who runs the woodwork shop with his brother Petros."

"I didn't know where he lived. I never realised he lived next door to you. I've got a bit of a bone to pick with him and Petros at the moment. But what should I know about him anyway, then?" I asked.

"He's been diagnosed with cancer. It doesn't look good. He's had to go to Athens for treatment and Petros hasn't been with it since he heard. He's been all over the place, not keeping appointments, forgetting to deliver stuff, he's beside himself with worry. They're very close. Yiannis is only 35 and he and his wife have a nipper.

"What was that bone you had to pick with Petros anyway?"

"I think what you've just told me has buried it." I replied.

The above tale well illustrates the unexpected about living here on Rhodes. Things frequently don't go to plan for reasons not always as sad as the one above; but nevertheless, if you don't adjust your way of thinking, you won't hack it here.

Still and all, when we bemoan the lack of recycling on the Greek islands, the bureaucracy which means that everything official moves at a pace similar to that of someone walking through knee-deep custard, when we wince at the cost of food in the supermarket here these days and the fact that in recent months the price of fuel for the car has gone up about 70%, we can also flop down on our patio chair with a frappe and stare up at the blue sky, which here on Rhodes we can do for over three hundred days every year, and think, as we also stare at the twinkling turquoise sea, "Yes, it's alright here really."

The secret really is, if you move here then don't expect anything other than a simple life. Tonight, before dark, we took an hour's stroll down the valley to the beach. We walked along past the clutch of tavernas here in Kiotari and thought, "It's late October now and approaching evening and it's still 22°C."

Moving out here a piece of cake? No, it's not in any way as simple. But if you experience a fair degree of luck, along with sensible planning, then it will work for you. But because it's worked for Yvonne-Maria and I, when for others it's turned into a complete nightmare, I suppose, *tzatziki* for me to say, isn't it.

And so, finally...

You'll have noticed having read my Ramblings, that I make scant reference to religion or to religious festivals and holidays. This is because I have an antipathy toward religion in general. Whilst others may see the processions where they carry an icon, or festivals where all the villagers kiss an image, or other activities like one here on Rhodes where a girl who wishes to conceive must walk up some three hundred stone steps to pray to the virgin at a particular monastery, as quaint, or even as part of the country's culture, I'm afraid I see it differently.

Every country on this small planet of ours seems to think that they have a monopoly on the creator's blessing, don't they? What was that superb observation on the subject that Bob Dylan wrote some decades ago? *"With God on Our Side"*, yea that was it.

The Greeks, as is the case around the world, can't countenance the idea that God is anything other than Greek Orthodox, their brand of religion. Jesus *must* have been Greek Orthodox, mustn't he? The locals in the villages, for all their kindness and warmth, often don't want to reason on the matter. But the fact is that the flag hangs from every church for every special occasion, demonstrating the fact that nationalism is inextricably linked to religion. Here in Greece the clergy are, to me, more pompous than in many other countries, with their ZZ Top beards *et al*, preening themselves at every possible opportunity beside the politicians and bigwigs of their country. The rituals and liturgy they practice have precious little to do with the man they claim to follow, as a brief scanning of the gospels and the books of Acts will confirm, and *everything* to do with promoting national pride and xenophobia.

I have never been a fan of either nationalism or patriotism in the extreme. Here are some of my favourite quotations:

"One of the great attractions of patriotism - it fulfills our worst wishes. In the person of our nation we are able, vicariously, to bully and cheat. Bully and cheat, what's more, with a feeling that we are profoundly virtuous."
 - Aldous Huxley

"So many of the problems that we face today are due to, or the result of, false attitudes . . . Among these is the concept of narrow nationalism—'my country, right or wrong.'"
 - Former United Nations Secretary-General U Thant

"The flag, like the cross, is sacred."
 - Encyclopaedia Americana

"Patriotism is as volatile as any emotion ... [since] once released, it can assume ugly forms."
 - The New York Times Magazine

"Patriotism is the last vestige to which a scoundrel clings."
 - Bob Dylan (possibly borrowing it himself too)

So, now you know why I have largely kept away from reporting on national or village religious observances and the like. You can read about such things in a plethora of other books anyway, whereas I prefer to concentrate on the essential humanity and dare I say - humour - of my experiences. Human contact and interaction are to me much more enriching than illogical superstitious enslavement.

Soapbox bit over.

Thanks. JM, Oct 2010.

Follow the author's regular diary from Rhodes at:
http://honorarygreek.blogspot.com

Printed in Great Britain
by Amazon.co.uk, Ltd.,
Marston Gate.